D0820905

Management Models
for Corporate Social Responsibility

Jan Jonker · Marco de Witte (Editors)

Management Models for Corporate Social Responsibility

With 57 Figures and 13 Tables

 Springer

Dr. Jan Jonker
Radboud University Nijmegen
Nijmegen School of Management (NSM)
P.O. Box 9108
6500 HK Nijmegen
The Netherlands
janjonker@wxs.nl

Dr. Marco de Witte
University of Groningen
Faculty of Management and Organisation
P.O. Box 800
9700 AV Groningen
The Netherlands
dewitte@hgrv.nl

ISBN-10   3-540-33246-4 Springer Berlin Heidelberg New York
ISBN-13   978-3-540-33246-6 Springer Berlin Heidelberg New York

Cataloging-in-Publication Data
Library of Congress Control Number: 2006927437

Springer is a part of Springer Science+Business Media

springeronline.com

© Springer Berlin · Heidelberg 2006
Printed in Germany

Hardcover-Design: Erich Kirchner, Heidelberg

SPIN 11732495   88/3153-5 4 3 2 1 0 – Printed on acid-free paper

Table of Contents

Organising Identity

Organising Transactivity

Organising Systems

Organising the Business Proposition

1 Finally in Business: Organising Corporate Social Responsibility in Five

Jan Jonker and Marco de Witte

Key words: Sustainability, responsibility, identity, transactivity, transparency, systems.

1.1 Introduction

Our society is fundamentally in transition. As a result, new and unforeseen demands are placed upon business. In the past decade it has become evident that business needs to find new ways to respond to these developments. The conventional balance between actors in society is under construction. Governments tend to retreat from their traditional governing role in many sectors. New (environmental and social) risks are apparent and the challenge of sustainability has to be taken up. What emerges is an image of a society in transition. One of the critical issues that becomes apparent is the changing interface between business and society. It is unclear how roles, responsibilities and functions of business should be defined and handled given this transition. The search for answers to these questions necessitates a corporate vision that goes beyond the conventional, economically driven business perspective.

In the past decade the search for these answers led to the development of the concept corporate social responsibility (CSR). This book contributes to this search in a hands-on manner, for it presents a wide range of tried and tested models and instruments that are developed to explore and organise CSR within organisations. In many ways, it is the result of the practical efforts of professionals that are engaged in finding ways for organisations to cope with their new roles and responsibilities in contemporary society. To structure the presentation of the models, the concept CSR is framed in a brief elaboration which results in a generic CSR management model. This management model serves as a framework for this book.

CSR is one of the 'umbrella' labels that has recently gained popularity. Many of the emerging issues are being addressed under this label. CSR indeed covers a wide range of issues and topics such as human rights, health, renewable energy, child labour and eco-efficiency. It is regarded positively, yet is often not integrated in the core business of an organisation. Despite ongoing promising debates, it is often not deemed urgent enough in the face of competitive pressure, changing demands or economic recession. As a concept CSR is often viewed as being too vague and complicated to be put into business practice. In the end, refuge is often sought in activities like partnerships, emissions reduction, stakeholder dialogue, reporting and the application of a new generation of standards. After a decade of various initiatives, it is time to ask whether these activities have fundamentally contributed to the demand for new approaches, new concepts and business strategies. Based on current results in research and practice the conclusion is that CSR still mainly remains a promise for the future.

1.2   The roots of the debate

It needs no profound research to be aware of the various debates taking place across society. Two key words seem to be central to these debates: sustainability and responsibility. Sustainability refers to a normative perspective on the internal and external environment regarding tangible and intangible resources. Tangible resources (e.g. water, oil, primary material etc.) should be used with explicit care and, if possible, replaced by alternatives and recycled. Intangible resources (e.g. know-how, competencies, qualifications etc.) should be identified and (strategically) maintained. It is in the interest of the organisation to carefully look after the combined tangible and intangible resources and to reflect this in its business strategy and positioning in the value chain. Responsibility nowadays refers not only to economic, but also to social and environmental responsibility. Corporations are challenged to go beyond the predominantly economic view and take into account a wider context. This challenge can be interpreted as (implicit and explicit) societal demands to incorporate social and environmental values into business practice. Recently, it has become quite common to refer to this responsibility on a corporate level as 'corporate social responsibility' (CSR). Undoubtedly CSR has become one of the (new) organisational challenges over the past decade, certainly when viewed from the perspective of the growing needs and obligations of sustainability. To grasp these developments one needs to briefly position these two key notions in the various debates.

Sustainability

The sustainability debate was ignited in the beginning of the 1970s with the release of the publication of the first report of the Club of Rome, The Limits to Growth. This report revealed the devastating impact of mankind on its natural environment. The shock that was provoked by this sudden awareness led to a whole range of technological and research activities. Since then, 'environmental management' or 'eco-efficiency' has led to well-established technological and managerial disciplines supported by laws and regulations. In turn, this has led to the broad acceptance of concern for the natural environment, be it in policy or business practice. Recent reports on the natural state of the earth show a dramatic decline in natural resources and an unavoidable and unprecedented rise in temperature which will lead to dramatic changes in the next decade alone. One hears a vast range of opinions on these findings and their possible impact in debates by academics, politicians and the man in the street, both on a local and global level. Who is shouting the truth remains unclear. Yet one thing is certain: the natural environment has become a firm issue on the agenda of companies and governments. In more recent years this has been increasingly backed by the demand for organisational responsibility.

Responsibility

For a long time, the traditional responsibility of companies has been very simple: economic 'survival' in a free market context. Its established mantra was: 'the only business of business is to do business'. In the past, several companies adopting a broader perspective on their responsibility were predominantly directed by self-interest. Health, education, sports or housing for employees were seen as areas that were justifiable and would bring a 'defendable' return on (social) investment. Highly motivated, well-educated and healthy employees mean prosperity and continuity for the firm. Nowadays society has changed fundamentally: local has become global, and what was closed is now open. Everything and everybody is interconnected and interlinked. Classical societal concepts no longer seem to suit the needs and problems facing society. As a result, more and more demands are being placed on the possible role and responsibilities of organisations. Organisations are not only held responsible for delivering high-quality and high-end products and services, they are also expected to meet the needs of internal and external stakeholders as well as to ensure that any negative social, environmental impact is reduced to a minimum. And what is more, society demands they operate in a way that will not damage future generations or people anywhere in the world. This requires a different perspective on what an organisation stands for, one that also does not lose sight of its primary economic objectives.

1.3   The strategic significance of CSR

The consequence of these debates is that willingly or unwillingly companies are fast becoming responsible for a wide array of issues. Their traditional role is being rewritten. It is clear that the present debate on CSR is still young, despite its strong roots. It is rapidly gaining momentum and impact in the international business arena supported by developments, incidents, publications, measures, governmental regulations etc. Sustainability and responsibility, under the 'um-brella' of CSR, are now part of an emerging global social movement. What seems to be at stake in the sustainability and responsibility debates is the role and function of the business enterprise in contemporary society, including the way business is driven in terms of values, strategies, business propositions, changing responsibility and accountability. The general view is that in the future generating economic value should go hand in hand with the development of social and 'natural' capital. This involves the growing strategic significance of CSR for companies. CSR seems to refer not so much to the qualities of an individual (organisation) but to the qualities of its relationship with the world (based on values and identity). It requires the development of an innovative vision of the world leading to the incorporation of externalities and a positive contribution to the social context. If CSR is really embedded in an organisation, it will be at the heart of the business, linked to every business proposition and added value in the value chains of various stakeholders. This makes it possible to view CSR as a part of a process of innovation and (social) renewal. The key point is the development of competencies and capabilities to connect the business approach with the needs and circumstances of the various stakeholders. It demands a commitment to reshape relationships within the business and social context. The key question is, therefore, how to organise CSR?

Organising CSR

The CSR perspectives are generally referred to as the 'triple bottom line' and are widely used in the contemporary CSR debate. 'Planet' refers to sustainability, 'people' to a changing social responsibility and 'profit' to the business results. Launched in the mid 1990's by John Elkington this typology has gained widespread acceptance and as such has been of great help in raising and positioning CSR in organisations. A decade down the line, semantically as well as conceptually, it seems as if the 'triple bottom line' has served its purpose. At best, it leads to a fragile balancing act suggesting some kind of optimum between the p's. The moment CSR really becomes an organisational issue, implementation problems arise for which this typology provides no clear directions. The core issue is to link different internal and external organisational domains in an integrated way. CSR needs to become an organised part of the business and linked to the value proposition; that is the real challenge lying ahead. At present that is generally not the case. One should not be surprised therefore when organisations simply put it to one side when preoccupied with 'priority' issues such as competition, changing demands or economic recession. The approach taken here is to involve CSR in all aspects of the organisation. This approach needs to be directed by the specific business strategy of the individual organisation. CSR only really becomes organi

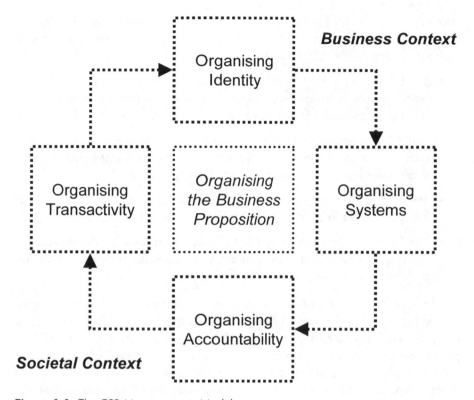

Figure 1.1. The CSR Managements Model

sationally embedded when it results in all-round added value. Based on this perspective an integrated management model has been developed which is depicted in Figure 1.1.

This model provides a generic approach to all the organisational aspects of CSR and the way they are interlinked. It has been developed based on the results of recent international research activities. It emerged during a project with the Corporate Citizenship Centre (CCC) of the University of South Africa (UNISA)[1] A central notion of the model is the Business Proposition (BP) of an organisation. The BP is what an organisation makes or sells; its 'raison d'etre'. This comprises mission, vision and the overall business strategy focusing on creating customer value. In order to effectively define the BP, four domains have to be organised: (a) the organisational identity, (b) the systems, (c) ac-

---

[1] This project was conducted in 2004 by Claudia Appels (Mscie) and Lisette van Duin (Mscie) both former Master students of the Nijmegen School of Management of the Radboud University of Nijmegen. Without their valuable support we would not have succeeded in coming this far with the model.

countability and finally (d) transactivity. These four interlinked organising activities take place in a business and societal context. These issues each entail a number of 'organising' activities:

- The BP and organising identity cover issues such as: core values, drivers, vision, branding, image and corporate identity. Depending on the chosen strategy, a specific identity and corresponding values are formulated;

- The BP and organising systems cover issues such as internal and external communication, design of primary and supportive processes, implementation, marketing, training, competence development, etc.;

- The BP and organising accountability cover issues such as auditing, reporting, accounting, monitoring performance and standards;

- The BP and organising transactivity cover issues such as stakeholder involvement, developing partnerships, procurement, organising dialogue and the supply chain.

The key point here is to develop those elements that are crucial for the individual company with a refined strategy based on the business proposition. If a company normally follows e.g. a strategy of innovation, emphasis should be placed on issues such as diversity, inclusion, room to manoeuvre, employee values, dialogue and communication. If, on the contrary, a company follows a more defensive cost-leadership strategy then it is all about zero defect flows, reuse and recycling, maximum waste avoidance and risk analysis. Whatever the strategy, a modern approach to sustainability should be a core element so that the result is the optimisation of eco-efficiency.

1.4   Experiences

So far we have used this model in a number of case studies. Analyses of these cases show that companies develop customised approaches for CSR. In addition, the results revealed specific focal points during the implementation of CSR. Based on these experiences it became apparent that the model is of most value when a company already has some kind of CSR strategy in place. This strategy – however modest it may be – offers ground for systemic improvement. Analysis also indicates a kind of 'hierarchy' in the model: organising identity leads the way. It's the identity that provides the strategic direction. These experiences have given support to the idea that this model is a highly valuable tool. We are presently engaged in additional projects in order to expand our understanding of the method's various possibilities in practice.

1.5   The quest for applicable management models

Over the past few years, impressive progress has been made in the field of CSR. As we knew this must have resulted in a number of tried and tested management models (concepts, tools, instruments etc.), models that have demonstrated added value in everyday (organisational) practice, we set out to harvest this progress in practice. As the result of an international email initiative more then 150 people from around the world agreed to participate. We then used the above outlined model to assess and structure the potential contributions offered. The final result led to the concise overview of models presented here. In this volume we offer this experience in a practical manner leading to an easily accessible, very readable volume. The result is a knowledge bank provided by people still struggling to an extent with various aspects of CSR. This hands-on experience is what makes this book so valuable. It is especially aimed at managers and consultants: people that have to deal with CSR in everyday practice.

References

Fussler, C., A. Cramer and S. van der Vegt (2004). *Raising the Bar*, Sheffield: Greenleaf Publishing.

Habisch, A., J. Jonker, M. Wegner and R. Schmidpeter (2005). *Corporate Social Responsibility Across Europe*, Heidelberg: Springer-Verlag.

Jonker, J. and M. de Witte (2006). *The Challenge of Organising and Implementing Corporate Social Responsibility*, Hampshire: Palgrave.

Website

www.corporateresponsibility.nl

Generic Models for the Business Context

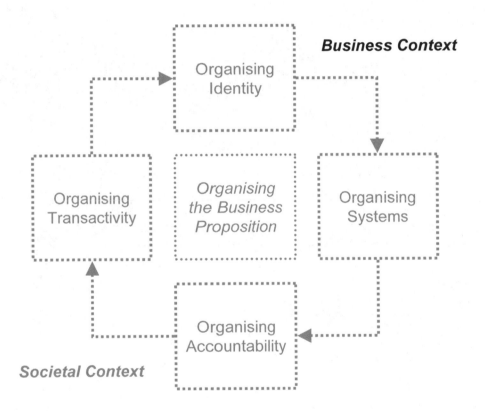

2 The SIGMA Management Model

Dave Knight

Key words: Sustainability, principles, the Five Capitals, accountability, management framework.

2.1 Introduction

The Sustainability – Integrated Guidelines for Management (SIGMA) are the key output from a four-year multi-stakeholder project to provide practical, yet comprehensive guidance to organisations seeking to improve their sustainability and CSR management and performance.

The core partners of the project were the British Standards Institution – the UK standards organisation, Forum for the Future – a leading sustainability charity and think-tank, and AccountAbility – the international professional body for accountability. The whole project was supported by the UK Department of Trade and Industry (DTI) and involved over 20 organisational partners, mainly companies. These companies piloted and helped develop the guidelines, together with a wide range of additional stakeholders who contributed to the project in various ways from the steering group to being interested parties.

The SIGMA Guidelines consist of two main parts:

1. Guiding Principles – support the development of organisation specific principles and enable practitioners to understand what their organisation might look like if it were sustainable.

2. Management Framework – enables a systematic approach to be taken to the development, delivery, monitoring and communication of an organisation's sustainable development strategy and performance.

The guidelines also contain an introduction to the SIGMA Toolkit, which provides advice and guidance on specific management challenges, such as stakeholder engagement and assessing risks and opportunities.

As Zadek and Ligteringen point out in their briefing paper on the Future of Corporate Responsibility Codes, Standards and Frameworks, the SIGMA guidelines are part of the emerging global architecture around de facto standards. Although there is a plethora of standards, guidelines and approaches, there is a notable trend towards convergence and integration, with SIGMA providing an integrated framework to guide the ongoing management of environmental and social impacts. As such, SIGMA utilises and highlights, for example the GRI Guidelines and the AA1000 Assurance Standard, as the detailed guidance for reporting and assurance and does not seek to recreate them. In fact, the SIGMA compatibility tool provides a guide to the alignment of 13 key management systems and approaches while another tool reviews and summarises 20 key standards and guidelines.

The key benefits of the guidelines are that they enable organisations to align their existing activities with a robust framework, yet are flexible enough to accommodate the specific circumstances of the individual organisation. They are not a prescriptive set of rules, rather a structure and guide for action and a way of assessing organisational CSR effectiveness.

2.2   The essence of the SIGMA management model

The SIGMA Management Framework is the core of the model and is shown in Figure 2.1. It follows the widely used 'Plan, Do, Check, Act' model, represented by four phases: Leadership and Vision; Planning; Delivery; Monitor, Review and Report. This enables alignment to established management processes, systems and standards. It does not specify a method of application; moreover, it provides a flexible, yet systematic structure for CSR management activity.

The leadership and vision phase activities support the development of an organisations identity and leadership needs, and enables it to understand and develop a vision of what it may look like if it were to be sustainable. The planning phase guides systems development and activity prioritisation, confirming the changes needed. The delivery phase is concerned with delivering the business proposition, implementing the CSR programme while maintaining and enhancing natural, social, human, manufactured and financial capital and being accountable. The monitoring, reviewing and reporting phase is about checking progress, learning and adapting as well as transparently reporting progress.

Tables in the guidelines for each phase provide the 'how, what, when, why and who?' of CSR management, including suggested activities to focus on: key questions to ask; suggestions for who needs to be involved; potential timing for activities; expected outcomes; further resources, as well as hints and tips to assist with implementation, mapping of what is already underway and establishing what is required.

The reality of CSR management in organisations is that many activities will already be happening, going at different speeds and involving different people. The actual activities will depend on the maturity of the CSR programme, resources available and existing strategies and approaches. The four-phase framework provides a structure to consider how these activities interrelate and

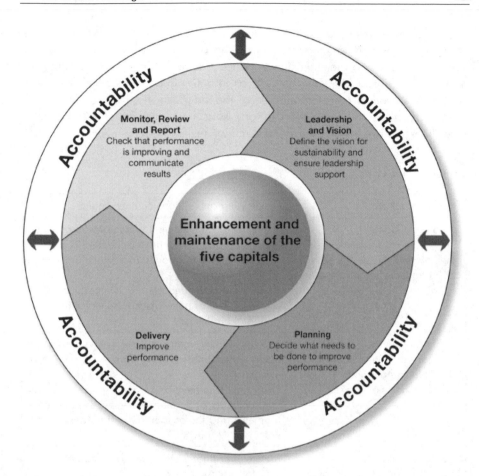

Figure 2.1. The SIGMA Management Framework

support each other as well as showing the process for how overall CSR management can be advanced.

The key differentiator of SIGMA from other management approaches is that SIGMA is underpinned by the guiding principles of the five capitals and accountability which provide the basis for all CSR activity. Many established management systems provide effective structures for the management of issues without questioning or guiding the user towards more responsible social and environmental performance. For example, many environmental management systems enable organisations to effectively manage their environmental impacts, however bad these impacts may be. The principle of continuous improvement may move the system user in the right direction but does not provide guidance on how far or how fast the organisation needs to go to become sustainable.

SIGMA goes some way to closing this gap. While working within any phase of the management framework to deliver the business proposition, the organisation is required to maintain and enhance natural, human, social, manufactured and financial capitals, as well as practicing accountability. The term 'Capital' is used to represent the use of the stocks of these five assets, which together provide the foundation of any successful enterprise and reflect its overall impact and wealth. Table 2.1 summarises the five capitals.

Table 2.1. The Five Capitals

The Five Capitals	Maintaining and enhancing each capital
1. Natural Capital The ecological foundation for the other capitals. Natural capital cannot be traded off against the other capitals	Understand, monitor and manage resource inputs and the outputs and impacts generated Operate within the boundaries of natural cycles and systems Consider resource reduction and substitution, eco-efficiency, use of renewables, respect for and protection of biodiversity
2. Human Capital The ability of the individual to contribute to organisational success and have their potential fulfilled	Aim for healthy, motivated and skilled workforces doing varied and satisfying work in learning environments Ensure fair treatment and wages, respect for basic human rights and cultural differences, safe environments and the encouragement of identity, empathy and creativity
3. Social capital The value added by relationships, organisations, networks, partnerships and collaboration	Maintain an organisations licence to operate within societal structures Work towards community development; ethical sourcing of supplies, consistent public policy positions, fair payment of taxes, respect for law, the rejection of corruption and the adoption of transparent and fair governance systems
4. Manufactured Capital Any fixed assets, such as buildings, goods and infrastructure owned, leased or controlled by the organisation	Utilise technology, infrastructure and systems in the efficient use of resources Consider closed loop manufacturing systems, leasing services, zero-waste and emissions approaches and sustainable design
5. Financial Capital Existing in the form of tradable currencies, it should reflect the value of the other capitals (rather than being a true capital in its own right)	Publish financial accounts Consider putting financial or 'shadow' values on other capitals wherever possible Recognise the importance of non-financial measures

All business activities use one or more capital during every management phase to deliver the business proposition. Therefore, following the SIGMA model, businesses seeking to improve their CSR will move towards integrated management approaches. This includes using broader measurement of performance and success, issue based and cross-functional working and by improving their ability to communicate the value of CSR.

Practicing accountability during every management phase is the other key SIGMA principle. As recognised in the introduction to this book, CSR refers to the qualities of the organisation to relate to the world around it – to its stakeholders who influence or who are influenced by it. Accountability secures a licence to operate and is fulfilled by being transparent and responsive to stakeholder needs and through complying with legislation and voluntary commitments.

Effective stakeholder engagement enhances accountability. In practice this means understanding who stakeholders are and how best to engage with them as an embedded part of the ongoing management of the enterprise, during all phases of the management framework, not as a separate exercise. This ensures, for example, that it informs the organisation's risks, opportunities and priorities in the planning phase, it stimulates innovation and efficiency gains in the delivery phase and helps inform performance measures in the monitor, measure and review phase.

The culture of an organisation is crucial in this area. Accountability is not a public relations exercise. It must be led from the top, through good governance and must be consistently implemented and communicated. This includes through the supply and selling chains such as in supplier relationships, lobbying, advertising and marketing activities.

To make a real difference to CSR performance significant capabilities and innovation are required. To help enable this, the management framework is supported by the SIGMA toolkit, a selection of tools and guidance available to support implementation and to tackle particular challenges at each phase of the framework. Many of the tools exist in their own right, like the Global Reporting Initiative (GRI) guidelines while others were developed during the piloting of the SIGMA guidelines. The tools available through the toolkit are just a selection and can be supplemented as appropriate by the many others that are increasingly available elsewhere.

2.3 Experiences of SIGMA in practice – case study, BAA Heathrow

BAA Heathrow is committed to working towards sustainable development and decided to use the SIGMA guidelines to manage other aspects of sustainability that were outside their existing environmental management system. Economic issues, like employment and the use of local businesses together with social issues such as community dialogue are considered alongside environmental issues in BAA Heathrow's Sustainable Development Management System (SDMS). This can be considered as the more integrated management of social, human and natural capitals as well as improving accountability.

Initially, as part of the planning phase, the SIGMA benchmarking tool was used to conduct an analysis of BAA Heathrow against the SIGMA management framework. This found that although BAA Heathrow had a clear sustainability vision and operating principles (Leadership and Vision phase), work was needed on longer term targets and strategic assessments of long-term developments (Planning phase). Incorporating wider sustainability risks into departmental operations and improvements to the compliance audit process were other areas for improvement (Delivery and Monitoring, Review and Report phases).

BAA identified ten significant issues from air quality to economic regeneration and developed five to ten year strategies for each. Eleven functional action plans have been developed to support delivery of the strategy. A Sustainable Development Board ensures that the significant issues are built into the airport's overall strategy and monitors delivery of the action plans. Operating at departmental level, the action plans review ways of working for consistency with BAA's sustainability strategy objectives and to deliver prioritised improvements. They also serve as a communications tool for sustainability issues with staff surveys showing they have led to increased awareness and understanding of the issues.

The functional action plans support accountability to and from employees and are the key mechanism for employee involvement in the SDMS. Teams work together to identify their impacts and to consider how they can amend their ways of working to improve sustainability performance. The overall sustainability strategy and the related targets influence the issues covered by the plans each year. Each plan is co-ordinated by a volunteer or appointed champion who has overall responsibility for keeping the plans up-to-date and for securing the resource to deliver them.

With the development of Terminal Five, BAA continues to work with its stakeholders to secure its licence to operate and grow. All personnel are encouraged to support accountability through their relationships with wider stakeholders. A stakeholder database records the issues that are of interest to stakeholders and the information they are requesting. The Sustainability Training and Communications Manager supports the programme through awareness raising campaigns and specialist training including at new employee inductions.

Allowing the SDMS to develop organically, being informed by, rather than rigidly following the SIGMA management framework and guiding principles has enabled it to be implemented in a manageable way. BAA has learnt to apply wider sustainability considerations to an enhanced environmental management approach, helping the business to change whilst moving to a more holistic and scientific management approach.

2.4   Some dos and don'ts when using the SIGMA model

One size does not fit all and the finest management models on their own do not deliver CSR performance improvements. Making any system live and work for each organisation requires translation. The culture, size and communications style of the organisation are all important factors to consider when making improvements. Any model needs adapting, using the language of the business and sensitive communication and engagement together with a careful roll-out to ensure effective and lasting change.

Organisations do not have to complete all potential activities listed in the Guidelines. They select the most useful and relevant aspects of the approach and make them work within their culture. As with any systematic approach, performance can be monitored and delivered through setting and managing against specific, measurable, achievable, realistic and time-based (SMART) targets.

For smaller or medium sized businesses, the guidance can appear complex and overcomplicated. This is partly as a result of the development focus on large and multinational companies during the piloting process and the need to cover the full range of CSR issues and management. Initially, selecting the area your business needs the most support with and simplifying the language and actions to a level appropriate for your organisation will ensure smoother, more effective use of the guidelines.

It has been widely demonstrated that team work and networking produce better results than tackling a problem individually. There are many networks offering support for organisations that are seeking to understand and improve their CSR performance. Get involved and use the learning to be gained from others while contributing your own.

2.5   Wrapping up

The SIGMA guidelines provide a principles-based framework to organise, understand and deliver more effective CSR management. They are designed to be drawn on as appropriate to the evolution and scale of CSR management within an organisation rather than to provide a prescriptive 'one model fits all' approach.

The four-phase management framework enables an organisation to align their existing management approaches and systematically and robustly manage CSR issues in an integrated way. Delivering the business proposition through each management phase should contribute to the maintenance and enhancement of the five capitals and the practice of accountability.

References

The SIGMA guidelines (2003). Available from www.projectsigma.com

Suff, P. (2004). *BAA's sustainable future for Heathrow*, Environmental Information Bulletin

Ligteringen. E. and S. Zadek (2005). *The Future of Corporate Responsibility Codes, Standards and Frameworks*, briefing paper.

Websites

The SIGMA guidelines and other project material are freely available from the website:

www.projectsigma.com (Permission to reproduce the Sigma Guiding Principles and Management Framework Model is granted by BSI.)

www.sd3.co.uk

www.baa.com

www.forumforthefuture.org.uk

www.accountability.org.uk

www.bsi-global.com

3 CSR in the Extractive Industry: An Integrated Approach

Monique de Wit and Esther Schouten

Key words: Extractive Industry, Shell, social performance, management system, CSR.

'There is no necessary connection between fancy programmes for consulting stakeholders, and stakeholder concerns being incorporated into how a company regulates itself. Shell learnt from the Brent Spar that its traditional, technical approach to environmental risk management was not effective at controlling the risk that people would perceive its actions as environmentally unfriendly and contrary to community values. There is a great danger that once external (and internal) stakeholders' values and perceptions are identified, they will be managed by public relations exercises that neutralise the possibility of protest and consumer boycott, rather than actively prompting internal organisational commitment to real change'. (Parker, 2004)

3.1 Introduction

CSR should be managed as any other business activity and its management model elements should therefore be easy to be integrated into existing structures. However, as Parker (2004) indicates, the important difference is that stakeholder engagement should be at the core of the management model. The CSR model that we present here contains the following elements (Wood, 1991):

- Social policies, stating the company's values, beliefs, and goals with regard to its social environment;
- Social programmes, specific social programmes or activities, measures, and instruments implemented to achieve social policies;
- Social impacts, looking at concrete changes the corporation has achieved through the programmes implemented in any period.

A CSR management model containing all the elements as described above with stakeholder engagement at the core and easy to integrate is applied to the energy company Royal Dutch Shell (in short, Shell). Shell energy producing companies operate in over 145 countries, and employ more than 119,000 people. The management model and experiences within Shell are described here.

An integrated CSR management model

The approach taken is in line with ISO 14000 and 18000 and follows the plan, do, review, and feedback cycle, ensuring continuous improvement. It can be graphically presented in many different ways, Figure 3.1 below gives one particular way. The key elements are based on leadership commitment (identity), continuous stakeholder engagement (transactivity), a policy, organisational structure, impact assessment, planning and implementation (systems) with monitoring, corrective action, audits and management reviews (accountability).

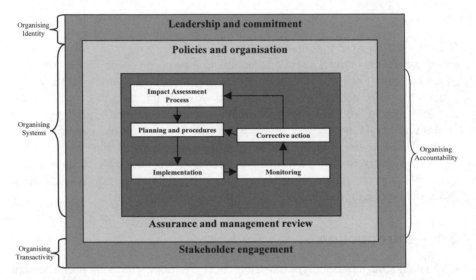

Figure 3.1. CSR management model in the extractive industry

3.2   Explanation of the CSR management models

A short explanation and the tools used are given per element of the CSR management model.

Organising identity: Leadership and commitment

The Shell General Business Principles (SGBP) apply to all Shell companies' business affairs and describe the behaviour expected of every employee. The Principles are based on core values of honesty, integrity and respect for people. In joint ventures, Shell companies use their influence to persuade partners to adopt and apply principles consistent with SGBP. Shell companies also expect contractors to conform to the Principles. For the successful implementation of

SGBP it is key that management is committed to achieving the highest standards of CSR performance by all staff and contractors. They are to be seen as providing a leading role towards continuous improvement through demonstrating leadership and active stakeholder engagement.

Organising transactivity: Stakeholder engagement

Similar to leadership and commitment, stakeholder engagement is needed in all CSR management model components. Stakeholder engagement is a continuous process and crosscutting aspect of the CSR management model. It starts when finalising the design of a facility and continues through to abandonment. Stakeholders should be engaged early to identify issues, agree approaches to manage these and review the outcomes. When dealing with key issues, both leaders and (technical) experts should actively participate in the stakeholder dialogue.

Stakeholder engagement is a key tool to focus management attention to the high risks and opportunities as perceived by stakeholders. The tools applied for stakeholder engagement vary and are dependent on the stakeholder groups. Some examples are one on one meetings, public meetings, thematic workshops, community panels and participatory assessment workshops.

Organising systems: Policies and organisation

Policies and objectives should support the overall business objectives. In setting objectives, management should consider the overall risk levels of its activities and identify those critical activities which require a fully documented demonstration that risks have been reduced to as low as reasonably practicable.

The organisation and resources should be adequate for its purpose. Responsibilities at all levels should be clearly described, communicated and understood and staff should be trained following structured competency assessment and training systems. Clearly defined CSR competencies are crucial, they should include stakeholder engagement, impact assessment, planning, measurement and reporting.

Impact assessment

The impact assessment process includes a) an inventory of the impacts to the environment and health, safety and security of people and communities of all the activities, materials, products and services during the project lifecycle; b) an assessment of the related risks and opportunities; c) implementation of measures to control these risks and realise opportunities.

Within Shell companies, two tools are used in this process:

1. Integrated Environmental Social Health Impact Assessments (ESHIAs) are required prior to all new projects and major facility developments, as well as prior to the significant modification or abandonment of existing facilities. ESHIAs provide a structured way of looking ahead at how both positive and negative impacts could arise throughout all stages of a project development from construction to operation and abandonment. It acts as a tool to aid design and decision-making. The different activities of an impact assessment include: a) scoping exercise b) baseline data collection, c) description of impacts and evaluation of their significance, d) mitigation of negative impacts and enhancement of benefits, e) evaluation of the positive and negative impacts left after mitigation, to enable decision makers to weigh the benefits against impacts of the project.

2. Social Performance (SP) plan for major operations. Social Performance, as defined in Shell, is about how to manage the impacts of the business on the communities and societies in which Shell operates. An SP plan includes a vision, description of business and social context, identification of stakeholders and issues, assessment of operational impacts and broader societal issues, and an action plan for stakeholder engagement, management of operational impacts and optimisation of community benefits.

Planning and procedures

Both the stakeholder engagement and the impact assessment process result in plans, a stakeholder engagement plan, an SP plan, and an Implementation Management and Monitoring Plan (IMMP) as a result of the ESHIA. These plans provide a delivery mechanism for commitments and undertakings made during the impact assessment process.

In addition, a crisis management plan explains how to manage unexpected incidents or events that potentially puts employees, local communities, the business and/or the environment at risk and requires rapid action and communication in the face of immediate and intense external scrutiny.

Depending on the type of impacts identified, various other plans are possible, e.g.:

*   Local content plan: local employment and supply chain opportunities provide income-generating opportunities for local stakeholders and a sense of 'ownership' in the project. It can also be an effective means of contributing to overall community capacity;

*   Biodiversity action plan: this is especially relevant when operating in a protected area or area of high biodiversity value. The plan is setting out how to manage the key biodiversity related issues;

- Resettlement action plan: this is a tool for systematically organising land acquisition, compensation calculation, relocation of people and livelihood restoration with participation of project affected groups. The steps in the resettlement process can be divided into three phases: resettlement planning, resettlement implementation and livelihood restoration.

Within Shell, guidance notes are developed in order to provide practical guidance to local managers on a number of key CSR themes. For example, impacts on vulnerable groups, operating in conflict areas, social issues along pipelines and managing grievances of communities.

Organising accountability: Implementation, monitoring and corrective action

In order to monitor progress, performance indicators need to be established. This should be done in consultation with the affected stakeholders and should also include other feedback like complaints. Results should be reported such that they can be externally verified.

Regular community surveys can help to track changes in community perception of the companies CSR management. The community survey should be based on independent and appropriate survey methods (such as interviews, questionnaires or Participatory Rural Appraisal techniques). The results should be used as input to the management system and should be fed back to those surveyed.

Assurance and management review

An assurance programme should be in place to assure the effectiveness of the management system. It can include a self-assessment and reviews by auditors independent of the facility. Appropriate assurance frameworks should also be implemented to ensure that the information that management and stakeholders base decisions on is complete, accurate and reliable.

A tool that is used in Shell is an (independent) Social Performance (SP) review to assess social performance in the company and assess the effectiveness of its implementation. SP reviews consist of the following generic steps: review of relevant information, internal assessment and external assessment including interviews with internal and external stakeholders, review of CSR tools and best practices that could be of potential relevance for the company, feedback and recommendations.

3.3   Experiences

The elements of this CSR model can be easily implemented in various management systems. Within the Shell group of companies, the elements are integrated in both the group Reputation management system and the HSE management system and there are examples of Social Performance management systems.

In which business management system the elements are integrated is not most important. It is more important that the people from different departments in the company (e.g. operations, external affairs, HSE) are involved in managing CSR. These people need the appropriate skills to ensure appropriate engagement and operational performance. In this regard some experiences, when implementing the elements of the CSR management model, are described below.

Historically, social investment projects have been focussed on general societal issues (e.g. health or education) and unrelated to the company's operational impacts. Experiences with CSR, as in Oman (see below), have shown that it needs to cover the full range from managing direct operational impacts (e.g. environmental pollution, resettlement), indirect impacts (e.g. payments to governments: www.shell.com/paymentstogovernments) to contributing to general societal issues (e.g. HIV-Aids: www.shell.com/hivaids). This also implies that people from the operations department need to be involved in managing CSR. In general, it is also the experience that good operational performance and managing direct operational impacts is for most neighbouring communities more important than philanthropy and social investment.

OLNG Impact on Local Fishermen

Oman LNG community assistance programme has built roads and given grants and donations. It also has a marine exclusion zone to enable LNG ships to safely collect LNG cargos. This represented almost a third of a community's fishing area. Moreover the cargo passing could affect local fishing. To manage the impacts, the community affairs department included measures to compensate the fishing community in their community assistance programmes. Moreover the operational department informed the community affairs department of LNG cargo routes and timing such that fisherman could be warned. (www.omanlng. com; Fossgard-Moser, 2004)

Strategic use of social investment is aimed at enhancing benefits that the company can bring, as demonstrated in Canada (see example below). The company can deliver capacity development such that local people and businesses acquire the right skills to work for the company. People from Human Resources and Contracting department need to be involved. Projects that are unrelated to business (e.g. primary schools in Nigeria) are likely to deliver goodwill, but can never be used to off-set bad operational performance. In these circumstances, it is preferred to work in partnership with other organisations that are able to provide additional resources or expertise to ascertain long-term sustainability.

Athabasca Oil Sands – Building working partnerships with the native community

Programmes were established to raise skills and help create local businesses. By 2003, over $20m in contracts had been awarded to new local aboriginal businesses in areas such as construction, earth moving, heavy hauling, bus services and catering. Source: http://www.shell.ca/code/products/oilsands/dir_oilsands.html

In the earliest stages of a project screening, environmental and social profiles are used to get an overview of the main issues. The next step is an ESHIA, this is best carried out during the selection and definition stages of the project, so that results can affect the design of the project. Experience in Sakhalin (Russia, see below) indicates that starting an impact assessment later or not involving project engineers and therefore not integrating it within the overall project design, will reduce its effectiveness and could result in higher project costs due to the need to make changes at a later stage in the project.

Sakhalin energy

'During detailed pipeline route surveys begun in 2003, we discovered that the noise impact on the whales' feeding area during construction could be greater than originally anticipated. In April 2004, we deferred laying the off-shore pipeline to allow further studies to take place. As a result, we will miss two construction seasons.' Source: Shell report 2004.

It is important to keep abreast of the local community perceptions in order to avoid surprises, as demonstrated in the example of Pernis (The Netherlands). Stakeholders change, their expectations change, operational impacts change so continuous identification and engagement and involvement of the operational department is a must.

Pernis residential advisory board

Martinus de Groot (Schiedam): 'Companies should make more effort to inform local residents about what is going on, and do their best to reduce smells and nuisance as much as possible.' In Shell Pernis Residential Advisory Board local councilors, government services, local people and businesses regularly met to discuss how to improve the quality of the surroundings in the Rijnmond area. The emphasis in these meetings is on nuisance, and on environmental and safety aspects. Source: http://www.shell.com/static/nl-nl/downloads/leidraad-burenraad.pdf

Finally, the quality of implementation is more important than the number of plans written. SP reviews are focussed on improving the system, more so than on checking results. The experience is that SP reviews lead to competence development, both for trainees included in the review team, as well as for management and others involved.

3.4   Dos and don'ts

From the above examples some dos and don'ts can be derived:

Dos:

- Close cooperation between the operations department and the stakeholder engagement and social investment department to manage operational impacts;
- Use social investment budgets strategically;
- Integrate CSR early in the lifecycle of a project and continue throughout;
- Remind that stakeholder identification and engagement is a continuous process;
- Ensure all appropriate people in the organisation have the right CSR skills and not only the CSR experts;
- Ensure to have a good audit/review system in order to improve the quality of CSR.

Don'ts:

- Assume that processes and procedures are sufficient to manage CSR. Employees need to understand why managing CSR is important to the business and commit to it.

3.5   Wrapping up

CSR should be managed as any other business activity and its management model elements should therefore be easily integrated into existing structures with stakeholder engagement at the core. The key elements of the CSR management model are based on leadership commitment (identity), continuous stakeholder engagement (transactivity), a policy, organisational structure, impact assessment, planning and implementation (system) with monitoring, corrective action, audits and management reviews (accountability).

Experience within Shell shows that it is important that people from various departments are involved in managing CSR and that they have the rights skills to do so effectively. This management model has proved its value, and when applied to other industry sectors, it can be developed further.

References

Fossgard-Moser, T. (2004). *Social Performance, key lessons from recent experiences within Shell.* http://www.shell.com/static/royalen/downloads/society_environment/SPinShell_0304%20_ss.pdf

Parker, C. (2004). *The Open Corporation, – effective self regulation and democracy,* Cambridge: University Press.

Wood, D.J. (1991). Corporate Social Performance Revisited. *Academy of Management Review* (16) pp. 691-718

Websites

Shell General Business Principles: www.shell.com/sgbp

Shell standards: www.shell.com/standards

Shell Social Performance: www.shell.com/social

Social Performance: key lessons from recent experiences within Shell: www.shell.com/interactingwithcommunities (refer to Shell's approach, bottom of page)

Shell report 2004 www.shell.com/shellreport

4 RainbowScore®: A Strategic Approach for Multi-dimensional Value

Elisa Golin and Giampietro Parolin

Key words: Multi-dimensional value, balanced scorecard, business strategy, Economy of Communion (EoC), accounting.

4.1 Introduction

RainbowScore is a management tool based on a balanced scorecard approach. Like conventional balanced scorecard approaches, RainbowScore goes beyond the financial dimension, taking into account other strategic aspects of the company and measuring the outcome of each. RainbowScore however goes one step farther. It assigns a value to each aspect which is not solely dependent on the effect on financial performance – financial performance being regarded as only a part of overall performance. It highlights and defines all forms of wealth produced, especially those supported by ethical motives or ideals. The company and its basic dimensions are viewed as a rainbow, i.e. a unique and rich phenomenon. Through the seven colour frame we describe seven business and people aspects and present an explicit value creation structure – both stock and flow – which can inspire effective strategies, managerial methodologies, accounting and reporting methods. Corporate social responsibility is thus embedded in the business model.

Economic dimension – Red

The economic and financial dimension is the first business aspect we consider: This indicates a company's health and is the combined product of the commitment, professional competence and skills of the entrepreneur and employees. We can include a financial analysis but we must also look at other processes and information involved in value creation.

Basic stakeholders are seen as:

- Internal stakeholders, employees together with their families who benefit from the financial, professional and human conditions of work;
- Shareholders, whose risk becomes a source of profit;

- Public administration, the first actor – through taxation – distributing financial resources locally and globally;
- Civil society, whenever business profits are used to support social or cultural initiatives.

Planning and accounting for healthy company growth requires us to consider different aspects beyond just profits and profitability:

- New job opportunities, considering quality and amount, salaries and benefits;
- The solidarity dimension inside and outside the company.

Relational capital – Orange

The second aspect is relational capital seen as the combination of all real and potential external relationships of the company. Here we highlight a basic dimension for the company – the customer and supplier network. Total Quality Management and Stakeholder Theory have already focused their attention, embedded in management practices, on various customer interests, indicating different ways of identifying and answering specific needs.

Relational capital can be considered in three ways:

- Direct relational capital, basically needed in trade exchanges, for instance when participating in fairs;
- Indirect relational capital, i.e. all the sets of relations which help develop the company reputation, e.g. public solidarity actions;
- Relational goods, referring to the contents of human relationships, independent from any immediate financial benefit, i.e. as in friendship between colleagues.

In this way, a company's relational capital helps identify all external stakeholders linked to:

- Market development, via client satisfaction;
- Production, with suppliers and business partners;
- The local community and civil society, where the company operates;
- The social and intercultural dimension.

Analysing the quality of external relations and the achievable reciprocity amongst the subjects makes it possible to achieve two objectives concurrently: Firstly, the identification of specific factors determining customer satisfaction, by developing a deeper understanding of customer choice patterns; and secondly, the establishment of a productive business network with suppliers, government and members of the civil society.

Corporate culture – Yellow

Corporate culture is the third aspect and refers to the defined set of principles which guide company activity and are followed by all people in the company. This aspect is generally taken for granted and often considered at an implicit level. Nevertheless, corporate culture is a milestone for spontaneously or intentionally building, motivating and supporting, what is called the corporate style.

Describing corporate culture is the first step towards rediscovering the original reasons behind the formation of the company and, by involving people, working at the company, in this process, arouses enthusiasm in the search for practical ways to align stated values with company life.

Managers know that value alignment and trust increase both efficiency and effectiveness, whilst controls and sanctions can fail and are costly. This is why it is worth evaluating ethical effectiveness by analysing whether managerial behaviour, strategic choices, internal and external relations are consistent with the business mission ethical commitments.

Key issues include the:

- Definition of distinctive strategic and operative elements of corporate culture;
- Actions taken for sharing these principles and training people involved in company life;
- Attention to substantial transparency and legality.

Social and environmental quality – Green

The fourth dimension represents elements referring to the social and environmental quality. It examines what contributes to well-being in the company and in some ways represents both welfare and a well-being health index. A challenge facing management lies in creating more responsible and less stressful workplaces. Empowerment and engagement can help generate organisational trust which results in real well-being in the company.

Moreover social quality is strictly connected to environmental quality: both need to be planned and accounted for to maintain deliberateness and continuity. In this way company initiatives can be models for the civil society.

Focal points are:

- Protection of psychological and physical wealth inside the company;
- Work climate analysis, indicating the quality of staff relations at the company;
- Environmental impact;
- Company and product quality certification;
- Production of social capital.

Human capital and working community – Blue

The fifth dimension considers human capital and the working community in all organisational forms and expressions, the ultimate aim being to harmonise them. The organisational setting through which the company outlines its manufacturing and working teams is not complete by itself but is already a clear expression of the value given to the people working within it. In this way the organisation has a strong influence on the company's development, not only regarding process efficiency but also process contents.

Moreover, the organisational style cannot be separated from the relational style and the corporate cultural identity, but expresses them in daily management: The organisational role might assume the functional role by allocating everyone to the right place so that everyone is at ease and can give the best of his professional and human competences and skills.

Dimensions of this aspect generating added value inside and outside the company are:

- Infrastructure and organisational processes;
- Working community, composition and the way it grows;
- Work places, context setting and facilities;
- Corporate image.

Intellectual capital: Education, training and innovation – Indigo

The sixth aspect refers to intellectual capital, training and the innovation processes to develop, improve and continuously upgrade this basic asset.

Intellectual capital is linked to talent exploitation and in the organisation evolves from the supply and demand of various stimulations oriented towards the development of the company which come from both external and internal sources. Frequently, the scenarios that managers deal with are those of innovation and know-how growth. It's a context exposed to risks of individualism and intellectual capital concentration on one or few people which can increase competitiveness and worsen the working climate.

Knowledge processes are active processes taking place in specific social situations. They totally engage the people involved. Such processes help increase intellectual capital and include:

- Every knowledge sharing experience, where sharing acts bring about the development of what is shared;
- All networking setups (i.e open space work layouts can help);
- Spontaneous and structured training activities.

Communication – Violet

Finally, the last dimension is a cross key to many of the topics discussed above: Corporate internal and external communication. The meaning of communication might sometimes seem to overlap with that of information so that one might be indistinguishable from the other. Nevertheless, etymologically, communication is more than just an exchange of information; when applied in its broadest sense it helps the information to become operational, eventually resulting in new behaviour.

Moreover, effectiveness in communication is due to the obvious possibility of speaking the same language and being in harmony with the addressee's aims and values. This demands a similar, shared experience to create the 'we' feeling. This might require adapting the language to that of the stakeholders involved. A result is seen in active feedback and general participation. Communication and information quality can be evaluated by considering:

- Internal dialogue forms and frequency;
- Partners and employees participation in the company's life;
- Outside communication activities.

Conclusion

Real and effective strategy becomes operational whenever it can be both a guide and a process of analysis. It can be independent of production and market constraints and of inner and external variables (though considering them). The same happens when applying this 'coloured' key: RainbowScore supports innovating and planning steps, making available figures to verify and check, tracing a path to achieving strategy.

When a company decides to run RainbowScore it needs to pursue this process:

- Divide business strategy into the 'seven aspect framework';
- Define objectives for each colour and stakeholder and choose those to be achieved or prioritised;
- Verify consistence of objectives related to each colour or stakeholder and among colours or stakeholders in order to enhance synergies and balance potential conflicts;
- Choose actions to achieve objectives and guarantee periodic monitoring.

From this perspective the seven colours reporting system, which is a natural implementation of RainbowScore, helps explain the reasons for the company's success and suggests actions to improve it. Meanwhile the inner connection among various aspects makes manufacturing processes and relational dynamics comprehensible.

Giving each aspect a value in itself permits us to consider every single aspect as a stepping stone to others. In the same way that the seven colours of the rainbow come from the same light, inside the company all choices, events and problems are integrated and inter-dependent with each other.

4.2   The essence: The figure

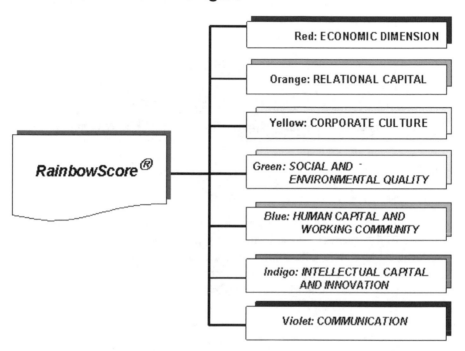

Figure 4.1. RainbowScore® Strategy and accounting for multi-dimensional value

4.3   Experience with the model

RainbowScore has been developed based on the experience of companies belonging to the Economy of Communion (EoC) project. Since 1991, when it was started in Brazil to answer to the needs of the poor, EoC has spread worldwide and currently almost 800 companies of various sizes are involved in the process. The company owners participating in the project voluntarily share their profits in accordance with the project's three objectives of equal importance:

- Helping people in need – creating new jobs and intervening to meet their immediate needs;
- Spreading the 'Culture of Giving';
- Helping their companies to grow – so that the companies remain both efficient and open to giving.

The identity and behaviour of the EoC companies are analysed according to the seven colour scheme outlined above. RainbowScore systemises the EoC company culture and translates it into an analysis and managerial tool useful to any company. As a result new organisational forms, training activities and employee involvement activities develop.

> Company information:
> Tessitura Grandi e Rubinelli
> Cameri (NO) – Italy
> Sector: entirely 'Made in Italy' high quality shirt fabrics manufacturing

Main Rainbow aspects

Orange – client satisfaction

The company operates and finds its sense of purpose and satisfaction by sharing values and objectives and enjoying a reciprocal relationship with clients at every level. All exclusive collections are created reflecting this way of working together. Often this stance helps people within the company to understand potential customer needs making it easier to find winning solutions.

Blue – organisation structure

Since the adoption of RainbowScore in 2002, all decision-making processes within the company adhere to the group system, both practically and structurally. The result is that all decisions are shared and responsibly implemented by two working teams – a supervisory board made up of four people and the management staff, 8 people – avoiding the need for the general manager to make all the decisions alone.

Yellow – values statement

'People are the most important asset of the company, and work is effectively based on human sharing: From this point of view, being a company means taking care of staff and factory workers, of suppliers and clients, all of whom contribute to the product's success.' These represent the core experience of both managers and staff, who together elaborated a value card describing their business style, ideas and values, discussing it with their supervisory board. As a first step this card was presented and distributed personally to all employees. Subsequently all employees were involved in training groups to share ideas, ways of life and concrete proposals to ensure that the values decided were implemented and followed.

Benefits of the Rainbow approach

Effectiveness and the feeling of belonging increased concurrently in the managers and employees involved. Both clients and suppliers appreciated the contents and ideas of the Value statement, and their relationship grew in trust and transparency.

4.4   Some dos and don'ts

RainbowScore is a way of looking at companies which gives maximum freedom in devising strategy, accounting and reporting systems. It entails analysing the seven aspects, mapping actual business strategy and value creation using indicators for measurement. Some aspects will be easier to understand than others during the value creation, but the real added value is in discovering the missing or deliberately developed aspects, which help to devise the optimal strategy. At the same time strategy and value creation must be linked with the main stakeholders of the company by means of a stakeholder/aspect matrix.

The following step should be to define the priority aspects to be developed and to create a plan of action with dates. Obviously this means defining and checking annual targets and at the same time introducing indicators and a reporting system. Indicators should be kept simple and fully integrated into the budget system. It is an exciting approach that requires organisational learning and flexibility.

4.5   Concluding remarks

Naturally the commitment of the owners and top management are a basic requirement for the successful implementation of a new strategy. One cannot expect every aspect to be equally successful at the same time, but it is worth focusing on a few 'super-drivers' that can produce value on many fronts (i.e. employee satisfaction). Initially it might seem that RainbowScore complicates company life. This might be true, but ultimately the RainbowScore will create greater awareness and effectiveness, thus resulting in tremendous benefits for the company.

References

Ferrucci, A. (ed.) (2001). *Per una globalizzazione solidale – verso un mondo unito* / For a global agreement towards a united world. Città Nuova.

Gold, L. (2004). *The sharing economy*. Ashgate Economic Geography Series.

Golin, E. and G. Parolin (2003). *Per un'impresa a più dimensioni. Strategia e bilancio secondo l'approccio RainbowScore®*. Città Nuova.

Gui, B. and R. Sugden (eds.) (2005). *Economics And Social Interaction: Accounting For Interpersonal Relations*. Cambridge: Cambridge University Press.

Kaplan, R.S. and D.P. Norton (1996). *The Balanced Scorecard*, Boston: Harvard Business School Press.

Website

www.edc-online.org

5 COMPASS to Sustainability

Michael Kuhndt and Justus von Geibler

Key words: Stakeholder analysis, stakeholder dialogue, communication.

5.1 Introduction to the model

Nowadays, business is facing new demands brought on by globalisation, new information technologies, the idea of services, and a sustainable economy. In order to ensure a high level of competitiveness, more and more companies are searching for ways to:

- Pro-actively involve and satisfy stakeholder demands in daily business;
- Efficiently manage sustainability performance;
- Increase a company's / sector's transparency and accountability.

The sustainability COMPASS (COMPAnies' and Sectors' path to Sustainability) is a management tool designed to assist companies and sectors to meet these challenges (Kuhndt and Liedtke, 1999). Based on active stakeholder involvement, COMPASS helps a company/sector to understand its main sustainability issues and to develop a sustainability indicator set in order to measure and report on progress made towards sustainable business development. The main objectives of COMPASS are to:

- Help companies/sectors to translate the broad concept of sustainability into specific and measurable targets and indicators useful in day-to-day business decisions;
- Support companies and sectors in sustainability performance management;
- Increase transparency and accountability of companies and sectors through sustainability reporting;
- Pro-actively involve internal and external stakeholders in order to make better consensus-based decisions which increase credibility and facilitate action;
- Enable decision-makers to optimise processes, products and services throughout the entire value chain considering economic, ecological and social aspects.

The COMPASS methodology is based on a Plan-Do-Check-Act management cycle. It combines the following five elements: the four analytical and action orienttated elements which are COMPASSprofile, COMPASSvision, COMPASSanalysis and COMPASSmanagement, and a dialogue oriented element, COMPASSreport.

COMPASSprofile aims at describing the state of knowledge about economic, social and environmental performance issues within the organisation/sector and the expectations of different stakeholders facing the organisation/sector. The combination of available knowledge, the alignment of different levels of knowledge, the qualification and motivation of employees from different hierarchy levels, phrasing of visions, guidance and concrete targets is the aim of COMPASSvision. The company creates a picture of the future that it has to work towards. Examples are: high customer satisfaction, high productivity of resources and high health protection. Furthermore, relevant units of measurement are selected such as, for example, assessment of clients and companies or resource productivity, based upon which progress as well as stagnation can be traced.

COMPASSanalysis comprises the actual measurement of performance and thereby identifies particularly critical and important technical and organisational improvement areas. COMPASSmanagement finally ensures the translation of the target set and indicators selected into decision-making processes by providing suitable management instruments. In COMPASSreport a communication plan is prepared that helps to report (according to international standards and guidelines, like those provided by the International Organisation for Standardisation (ISO) and the Global Reporting Initiative (GRI)) to an internal or external audience on performance improvements and achievements.

5.2   The essence

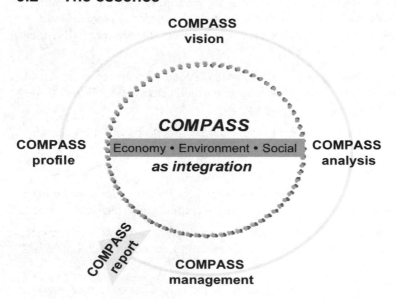

Figure 5.1. Elements of COMPASS

5.3   Experience with the model

In principle, the COMPASS methodology is suitable for any company or sector, regardless of size or sector. After successfully testing and fine-tuning COMPASS in about 40 companies covering different branches (manufacturing, food and service sector) the methodology has been adapted to the specific needs of a selected business sector. Within a four-year project the European Aluminium Industry together with the Wuppertal Institute and triple innova, developed a stakeholder based sectoral sustainability indicator set following the COMPASS methodology that finally resulted in the publication of a first sectoral sustainability report in 2004. The tailor-made COMPASS for the European Aluminium Industry comprised a systematic approach consisting of three core tools of COMPASSprofile:

- A sustainability agendas review;
- A sectoral focus area analysis;
- A consideration of stakeholder expectations.

The research based review of current sustainability agendas and trends evolving at different levels (governmental, NGO, business, multi-stakeholder etc.) provided an overview of the prevailing topics in the international sustainability debate. The focus area analysis helped to identify key sector-specific issues. The results from the agenda review and the focus area analysis served as essential input for the initiation of a wide stakeholder involvement in dialogue.

Further on, in order to gather first data on the opinions, expectations and demands from internal (aluminium companies and associations) and external stakeholders (labour organisations, academic/research institutes, government, related social and environmental NGO's) regarding sustainable development of the European Aluminium Industry, a stakeholder survey was conducted. The selected survey participants were asked to evaluate sustainability categories and aspects identified in the agenda review and pinpoint additional categories and aspects they considered important (see Figure 5.2).

The survey helped to identify stakeholder consensus and dissent areas concerning environmental, social and economic aspects along each life-cycle phase of aluminium production and consumption.

Based on the stakeholder survey, the area analysis and the agenda review, a first draft indicator set was developed. This indicator set was then put into a stakeholder discussion process to acquire feedback and to improve it. Two workshops with internal and external stakeholders were conducted. The first workshop was carried out targeting the stakeholders, who participated in the stakeholder survey and expressed their interest in an involvement in further

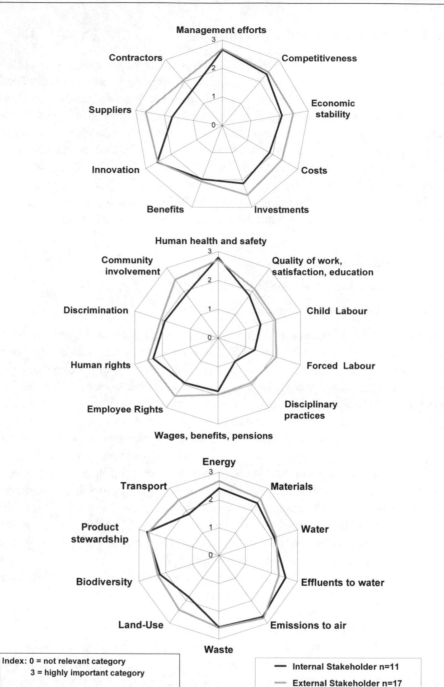

Figure 5.2. Survey results related to the question: 'Which type of information do internal and external stakeholders expect from the aluminium industry?'

activities. Besides the project partners, participants from different companies and institutions joined the workshop. Among the external stakeholders, were participants representing research, consultancies, training and development agencies, sustainable and ethical investment organisations, environmental NGOs and intergovernmental organisations. The second stakeholder workshop aimed at gathering previously uncovered issues and including underrepresented stakeholder groups, for example, civil society, suppliers, academics (in the field of sustainable consumption), governmental representatives (regarding Integrated Product Policy (IPP)), trade unions and development-aid agencies.

The workshops provided the opportunity to take up a number of additional stakeholder demands for further content improvement and the use of the indicator set. With respect to the content of the indicator set, the stakeholders expressed the need for broad but prioritised coverage of the indicator set. In this context, the importance of specific sustainability aspects has been mentioned, such as human health and safety, research and development, implementation of best available technology, air emissions, pot line management, sustainability standards in entire supply chain, impacts of mining, ecologically sensitive 'No Go Areas', energy demand, and sources and recycling. Furthermore, the stakeholders also demanded a reduced number of indicators.

Also the importance of governance within the sector has been highlighted. Related specific aspects are, for example, the long-term sustainability vision of the sector, the provision of concrete targets per indicator, and the regular updating of indicators. Most of these issues in the indicator set have been elaborated during the course of the project. Regarding use-related issues, stakeholders expressed the areas for which the indicator set should be used once it is established. Both internal and external benchmarking are promising applications. A wide range of firms can use the indicator set for their external reporting, including the SMEs within the sector.

Throughout the project, the objective was to develop a sector-wide sustainability report at the European level. To provide aggregated figures in the report, the European Aluminium Industry Association (EAA) has started to collect detailed data from the production sites and from company level. For the collection of data, methodological sheets were used, which describe the single indicators more comprehensively. Hereby, the EAA used the initiative to reach out to more than 700 production plants. Consequently, in October 2004, an indicator set for external reporting was released by the European Aluminium Association, covering 34 indicators for the whole sector.

5.4   Some dos and don'ts

Understand stakeholder demands as a starting point for business action

The process of active stakeholder consultations and review of stakeholder initiatives has been valuable for the actors within the project to improve the awareness and understanding of sustainability within the sector and within member companies. With reference to increasing networking (campaigning) power of NGOs, the early involvement of stakeholders can promote the anticipation of future business risks and is hence a crucial starting point for today's management decisions. Integrating and addressing external stakeholder demands into corporate decision making will help to capture intangible value (e.g. strengthening image, acquiring new knowledge, improving satisfaction of employees) and increase the companies' shareholder value.

Consider supply chain management and product stewardship

For improved corporate sustainability performance and improved reputation, sector organisations and larger companies can engage actors along the product chain. Within the supply chain the challenge remains to engage SMEs in reporting activities, as they face a number of barriers for improved external communication. Examples of those barriers are limited financial and human resources or external demand for information. In that respect, the data collection process for the sectoral sustainability report might be a way to engage and help more SMEs to work on sustainability issues. Regarding product stewardship, multiple approaches can be taken by companies to address sustainable consumption, namely: Responsible marketing guidelines, customer advice, product pricing, functional product design, specific services for minorities and consumer protection.

Ensure a consistent data gathering process for external reporting

A precondition for the aggregation of the indicators on the sectoral level was the consistency in the data-gathering methodology. Methodological sheets can be used, to provide a uniform and consistent database as bottom line for aggregation and further application of the indicator set. The sheet covered aspects like indicator description, linkages to sustainable development and other indicators, methodological description, assessment of data or agencies involved in the development of the indicator, and references.

Don't stop walking towards sustainability

Sustainable development relates to an unlimited time horizon and is an ongoing dynamic process. The dynamic character of sustainability has been considered in project through the sequence of workshops, which allowed learning processes over time, and the indicator set which includes flexible timeframes for phased implementation. The flexible implementation considers differences of the companies within the sectors, such as size, organisational capabilities or position in the supply chain. The indicators need to be revised from time to time to adapt the indicators to changing conditions, such as stakeholder demands, significant modifications in the underlying sector, e.g. technological innovation, or progress made in research on sustainability indicators. Over time, single aspects might be added if stakeholders demand information on additional issues. Some (smaller) companies, might start with a limited number of indicators and increase the number of issues covered over time.

5.5   Wrapping up

The COMPASS methodology offers a methodological framework for operationalising the normative concept of sustainability at the micro-level. The presented approach aimed at methodological innovation through a sectoral approach towards sustainable industry development. The outcomes can be used at the corporate level as follows:

Internal Benchmarking: Companies can use the information from the companies' performance aggregated at a sectoral level as a base line for internal benchmarking processes. Based on the knowledge of their own performance it becomes apparent where the companies perform well and where there are opportunities for improvement.

Product and process innovation: Continuous monitoring can aid in recognition of opportunities for improvement both at product and process level.

Monitoring value creation: As partly intangible aspects, improvements in environmental and social aspects can affect the value drivers and lead to increased value of a company. The extent of this relationship may vary from one company to the other. In order to get a better understanding of the value creation process, companies can investigate what types of performance improvements are significant in affecting the value drivers. In this respect, companies would be identifying priority themes for value creation.

Concluding, sustainability reporting as well as the related processes of identifying the relevant indicators and data gathering can improve the ability of an industry sector to respond to increasing demand for transparency and accountability. In order to support the continuous use and development of the indicator set, a management structure and an interdisciplinary sustainability team that supports decision-making towards sustainability need to be set up on a sectoral and company level. Such a structure and team will also assist in developing sector-wide sustainability visions and targets. With these visions and targets, the sustainability indicator set can be built into a long-term framework.

References

Kuhndt, M. and C. Liedtke (1999). *Die COMPASS-Methodik, COMPAnies and Sectors path to Sustainability*. Wuppertal Papers Nr. 97, Wuppertal Institut.

Kuhndt, M., J. von Geibler and C. Liedtke (2002). *Towards a Sustainable Aluminium Industry: Stakeholder Expectations and Core Indicators. Final Report for the GDA* (Gesamtverband der Aluminiumindustrie) and the European Aluminium Industry. Wuppertal Institut.

Kuhndt, M, J. von Geibler and A. Eckermann (2004). *Towards a Sustainable Aluminium Industry: Stakeholder Consultations. Final report*. Wuppertal Institute for Climate, Environment and Energy and triple innova. Wuppertal.

Kuhndt, M, J. von Geibler and A. Eckermann (2004). *Reviewing the journey: Towards a Sustainable Aluminium Industry: Stakeholder Engagement and Core Indicators*. Wuppertal Institute for Climate, Environment and Energy and triple innova. Wuppertal.

Kuhndt, M., B. Tunçer, C.S. Andersen and C. Liedtke (2004). *Responsible Corporate Governance: An overview of trends, initiatives and state-of-the-art elements*. Wuppertal Paper.

Websites

http://www.sustainability-compass.net
http://www.wupperinst.org
http://www.triple-innova.com

6 sustManage™ – Integrating Corporate Sustainability*

Oliver Dudok van Heel and Will Muir

Key words: Sustainability management, KPI, efficiency, cultural change, software.

6.1 Introduction

Over the last 3-5 years, corporate sustainability has become an integral part of companies' strategy, with many new initiatives developed to help companies embrace this important agenda. In spite of this, one thing has become apparent: Existing models fail to integrate sustainability into everyday business operations as well as businesses and external stakeholders might hope. Most corporate sustainability initiatives get benefit from little input – or enthusiasm – from those middle managers whose role it is to implement commercial or operational strategies.

This has two main consequences:

1. Sustainability initiatives fail to deliver the direct and indirect business benefits that good sustainability management promises. This is a concern for the business involved;

2. Corporate sustainability initiatives have little positive impact on the social, environmental and economic concerns they are set up to address. This is a concern for all.

This implementation issue is one of the main challenges in delivering any corporate initiatives across large businesses. We have experienced this issue in the past in implementing some of our major environmental management programmes, especially with regards to energy efficiency. While the benefits of energy efficiency are clear – less energy use, lower emissions and lower costs – this did not automatically translate into broad-scale acceptance of energy efficiency projects within businesses. Analysing this paradox, the underlying reasons for this became clear: Operational managers are focused on delivering against their performance objectives, and do not have the time to devote to corporate initiatives that distract them from their performance objectives. Armed with this experience we devised a management system that would be embraced

---

* sustManage is © 2005 and TM of Enviros Consulting Ltd.

by operational managers because they helped them achieve their objectives, instead of being an unwanted intrusion upon them. This was based upon 3 separate but complementary pillars:

1. People;
2. Systems;
3. Opportunities.

Table 6.1. sustManage triple focus

Focus	Process
People Staff and management buy-in, motivation, awareness, training and development in line with operational objectives.	Create a shared vision to focus on sustainability performance Ensure management buy-in Identify, train and coach improvement teams Establish clear accountability
Systems Visibility of good and bad practice is critical – if you can't measure it you can't manage it.	Driven by web-based software Establish correct key performance indicators Determine internal accountability for KPI performance Enable quick and accurate reporting of sustainability
Opportunities Specific opportunities that can deliver rapid and tangible improvements are a key focus point of delivery	Assess current performance Identify low/no cost improvement opportunities Value other identified opportunities Project manage the implementation of opportunities

The strength of sustManage lies in its ability to deliver corporate sustainability performance while achieving real and lasting cost savings through energy and resource-efficiency initiatives. The importance of the financial savings brought by sustManage cannot be over-stated; it is these financial savings which align to the priority objectives of site management, to ensure their commitment to the process. In a nutshell, organisations get a fully functional sustainability management system with a substantial reduction in operating costs.

Site focus

sustManage has been designed to be delivered at individual sites as opposed to at the corporate level for the following reasons:

- Most company impacts are local;
- Implementation challenges are at the operational – site – level;
- Resource efficiencies are most likely to be found at the site level;
- The latter point is also why sustManage is most likely to succeed in organisations that have large natural resource costs, as that is where most savings are to be made.

6.2   The sustManage building blocks

The sustManage programme has a number of 'building blocks' which collectively form the basic structure of the Methodology.

The sustManage scoping study

The scoping study is an assessment carried out at the outset of the project to determine sustManage's ability to achieve its financial and sustainability objectives.

Strategic analysis

To ensure that sustManage has an appropriate corporate fit with an organisation and that it tackles the main issues affecting that organisation, a strategic analysis is carried out during the scoping study to evaluate the internal and external drivers of an organisation related to sustainability and assess the impact of these threats and opportunities on the organisation's competitiveness.

Performance, risks and opportunities assessment

Building upon the Strategic Analysis, the sustManage scoping study is an initial investigation of the site that will identify areas of potential risk, opportunity, inefficiencies and/or savings through visual inspection of existing plant and equipment, interviews with key staff, a comparative assessment of processes and procedures against industry 'best practice', and an evaluation of the organisations exposure to current and impending sustainability issues and legislative standards.

Furthermore, the scoping study presents the business case on which the adoption of a sustManage programme hinges. It will quantify the financial case for the adoption of sustManage – a key component to achieving buy-in of operational managers – as well as outline the less tangible sustainability benefits the programme can help deliver.

Once the scoping study has been completed, the actual implementation can begin. This will follow the 3 pillars of sustManage – People, Systems & Opportunities – complemented by sound Programme Management.

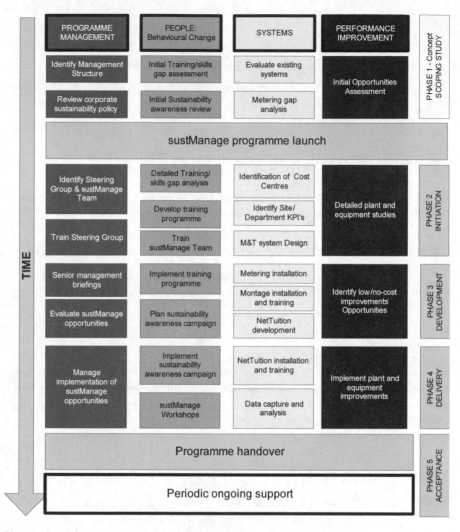

Figure 6.1. The sustManage building blocks.

A – programme management

To ensure that all the impact of all programme components is maximised, the implementation of sustManage depends upon a rigorous implementation process, with very clear steps and deliverables for each step. The total methodology document is over 100 pages long, with detailed explanations of all the process components. This level of detail is key to the programme's successful delivery.

Governance structure

The first step in the implementation process is to put a Steering Group together. The Steering Group will have overall responsibility for the programme, setting programme objectives in line with corporate initiatives, assisting with pro-gramme communications, developing an accountability strategy, monitoring progress in line with objectives, and assisting with the removal of barriers that have a negative impact on performance. At an operational level, a sustManage Team is created, comprised of a cross-section of departments, who have a more direct responsibility for the day-to-day management of the programme. The focal point of any sustManage programme is the sustManage Champion. This will be a nominated member of the sustManage Team with overall respon-sibility for internally driving the programme forward.

B – People

The people component of the programme focuses on making sustManage rele-vant to operational staff by making it clear how sustManage contributes to helping them achieve their objectives. This understanding is at the core of sustManage's success. Once operational managers see sustManage as facilitating their work, the crucial buy-in is achieved.

Programme communication, training and awareness

Good communication is a powerful tool for motivating people. The sustMan-age programme will deliver regular training, development and general aware-ness sessions to the staff at the site, using varying methods adapted to the ob-jective, audience, required impact and timescale. The programme will also de-liver more formalised training and development to the sustManage Team and where appropriate the Steering Group. Educational workshops will focus on building awareness within the sustManage Team and provide educational ma-terial on key aspects to improve the environmental, economic and social as-pects of the organisation.

Communication and Training Needs Analysis & Development Programme

The sustManage programme is geared towards identifying communication and training needs and areas of best practice that need to be shared within the group. This will ensure that all those involved in sustManage have a common understanding of its role and importance, and are equipped with the skills nec-essary to deliver them.

Accountability

Accountability of key personnel is essential if resource efficiency is to be achieved and improvements made towards achieving sustainability. Key personnel such as those responsible for sustainability aspects must be held accountable for performance and project delivery. The systems component will deliver measurable targets for the performance of individuals at all levels of the site. These targets are set in conjunction with the individuals affected and significant effort is made to ensure that these are achievable from the outset.

Encourage involvement of all

The programme is keen to provide a voice to all employees and encourage individual contribution and ownership of the programme within the site. The programme will develop staff awareness campaigns and implement systems and policies that enable suggestions for performance improvement to be introduced and policies such as rewards and recognition schemes to identify positive contributions.

C – Systems

The role of the systems component of a sustManage programme is to put the appropriate information into the hands of all the participants in sustManage (potentially including external stakeholders). The systems component thus consists of creating the appropriate information infrastructure:

- Establishing the appropriate indicators and KPIs to report;
- Establishing the source of data to inform those indicators and KPIs;
- Establishing the systems to capture the source data at the appropriate frequency;
- Modelling the KPIs in software and establishing core performance metrics by:
  - Establishing the improvement goals (targets), often as a result of a data analysis process;
  - Identifying the appropriate outputs (reports, data export, display boards) and systematising this reporting.

Indicators and targets

The success of any management system relies on the selection and use of quality indicators. Where appropriate, we will utilise the KPI's that the organisation has already developed. If no indicators are in place, or the indicators prove inadequate for the objectives of sustManage, we will use the Indicator Database we developed in preparing the methodology to select the most appropriate KPIs. It is important that these KPIs are held at departmental level and accountability for performance is shared.

The role of software

Software is the glue that holds sustManage together. sustManage was developed at the outset around Montage, Enviros' Monitoring and Targeting (M&T) software, and good M&T software is a necessary component of the programme, as it allows for the continuous monitoring of performance and the setting of targets. Applications of M&T software include the ability to discern underlying performance, which allows targets to be set, poor performance to be eliminated and good practice repeated. For instance, the M&T software could tell us that:

- Site A has a larger energy bill per unit production than site B;
- Employee satisfaction is lower this month than last;
- There are more injuries in product line X than in product line Y.

While all the above points may have very valid explanations, without the clear definition of indicators and the application of the software, the differences would not have been apparent. Once these are apparent, an organisation can explore the reasons behind them and develop corrective action, where appropriate.

This information is made available to all managers who have responsibility, either directly or indirectly, for the indicator in question. Each user of the system will have a homepage developed that will summarise the performance for those indicators for which he or she is responsible. This will allow them to monitor key performance each time they log on to the corporate network. Where appropriate, an email can be triggered to warn managers if performance falls outside a pre-arranged range. These systems underpin the whole sustManage programme and will provide the platform upon which to drive sustainability through availability of quantitative and qualitative data.

D – Performance improvement and specific projects

One of the main objectives of any sustainability programme is to introduce new methods of working that have a positive impact on the environmental, economic and social performance of an organisation. Having introduced the foundations for achieving sustainability through cultural change and improved management information, the emphasis now focuses on project identification and delivery.

Review existing opportunities

All performance improvement opportunities identified in the initial scoping study will be captured in a software tool, which we call the Opportunities Manager. Where feasible, the extent of the performance improvement resulting from implementing the opportunity project will be quantified using a regression analysis to calculate the impact the project will have on actual performance and allow for targeting through project implementation to monitor overall performance.

Evaluate and select sustManage opportunities

Together the team will decide acceptable criteria to assist in prioritising the projects using the matrix structure below. Those projects with little or no capital investment tend to take priority over the medium to large capital investment projects. Those projects that require a medium/large capital investment will be further analysed and a business case produced to assist with the project justification and company's financial planning.

Project sign-off

At the end of the programme, a review of the programme will be carried out by the Steering Group, sustManage Team and other key players. The software data will indicate the programme's success and plans made to future-proof the programme.

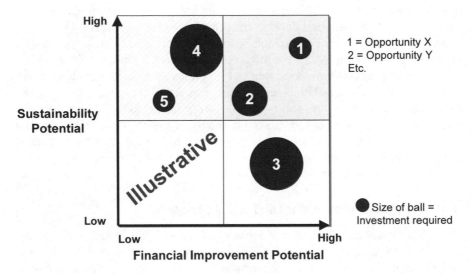

Figure 6.2. sustManage opportunity matrix

6.3   Practical applications of sustManage

At the time of writing we are in the process of implementing the first sustManage project across a number of sites of a large multinational brewery. As mentioned in the introduction, we have ample experience in using this methodology to help companies deliver resource efficiency improvements in a similar process called enmanage. We have implemented this system in a number of organisations over the years, fine-tuning the methodology to the process it has become today.

BP

Enviros has been working with BP, providing systems and people to support BP's energy efficiency programme. Our work has taken place at many of BP's largest refineries and chemicals complexes, in Europe and North America. 'The key to enmanage is that it starts at the operating level of a company and drives local value creation' says Kevin Ball, Director for Energy Efficiency at BP. 'It then rolls that information up to provide insight to the corporation'.

The enmanage approach is powerful, because it allows companies to create a holistic picture of interrelated factors once managed separately. 'We worked together with Enviros to take our energy consumption, our energy spending, and put it together with plant processes and our greenhouse gas impact to see a complete picture'. BP's Coryton site in the UK, a pilot for the enmanage team, lowered its CO_2 emissions by 40,000 tonnes at no cost through increased monitoring and operational focus.

Unilever Canada

Unilever Canada was an enmanage project that focused on a culture change process led by the team on site, which delivered a wide range of savings through individuals recognising areas for improvement. They have achieved over £1m ($3m CAN) pa of savings with an average payback of 6 months – representing a considerable proportion of the sites utilities:

- Natural Gas use is down 39%;

- Electricity use is down 24%;

- Steam use is down 50%;

- Air use is down 27%;

- Water use is down 52%;

- Over 100 individuals have contributed to the programme and are called 'Watt Watchers'.

6.4   Dos and don'ts

The nature of the sustManage programme implies some ground rules which need to be followed:

Table 6.2. Some dos and don'ts

Dos	Don'ts
• Plan, plan and plan again.	• Don't dive straight into 'doing' without getting full support & engagement from senior team.
• Ensure you have management commitment to the process at every level. If management are not engaged, then staff will not follow. Don't progress with the project until this is in place.	• Don't focus on technical fixes, information systems, etc. at the expense of people engagement.
• Ensure everyone in a 'chain of command' has a target – i.e. don't break the link of responsibility between top person and the shop floor.	• Don't throw money at capital projects if you want sustainable improvement – even the most efficient piece of kit can be badly operated.
• Ensure ownership lies with the operational staff.	• Don't put into place monitoring without targeting and ownership of the target.
• Publicise the effort effectively using every available communications medium – time & time again.	• Don't be afraid to ask stupid questions – the best ideas come from challenging the basics.
• Celebrate success & give public recognition for individual contribution.	• Don't use the wrong unit of measure: if people are motivated by money then talk in those terms, if people are motivated by reducing pollution then talk in those terms.
• Measure your performance regularly but ensure that you set targets that are achievable.	
• Recognise that change can be difficult – persevere in the face of challenges.	• Don't do it alone, it is always a team effort.

6.5 Wrapping up

The reason for the methodology's success lies in its ability to combine a 'hard' systems approach with a 'soft' people approach, thus providing operational managers with both a carrot and a stick that will help them deliver sustainability. The very considerable financial returns of a sustManage programme ensure site buy-in and the approval of hard-nosed financial personnel for whom the sustainability agenda is not necessarily a priority. Finally, an emphasis on measurable performance changes and creation of a culture of continuous improvements creates a process that is, in itself, genuinely sustainable.

Websites

www.enviros.com/sustManage
www.enviros.com/montage

7 The Molecule Model

Henk Folkerts and René Weijers

Key words: Sustainable, economy, business, molecule, leadership.

7.1   Introduction

The Molecule Model is designed to help firms integrate the concept of sustainable development into their strategies and day-to-day operations. The model (see Figure 7.1) reflects the fundamental shift currently taking place in the debate on sustainability and forms the basis for the development of a sustainable company.

The model is based on the following principles. Firstly, an acceptance of the strategic role played by corporate social responsibility (CSR). The model combines pointers for a long-term strategy with specific indicators paving the way towards a concrete plan of action. It starts with the business owner's conviction that sustainability forms the core and anchor point in a renewed competitive, distinctive and defensible position. In the current business environment, we believe that CSR is not just a necessity. It is also a personal choice and an inspiring opportunity.

Secondly, CSR is part of a long-term process of societal and corporate development. There have been three distinct waves of economic development to date: the agricultural economy (during the period up to 1660), the industrial economy (1660-1960) and the information economy (1960 to the present). A fourth wave is now emerging: the sustainable economy, riding on a sense of urgency coupled with new needs, demands and ambitions. This trend is fostered by the availability of new, clean technology together with sources of alternative, sustainable energy. There has been a shift in the past three decades away from 'end-of-pipe' solutions based on limited investments towards systems and cyclical solutions based on inter-company and community investments. In short, we are entering a period characterised by an emphasis on renewal rather than repair.

7.2   The essence

The model consists of seven related key words that can be developed step by step. It is symbolised by a molecule consisting of seven atoms. The model gives companies a better understanding of sustainability, and helps them to define their position and develop their strategy. In particular, it challenges firms to explore new business propositions.

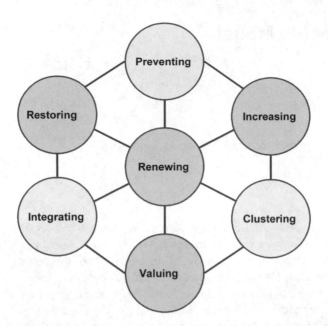

Figure 7.1. The Molecule Model: A strategic model for developing a sustainable company (Folkerts and Weijers, 2004)

The model consists of the following 'atoms':

Restoring

The first atom is all about restoring the damage caused to natural, social and economic capital and resources. Such damage is caused because the wrong choices were made in the past. Many current activities, such as reductions in carbon dioxide emissions, still focus on the need to reduce damage. Although this is a huge challenge in itself, restoration goes beyond that. More and more business activities are being conducted with the aim of restoring natural and social capital; these include the restoration of water quality, ecosystems, wetlands, etc. In the past, this was a cost-driven activity undertaken by governments and the public sector, but private firms are now gradually assuming responsibility for them and turning them into yield-driven activities. An example is Scandinavian paper manufacturers, who plant more trees than are strictly necessary for the purpose of paper production in order to reduce the amount of carbon dioxide emitted into the atmosphere.

Another trend is for firms and public-sector organisations to cooperate in performing restoration activities. For example, TNT and the United Nations formed a partnership in order to set up a distribution network for the UN's food aid programmes. Similarly, Unilever supplied the UN with consumer and marketing information for its aids prevention programmes.

So restoring the damage caused to natural and social capital gives firms more and new opportunities to develop new business activities and concepts. This is why restoration has a place in strategic corporate dialogues.

Preventing

The second atom guarantees that no damage will be caused in the future. The emphasis is on preventing damage in the first place rather than on reducing the amount of damage subsequently caused. This means that firms take account of sustainable energy sources, efficiency in resource use, emissions, re-use and waste when taking decisions on corporate strategy, technology, and product and process design. For example, a firm may decide to use sustainable energy resources (such as solar or wind energy) so that fossil energy resources are not exhausted and so that no carbon dioxide emissions are produced. Herman Daly, an economist formerly employed by the World Bank, has proposed the following rules in the domain of resource efficiency:

- The quantity of renewable resources used each year should not exceed the quantity produced by nature that year;
- The speed at which not-renewable resources are used should not exceed the speed at which substitutes or sustainable resources become available;
- The quantity of polluting resources discharged into the environment should not exceed the quantity which the same environment is able to process or render harmless.

Whilst the above rules are not easy to apply, they are becoming increasingly necessary in the light of the rapid pace of economic development and the demand for resources emanating from Asian countries such as India and China.

Increasing

Increasing, the third atom, means exploring activities that simultaneously consolidate and increase the social, ecological and economic capital. The focus is on identifying new business propositions and increasing the overall 'cake' with respect to the different forms of capital instead of just shifting between them. This may mean, for instance, making less profit but at the same time doing more for the natural environment and people. The challenge is to increase the aggregate yield in terms of people, planet and profit. This is illustrated by the Hypercar project, which seeks to develop a completely new type of car that is lighter and safer than current car designs and is fuelled by sustainable energy.

An investment in a new fuel, hydrogen, utilises an inexhaustible resource, appeals to new knowledge, skills, talents and technology and has an enormous potential profitability. Thomas Gladwin (2000) claims that a stable society lives from the 'income' generated by its primary supply of capital and should not fully deplete that supply. He distinguishes four types of capital:

- Ecological capital: replaceable, cyclic, biological resources, processes and functions;

- Material capital: irreplaceable or geological resources such as minerals and fossil fuels;

- Human capital: knowledge, skills, health, safety, security and motivation;

- Social capital: the civil society, social cohesion, trust, values, norms and justice.

The different types of capital should be complementary to each other and may not replace each other. They should stay intact separately, because each one's productive power is dependent on the others' availability. A sustainable society organises itself in such a way as to assure its supplies of ecological, material, human and social capital.

Integrating

Integrating, the fourth atom, supposes an ability to cope with different and partially conflicting political views on sustainable development, i.e. liberal, socialist and 'green' views. Paul Hawken et al. (1999) distinguishes three frequently encountered views on sustainable development:

- The 'blue' approach: espoused by supporters of a free market economy that is capable of solving all problems, including those relating to sustainable development;

- The 'red' approach: adopted by supporters of a socialist model. They reject capitalism and the resultant gap between rich and poor, and consider sustainable development to be part of a wider structural problem;

- The 'green' approach: the greens perceive the world in terms of ecosystems. They emphasise pollution, population growth and so forth. They sometimes appear to care less about people than about animals.

Hawken c.s. advocate a 'whiter' approach. Rather investing in the political debate on the merits of the respective views, Hawken and his supporters opt for synthesis, integration, coherence, respect and trust. They make use of all the positive elements supplied by the various colours. Successful sustainable companies focus on this integrated 'white' approach.

Renewing

The fifth atom represents the renewal of a firm's philosophy, the introduction of new business concepts and the relationship with the environment and stakeholders. It focuses on new business principles. It results in a new identity and a more proactive and open relationship with customers, employees, suppliers, shareholders and human-interest groups. A knowledge of living systems and natural principles leads to new insights, a new logic and other strategic choices. This new approach has the following fields of application:

Combining different technologies, leading to the development of completely new sustainable products and services. An example is the Hypercar project (already mentioned above), in which ICT, materials and fuel (i.e. hydrogen) technology are combined to produce a new sustainable car design.

From linear management to life cycle management. This means business concepts that accept a responsibility for producing, selling and recycling materials, including waste. For instance, a company called Interface takes back carpets after they have been used by its customers, recycles them and sells them again.

From selling to hiring. Hiring products and services is more sustainable than selling. Rifkin calls this a shift from a 'possession society' towards a 'use society'. Elektrolux, which hires out kitchen equipment instead of selling it, is an example of this.

Sustainable product development. This includes measures based on the avoidance of environmental damage, resource efficiency principles, extending product lifetimes, re-use and recycling, and the use of renewable energy resources.

All these principles have many of the following aspects in common. They offer advantages for both suppliers and customers, they improve a company's economic, social and environmental performance, they change market and competition ratios, they result in new knowledge and employment and, finally, they strengthen ecological and social capital.

Clustering

The sixth atom is clustering. This means intensive cooperation between firms: vertically in the supply chain between suppliers, producers and customers, and/or horizontally among firms supplying similar or complementary products or services.

This cooperation may take place either in a particular region or at a global level, within the same industry or among different industries. Clustering creates opportunities for combined sourcing, shared facilities, joint innovation, combined transport, matching supply and demand, using each other's residual products and overarching life-cycle management. For instance, glasshouse growers heat their glasshouses with the aid of residual heat or carbon dioxide from a neighbouring factory. Clustering can help to reduce waste, energy use and traffic congestion.

Valuing

The last atom is valuing, which means more than just money. Of course, profitability remains important in both the short and the long term, but it is not the only and predominant consideration. Profit is an important condition as well as the result of a sustainable and defensible strategy. It is an indicator of success that is visible in the viability of a firm's day-to-day operations and in its value.

The emphasis on value and money is intended to make sustainable business practices better balanced. Both short-term and long-term yields are important. This means exploiting current activities as well as exploring and developing new business propositions. That is the challenge for present and future profitability. It also implies an awareness of the value of other, immaterial yields such as people's commitment and loyalty, social respect and reputation and the conservation of the natural environment. In short, it means governance for a wide variety of yields.

7.3   Experiences

As a first experience, the model leads to an increasing awareness in a company of the strategic importance of CSR. It helps both managers and employees to understand sustainable development and gives them more fun as well as a sense of purpose in their work. In addition, a dialogue with suppliers, customers, local society and government broadens their horizons and increases their commitment to sustainable development.

Secondly, the Molecule Model forms a good starting point for developing or renewing a firm's strategy. By analysing the different atoms, a firm can make better and more complementary strategic decisions and develop a unique market position.

Thirdly, whilst working with the Molecule Model is inspiring, it can sometimes be frustrating too. We encountered the following obstacles. Firstly, a narrowly defined scope solely on economic and technological dominance prevents the discovery of new values and yields. Secondly, legislation can discourage sustainable activities and business propositions. Another obstacle is power structures, which can hamper the development of new sustainable activities. Finally, existing infrastructures, for instance for energy supply, require large financial investments and sometimes lead to divestments. As a result, the process of infrastructural innovation takes time.

The fourth and possibly most important experience is that sustainable firms are always led by managers with a sustainable mindset. A leader's influence is undeniably great. Sustainable managers have a strong external orientation, show respect for their employees, customers, shareholders and the environment, but are hard on anyone who hinders them in their quest for sustainable development. Sustainable managers are curious, open, good at building relationships and starting a dialogue. They are 'bridge builders', connecting people and cultures.

The atoms and the relationship between them are fundamental and make it possible to connect strategic decisions with operational activities.

7.4   Some dos and don'ts

Our Molecule Model is not a 'how to' model, but more a coherent set of key words that can be used by firms in various ways and circumstances to find their own path to sustainable business propositions. We are on the threshold of a sustainable economy. Simple 'how to' approaches deny the wide variety in and richness of sustainable development and hamper more than they encourage. Having said this, we have often encountered the following five aspects when working with customers:

- A description of the internal situation;
- Involvement of the firm's external stakeholders;
- A desire to integrate sustainability with corporate strategy;
- Carefully defined targets;
- Accountability to stakeholders and shareholders.

Using the model also means being alert to various pitfalls. It is important to try and avoid:

- Going too fast;
- Falling back on old methods and systems;
- Overdoing, for instance by neglecting customers or the importance of money;
- Waiting for other people to take the initiative;
- Developing 'grand designs' without consulting the people working on the shop floor.

7.5 Wrapping up

The Molecule Model for CSR represents a paradigm shift and forms a coherent approach to sustainable development. It provides a starting point for a firm to renew its strategy and redesign its operations, and hence to find and achieve new, distinctive business propositions.

References

Collins, J. (2001). *Good to great*, London: Random House Business Books.

Cramer, J. (1999). *Towards sustainable business, connecting environment and market*, Society and Enterprise Foundation (SMO).

Folkerts, H. and R. Weijers (2004). *De winst zit in de opbrengst, naar een duurzame economie*, Assen: Koninklijke van Gorcum.

Gladwin, T.N. (2000). *Strategie en de externe omgeving, een pleidooi voor duurzame ontwikkeling*, in: Mastering Strategy, Het Financieele Dagblad.

Hawken, P., A.B. Lovins and L.H. Lovins (1999). *Natural Capitalism; the next industrial revolution*, London: Earthscan.

Rischard, J.F. (2002). *High Noon – Twenty Global Problems, twenty years to solve them*. Basic Books, member of Perseus Books Group.

Websites

www.csreurope

www.rischard.net

Global Compact Performance Model

Ursula Wynhoven[1]

Key words: Principles, ethical framework, performance, implementation, tools.

8.1   Introduction to the model

This chapter is about the Global Compact Performance Model. The Performance Model is a kind of toolbox for responsible corporate citizenship. It proposes a map to help guide businesses through the continuing improvement process of implementing the Global Compact principles without distracting from their other business goals.

The Global Compact is the United Nations' voluntary corporate citizenship initiative in the areas of human rights, labour standards, the environment and anti-corruption. It revolves around a set of ten universal principles derived from instruments that enjoy international consensus: The Universal Declaration of Human Rights, the International Labour Organisation's Declaration on Fundamental Principles and Rights at Work, the Rio Declaration on Environment and Development, and the United Nations Convention Against Corruption. The initiative has two objectives: Making the Compact and its principles an integral part of business operations and activities everywhere, and encouraging and facilitating dialogue and partnerships among key stakeholders in support of the ten principles and broader UN goals, such as the Millennium Development Goals.

The United Nations Secretary-General launched the Global Compact at the World Economic Forum in 1999 and the initiative entered its operational phase in 2000. Companies initiate their involvement with a leadership commitment by their Chief Executive Officer expressing support for the principles and the intention to implement them within the company's own operations and activities. The rationale for this requirement is our experience that effective organisational change requires the support of the organisation's leaders. With an explicit commitment on the part of the company's leadership, change agents inside the company should find it easier and faster to make the necessary changes to improve the company's social and environmental performance. A study under-

[1]   The author thanks Claude Fussler, Senior Advisor to the Global Compact Office, who developed the Performance Model and on whose work this chapter is based.

taken by McKinsey & Company in 2004 concluded that the Global Compact had indeed helped to accelerate and ease change in a significant number of participating companies.[2]

As a voluntary multi-stakeholder initiative, the engagement opportunities that the Global Compact offers are dialogue, learning, partnerships, initiatives and a variety of networks. From dialogue in 2002 on the topic of business and sustainable development with business practitioners, UN representatives, and representatives of civil society and labour organisations familiar with the Global Compact, a degree of consensus began to emerge around what are the key elements of business practice that are relevant to the process of internalising the principles. Knitting together these elements, Claude Fussler, Senior Advisor to the Global Compact Office, constructed the Global Compact Performance Model.

The Performance Model was built on lessons learned, including what the first companies participating in the Global Compact felt, after more than two years of working with the principles, had enabled them to begin the process of mainstreaming them within their own business operations and activities. One of the most fundamental lessons was that the methods and terminology of the 'total quality management' and 'managing excellence' approaches had proven helpful. Thus, the Performance Model was firmly grounded in this work.[3] Other key success factors identified were the presence of clear commitment and expectations from the company's leadership, a high level of employee support for and awareness of the principles, clear priorities, a favourable environment for the stimulation of new ideas and business innovation, measurable targets for benchmarking and communicating progress, ability to learn and adapt, and preparedness to engage with the company's various stakeholders.[4]

Because the ten universal principles are applicable everywhere and the Global Compact is a global initiative, the Performance Model has been designed to appeal to the widest number of businesses, from large multinational corporations to small and medium sized enterprises, wherever they are based or are operating, and regardless of their industry sector. Similarly, since the Global Compact is open to companies at all levels of experience with responsible corporate citizenship and it is a continuous improvement model, the Performance Model does and must have a relatively low barrier of entry. Use of the Performance Model is, of course, optional. There are other management approaches and models that can assist with the process of implementing the Global Compact principles.

---

[2] Assessing the Global Compact's Impact, May 11, 2004, McKinsey & Company.

[3] In developing the Performance Model, Claude Fussler found the Malcolm Baldridge Quality Award and the work of the European Foundation for Quality Management particularly helpful.

[4] C. Fussler, A. Cramer and S. van der Vegt, *Raising the Bar, Creating Value with the United Nations Global Compact*, Greenleaf Publishing, 2004, p. 53.

The ten principles of the Global Compact

The Global Compact asks companies to embrace, support and enact, within their sphere of influence, a set of core values in the areas of human rights, labour standards, the environment, and anti-corruption:

Human Rights

1. Businesses should support and respect the protection of internationally proclaimed human rights; and
2. Make sure that they are not complicit in human rights abuses.

Labour Standards

3. Businesses should uphold the freedom of association and the effective recognition of the right to collective bargaining;
4. The elimination of all forms of forced and compulsory labour;
5. The effective abolition of child labour; and
6. The elimination of discrimination in respect of employment and occupation.

Environment

7. Businesses should support a precautionary approach to environmental challenges;
8. Undertake initiatives to promote greater environmental responsibility; and
9. Encourage the development and diffusion of environmentally friendly technologies

Anti-Corruption

10. Businesses should work against all forms of corruption, including extortion and bribery.

Figure 8.1. The ten principles of the Global Compact

8.2   The Global Compact Performance Model

The Global Compact Performance Model is composed of ten elements of business practice (see Figure 8.2), each of which is represented by a separate segment of the diagram. It is a company driven continuous improvement process that begins with the organisation's vision and proceeds through each element represented in the diagram below and then, based on the results obtained, begins again taking on board lessons learned to make further improvements to the company's social and environmental performance. Each element has tools and techniques associated with it, which the Global Compact has identified and

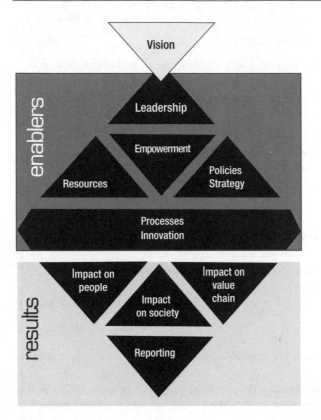

Figure 8.2. The Global Compact Performance Models (Source: Claude Fussler, 2004)

catalogued, and which companies might find helpful as they move through the process. Some tools and techniques are relevant to more than one element. The search for tools that have proven to be helpful is ongoing. Although some tools have been developed by and for the Global Compact, in general, rather than 'reinvent the wheel' by developing new tools, the Global Compact typically makes use of the convening power and communications machinery of the UN to leverage and promote proven tools and techniques developed by others. Tool developers are also encouraged to incorporate the Global Compact's universal principles within their existing and new tools.

The elements can be divided into two categories: 'enablers' and 'results'. Enablers are the foundational elements that help create an enthusiastic, focused, winning organisation capable of achieving its vision. The remaining elements – the results – define the key outcomes sought. The ten elements are:

Vision: This element involves integrating in the company's vision (of how it sees itself and what organisation it wants to become) a commitment to responsible corporate citizenship. In addition to looking at the ten Global Compact principles, this may include such efforts as reviewing major economic, social and environmental world trends, understanding potential risks, undertaking scenario planning and dialoguing with stakeholders, including employees, about their expectations of the company.

Leadership: This step is about driving the revised vision throughout the entire company. Commitment from the top to improve social and environmental performance is crucial in effecting sustainable and effective change. Leadership commitment is desirable not only from the highest levels of the organisation, but also from the leaders of each team and function. For a leadership commitment to responsible corporate citizenship to have its maximal effect, it must be widely communicated throughout the organisation and beyond. For this reason, the leadership of each Global Compact participant is expected to make one of their first acts after engaging in the initiative to communicate the company's engagement to their employees. Leadership is also important in overseeing the whole continuous improvement process. Momentum needs to be maintained and, sometimes, tough decisions will need to be made. Increasingly, we are seeing that some companies are treating responsible corporate citizenship as a corporate governance issue and are establishing board level oversight for the company's efforts to implement the Compact's principles. Effective leadership is not necessarily a top down only affair. Dialoguing with stakeholders and listening to others is important and may be a key indicator of strong not weak leadership.

Empowerment: Empowerment is about releasing the full potential of the organisation's people in line with the company vision and defining their role in relation to it. It is about organising, informing, showing, motivating, training, rewarding, listening to, consulting, and trusting staff so that they can play their role in helping the organisation to achieve its vision.

Policies and strategies: This element entails reviewing the company's existing policies and strategies and incorporating within them, or developing new ones consistent with, the Global Compact principles. Some companies have integrated corporate citizenship policies. Others have, or supplement these with, specific policies and management guidance materials on topics such as human rights and anti-corruption. Some companies post their corporate citizenship related policies on the Internet and some websites collect company policy statements, see, for example, the Business and Human Rights Resource Centre's website (www.business-humanrights.org). These may be a useful reference or starting point for a company updating its own policies. Some companies find it fruitful to engage in stakeholder dialogue as part of the process of revising their policies. Once policies are in place, it is crucial that they be rolled out throughout the organisation so that all employees and other relevant persons are aware of them and understand them.

Resources: This step is about managing the means to implement the company's policies and strategies and equipping employees with what they need to achieve their targets in a way that does not compromise the company's commitment to the Global Compact principles. It includes ensuring that financial, human, informational and other resources are distributed in such a way that is consistent with and will not undermine the company's corporate citizenship policies and commitments.

Processes and innovation: This element is about confronting dilemmas that may be posed by implementation of the Global Compact principles and turning them into innovative solutions and business opportunities. It includes understanding the key processes that can create improvements, setting targets and communicating them throughout the organisation. A thorough risk and opportunity assessment may be particularly useful here.

Impact on the value chain: This step is focused on how the company manages its relationships with its commercial partners, including its suppliers, and the influence and impact that it has on the operations and activities of these partners. How suppliers and sometimes also customers conduct their business can have a significant impact on a company's own reputation, including how the company's social and environmental performance are viewed. A company's suppliers and sometimes also its customers will often fall within its sphere of influence. Many companies take the step of communicating their corporate citizenship policies and expectations to business partners. Some even incorporate these into their contractual arrangements. Some companies review the social and environmental performance of their suppliers using audits. Some go further and assist suppliers to raise the level of their social and environmental performance through actions such as training and sharing of expertise.

Impact on people: This step is about the impact on the company's workforce, including employee morale, of its efforts to implement the Global Compact principles. The general wisdom is that there is a positive relationship between good social and environmental performance and the company's ability to recruit and retain high quality talent, as well as higher employee productivity. Some companies conduct employee satisfaction surveys and/or hold dialogue sessions with employees to obtain feedback on the company's performance and to help identify potential risks and dilemmas.

Impact on society: The impact of the company on the communities in which it operates as well as society at large is also a key element of the Performance Model. It is about how society perceives the company. Society here encompasses local communities where the company operates, civil society organisations, rating organisations and others. It will typically be easier for a company to operate smoothly and maintain its license to operate when local communities do not have a negative opinion of the company and instead feel that it responds favourably to their concerns and needs. Organisations that monitor social and environmental performance can affect, both negatively and positively, the company's operations and activities in a number of ways, including through their impact on the cost of capital. Depending on the scale and nature of the activities concerned, some companies perform impact assessments and use community opinion surveys to help gauge their impact on society. Many companies also study rating organisation's reports and benchmarks.

Reporting: This step is about reliable measurement and communication of the company's economic, social and environmental performance. Specific measurements that show actual performance are essential for ensuring continuous improvement. The Global Compact has developed guidelines on how it expects companies to communicate with their stakeholders about their progress in implementing the Global Compact principles and introduced consequences for companies that do not regularly communicate their progress. At least on an annual basis, participating companies are expected to include the following in their communications with stakeholders: (1) A statement of continued support for the Global Compact from the company's Chief Executive Officer, Chairman or other senior executive, (2) a description of the practical actions that the company has taken to implement the Global Compact principles during the previous fiscal year, and (3) measurement of outcomes or expected outcomes using, as much as possible, indicators or metrics, for example, those developed by the Global Reporting Initiative.

Stakeholder engagement and dialogue is essential to effective use of the Performance Model. In our experience, it is particularly relevant to the following elements: vision, leadership, policies and strategies, impact on society, and reporting. For example, the company's leadership may decide to seek stakeholder input as part of the process of evaluating its vision and then take the input received on board in fine-tuning the vision. Dialogue with stakeholders may also be fruitful in the context of reviewing existing company policies or developing new policies in areas such as human rights, labour standards, the environment and anti-corruption. Stakeholder dialogue is also important in understanding the actual and potential impacts of the company's operations on society, both positive and negative. Sometimes, dialogue with stakeholders can also help a company to find constructive solutions to dilemmas that it is facing. Finally, increasingly, many companies are involving a wide variety of their stakeholders in the reporting process and in helping to assess company performance more generally.

8.3   Experience with the model in practice

More than 2400 company participants from more than 85 countries are now involved in the Global Compact's multi-stakeholder effort aimed at underpinning global markets with universal values to render them more sustainable and inclusive. Global Compact participants and other stakeholders, often with the support of UN agencies, have also established local networks in more than 40 countries to help carry forward the Global Compact at the country level. Among other things, local networks engage in learning and dialogue activities aimed at helping their participants implement the principles.

Companies that have signed onto the Global Compact are expected to work towards implementation of the ten principles and to communicate with their stakeholders on an annual basis about their progress. The accessibility and relative simplicity of the Performance Model are particularly useful for companies that do not know where to begin in translating the principles into practice. It also helps organise and understand the myriad tools and techniques available to help companies become more responsible corporate citizens.

In 2004, the Performance Model was used as the organising framework for a publication called Raising the Bar – Creating Value with the United Nations Global Compact, which is a comprehensive catalogue of tools, techniques, case studies, information and other resources to help companies and other organisations implement the Global Compact principles. The Performance Model was used to contextualise available tools and resources. Each element of the Performance Model is given its own chapter in the publication, which elaborates the element and then outlines the existing tools and resources most relevant to it. A multi-stakeholder editorial team comprised of individuals from CSR organisations, UN agencies, and Amnesty International considered submissions received from tool developers, providers and users all over the world for inclusion in the book.

The framework of the Performance Model has also been employed in the preparation of many Global Compact case studies about individual company's implementation efforts. These case studies are publicly available on the Global Compact website: www.unglobalcompact.org. The framework has proven helpful in dissecting, for learning purposes, the major steps taken by companies in internalising the principles. Many of the case studies have been included in Global Compact publications, which are also available free of charge on the Global Compact website.

In 2006, another publication will be released utilising the framework of the Performance Model. This publication, a joint effort of the Business Leaders Initiative for Human Rights, the UN Global Compact Office and the Office of the High Commissioner for Human Rights, will aim to promote learning around how to implement human rights principles within business. It will be a free publication available for download on the Global Compact and BLIHR websites.

8.4   Conclusion

The Global Compact Performance Model is a framework to systematically guide companies in their ongoing efforts to implement the Global Compact's ten principles in the areas of human rights, labour standards, the environment and anti-corruption. It evolved from analysis of and dialogue about company's actual experiences in trying to internalise the principles. From this analysis and dialogue a degree of consensus emerged around what were the critical factors for successful implementation of the Global Compact. Use of the Performance Model is not mandated, but it has proven to be a helpful framework in understanding how companies are trying to implement the principles. The framework has been used in preparing many case studies about Global Compact participating companies. The Performance Model may be particularly useful for companies that are not sure where to start in embarking on the continuous improvement process that is a key expectation of engagement in the Global Compact.

References

Fussler, C., A. Cramer and S. van der Vegt (2004). *Raising the Bar, Creating Value with the United Nations Global Compact,* Sheffield: Greenleaf Publishing.

Website

www.unglobalcompact.org

Generic Models for the Societal Context

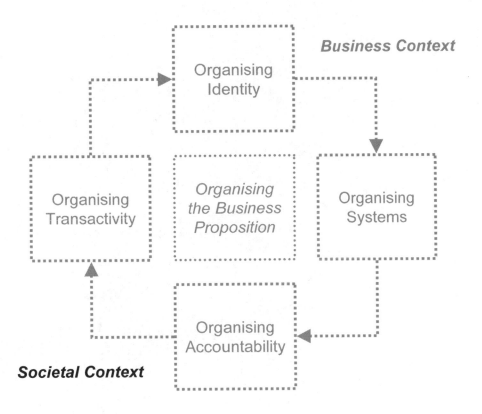

9 WEV: A New Approach to Supply Chain Management

Alex H. Kaufman

Key words: Labour standards audits, empowerment, voluntary.

9.1 The Model: Worker Empowered Voluntary Labour Standards (WEV)

The labour standards conundrum is an intricate web of local government regulations, trade agreements, international sourcing and globalisation. Western NGOs and organisations developed voluntary labour standards as a means to monitor working conditions in multinational corporations with suppliers in developing countries. Although the progress of these standards in recent years is a positive sign, the requirements of each standard are different. Additionally, all of these voluntary labour standards claim to uphold the core conventions of the International Labour Organisation. Furthermore, these voluntary labour standards (VLS) rely on government enforcement of the labour laws, a workers' understanding of their legal rights, and a strong set of occupational health/safety regulations. However, these VLS commonly referred to as 'codes of conduct' are largely designed by both U.S and European based organisations without the input of the key stakeholders, the workers. Factory workers are largely removed from the implementation and design of codes that govern their working lives. This problem is compounded by a lack of professionally trained 'social auditors' and the financial constraints which reduce the thoroughness of each audit. Lastly, a successful programme to improve working conditions requires the collaboration and support of workers, factories, buyers and government inspectors.

Although comprehensive in scope, the aforementioned systems of monitoring voluntary labour standards fail to engender sustainable improvements or collaborate with workers in the process. The solution is a new system of Worker Empowered –VLS (WEV), whereby workers participate in the monitoring and improvement of workplace conditions. WEV requires that factories and brands focus on educating the workforce to understand their rights under the specified code of conduct and jointly contribute to long-term improvements in their working environment.

9.2   The essence of the WEV model

Firstly, WEV is not another voluntary labour standard. WEV does not represent any one standard or code, WEV attempts to encompass all applicable customer codes through improved worker education. WEV simplifies the process of VLS implementation by allowing workers to assist in monitoring their own working conditions.

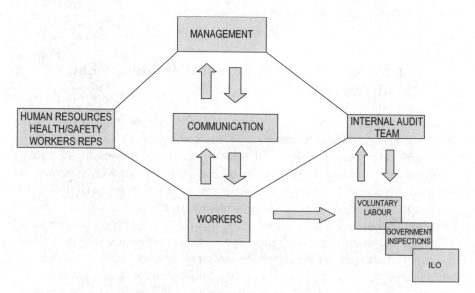

Figure 9.1. Worker empowered voluntary labour standards

In order to implement WEV, the workforce and management need to under-stand the intent of the particular standards set by their customers. Large gar-ment factories often post codes of conduct for several Western buyers, which confuse supervisory staff and workers. Additionally, the management must en-sure that the internal policies and regulations do not conflict with the key ele-ments of the codes.

Subsequently, the first task is how to communicate WEV to the workforce. Professional auditors know that most of the factories certified under various workplace standards tend to be particularly weak in terms of worker training and worker representation. If workers are empowered under WEV they need to understand the brand's code and local labour laws. This undertaking requires a substantial effort to transform factories into open-learning forums. Additionally, the factories need to allocate budgets and time to conduct worker training.

Ultimately, WEV requires proper enforcement of government regulations, consumer pressure, and a convergence of worker-centred codes to improve factory conditions in developing countries. Long-term relationships with multi-national buyers, factory owners, and workers can provide incentives for improved performance. These structural changes coupled with greater worker participation will translate into sustainable improvements in the workplace.

The final challenge of incorporating the WEV system into the current monitoring schemes is the availability of well-trained consultants, who can help to build a bridge between management and workers. The principal task of these consultants is to train management and workers to carry out a process of continuous improvements in working conditions. The implementation of continuous improvements under this process requires additional support through funding, technical support and incentives to the factories.

9.3   The implementation process: WEV in action

The bottom up – Top down approach

The first step in the process is sitting down with management to develop a mutual understanding of the WEV approach. The factory management chooses a team of management representatives and evaluates the varied VLS elements required by their customers. Subsequently, the codes are incorporated into the factory regulations and policies.

Secondly, the factory needs to accept the terms of the process. The third challenge is for the factory to see this as a tool for effective risk management and for the workers to understand WEV as a means whereby they can communicate grievances constructively and effectively.

Workers in the process

After the introductory meetings are conducted – a group of workers receive training in the process and then are chosen through an election to carry out various roles within the monitoring process. All meetings with the WEV Consultant require the attendance of both the workers and management committee. Together the staff decides how and when the first audits occur. At the onset the team conducts an audit based on the designated code through worker interviews, a document review and visual inspections of the facility.

A key weakness of factories is their inability to communicate code requirements to workers. Therefore a strong compliance programme requires the widespread education of workers. By educating the workforce the factory can avoid the recurrence of poor management practices and encourage workers to report areas for improvement to the audit team at regular meetings. Subsequently, the minutes of these meetings are translated into corrective actions on the factory floor through the joint working team.

In order to successfully implement WEV the support team sets objectives based on the current compliance strengths and weaknesses of the facility. Once these new objectives are set they are communicated to the factory management. The successful remediation tasks are noted down and included in a monthly or quarterly report.

Nuts and bolts

Both workers and management receive ongoing training on the three most important facets of auditing workplace conditions: basic human resource policies, health/safety and local labour laws. Moreover, training is offered in areas of particular weakness either through a WEV specialist or an external trainer in more sensitive areas such as sexual discrimination and labour relations. If workers and management have the opportunity to attend joint trainings, there is opportunity for further dialogues and common understanding of each others job functions. On top of the core subjects mentioned, trainings on productivity and quality control are of added value to the WEV process.

The internal WEV audit

Once the proper mechanisms are in place, the WEV Team carries out internal audits on a routine basis as set by the factory and workers. Different members of the WEV Team are assigned to specified areas of the audit. The factory then sets up audit teams made up of both management and workers. After carrying out the physical audit and interviewing workers the teams report back their findings to a central committee set-up specifically to act upon the findings. One of the major challenges at this step is the so called 'paternal leader', for this reason a comprehensive introduction of the process is integral to overall success of the programme. Without appropriate buy-in from management WEV can easily stall at this stage.

Total stakeholder commitment

The contribution of all stakeholders going forward shall bring about continuous and sustainable improvements to the factory's working conditions. Training and technical support are the key to attaining continuous improvement. Furthermore, as cooperation between workers, management and buyers improve, the factory sustains a high level of compliance without the assistance of outside consultants or auditors. Lastly, as the programme becomes part of the factory routine, the compliance process is no longer viewed as an added cost or an unnecessary disruption of their production targets.

Stakeholder participation and the development of WEV

The theory of WEV evolved over several years of audits and meetings with a wide variety of stakeholders, which included workers, supervisors, factory managers and compliance officers. Input from these key stakeholders provided the foundation for WEV theory and its implementation in factories. These discussions focused on the impact of voluntary labour standards on working conditions, human resource practices, and compensation methods. Workers need a living wage and management needs the productive labour of workers for their long-term success. VLS provides a tool to measure and verify internal cooperation (within an organisation) in cooperation with workers. The participation and collaboration of workers in VLS presents an opportunity to provide benefits to both workers and factory management. The development of a cooperative monitoring programme utilises the knowledge of the real experts, the workforce. WEV can be further defined as a method to bring workers into the process and evaluate their own environment.

Initial experiences in WEV Implementation

The author had the opportunity to test portions of the WEV theory in Thailand in 2002, through a government supported project aimed to assist Thai garment factories in acquiring certification in SA8000 and other voluntary labour standards. As various sections in the SA8000 standard refer to worker participation, this presented a useful platform to engage management in this model. We decided to initiate the process by suggesting the formal inclusion of workers as well as management representatives from the onset of the programme. The model was presented at three different factories over a six month period, we requested that workers be present at all the training sessions and be involved in the monitoring of working conditions.

9.4   Dos and don'ts

The following are recommendations on how to ensure the process is successful:

- Provide a detailed explanation to the factory management at the onset;
- Take time to write training materials in simple language that can be understood by participants with limited formal education;
- Use plenty of visual aids and photographs to accompany training materials;
- Plan the schedule in advance and have management sign off on the training dates;

- Conduct an evaluation of working conditions in the factory prior to the start of the programme;
- Develop role-play exercises, which allow the factory management to better understand the workers perspective.

The following are 'don'ts' seen from the perspective of the participating consultants:

- Do not assign employees to the VLS committees who are too busy with other tasks and cannot regularly attend training sessions;
- Ensure the factory does not send mainly administrative and human resources staff, their must be a considerable share of production people;
- Make sure the factory management does not exclude the actual workforce from the committees;
- Do not force workers paid on a piece rate to attend as participation means lost wages (try to get management to ensure them adequate compensation for training time);
- The management may be concerned that the monitoring committee might transform itself into a trade union. Ensure to explain the process to them thoroughly;
- Do not rush the process, it takes at least 3 months for most factories to make substantial improvements.

The points above further emphasise that the overall success of WEV lies in the initial introduction of the programme. Factory management needs to thoroughly understand the objectives of the programme and must encourage the participation of their employees at all levels. Otherwise, the process offers nothing different from the plethora of codes that fail to engender sustainable improvements in the lives of workers.

9.5   Facing the challenge

Firstly, the multinational corporations participating in these monitoring schemes need to take a greater financial responsibility. Under VLS and government inspection systems, factories rarely receive more than one audit per year, unless of course if there are multiple U.S. or European buyers involved. To develop a programme where workers are trained to monitor and report on their working environment requires funding for multiple visits by highly skilled trainers.

Factories also need to allocate resources for an individual who can designate a sufficient part of their working hours to support the WEV system. The individual or team in charge of maintaining and improving working standards in the factory needs to closely cooperate with line workers, supervisors, management and the WEV Team. This process requires the resources to educate and disseminate the programme to the workforce.

In summary, internal monitoring through strong worker-management teams can add value to the firm. A process of Worker Empowered-VLS can reduce accidents, decrease turnover, increase productivity and improve the quality of output. The success of the WEV approach depends on the support of buyers, management, government officials, and workers.

Although this paper advocates Worker Empowered –Voluntary Labour Standards, the possibility of its widespread implementation will require a dramatic paradigm shift in the actions of all the key stakeholders. A joint consensus of key stakeholders is necessary in order to implement new methods of monitoring and improve workplace conditions. While NGOs, academics, and activists criticise formal VLS programmes, there are no other formal structures available that can obtain the financial support of the major brands, buyers, and marketing companies.

In conclusion, an improvement of working conditions is best served by proper enforcement of government regulations, consumer pressure, and a convergence of codes of conduct in multinational supply chains. Furthermore, these factories depend on long-term relationships with multinational buyers, and financial incentives for improved labour standards. The current process of outsourcing is based on a lack of commitment with short-term profits as a driving force. The purpose of WEV is to establish a set of norms for labour practices with the involvement of local actors through a cooperative and self-sustaining system. Lastly, WEV empowers workers and factory management to jointly evaluate and improve working conditions under the guidance and support of their multinational buyers.

References

Bendell, J. (2001). *Towards Participatory Workplace Appraisal: Report from a Focus Group of Women Banana Workers*, New Academy of Business.

Chambers, R. (1997). *Whose Reality Counts?*, London: ITDG Publishing.

Reason, P. and H. Bradbury (eds.) (2001). *Handbook of Action Research*. London: Sage publications.

Estrella, M. (ed.) *Learning from Change: Issues and experiences in participatory monitoring and evaluation* (http:www.ids.ac.uk/ids/bookshop/).

Meadows, D.H. (1999). *Leverage Points: Places to Intervene in a System*, The Sustainability Institute.

Senge, P. (1990). *The Fifth Discipline*, New York: Doubleday/Currency.

10 A Model for Multi-stakeholder Partnerships on Human Rights in Tourism

Camelia M. Tepelus

Key words: Sustainable tourism, children's rights, child sex tourism, social responsibility.

10.1 Introduction

Tourism is one of the world's largest industries, increasingly promoted as an engine for development and poverty alleviation. According to the World Tourism Organization (WTO), a UN specialised agency and leading organisation in the field, tourism represents approximately 7 percent of worldwide exports of goods and services. This share increases to 30 percent when considering service exports exclusively.

This paper presents a model for corporate social responsibility (CSR) created to integrate human rights issues in sustainable tourism, through public-private partnerships between the industry, non-governmental organisations (NGOs) and international governmental organisations (IGOs). The experience with the model in practice is described in a case study presenting a voluntary code of conduct adopted by the industry to prevent child sex tourism.

10.2 A model of inter-stakeholders' partnerships against child sex tourism

How the model works and what it does

At the core of the model presented is the tourism sector's acknowledgement of accountability on the human rights impacts of its operations. The tourism industry is not accused of fomenting development of abusive situations. However, the private sector is asked to react against the use of its networks and establishments in circumstances leading to human rights abuses, such as in the case of child sex tourism.

Responsibility of the tourism sector in this field has been defined as direct, or indirect, potential. Direct responsibility corresponds to those businesses who knowingly publicise, promote, and receive sex tours, as well as to the operators of establishments and premises where abusers meet and sexually exploit children, namely, accommodation facilities, entertainment centres, leisure areas, etc. Tolerating such activities implies complicity and complacency of the private sector.

Indirect or potential responsibility also corresponds to tour operators, travel agents, other carriers and airlines, who become aware that they are used as vehicles carrying declared or potential sex offenders to the destinations.

The model for socially responsible behaviour calls for a public commitment of the company to support awareness raising, and to have a preventative approach to situations of abuse. This is particularly called for in poor countries of the developing world. The model intervenes at key points within the tourism supply chain, and sets in place tools empowering the private sector to prevent child sex tourism while simultaneously improving the quality of the tourism product.

This process takes place at different levels in the tourism supply chain (see Figure 10.1):

- At corporate level, through ethical policies and staff training;

- In relation to suppliers, by introducing specific clauses in commercial contracts;

- In relation to the customers, through awareness raising and by providing relevant information;

- In relation to civil society, by empowering local stakeholders through direct capacity building and annual reporting.

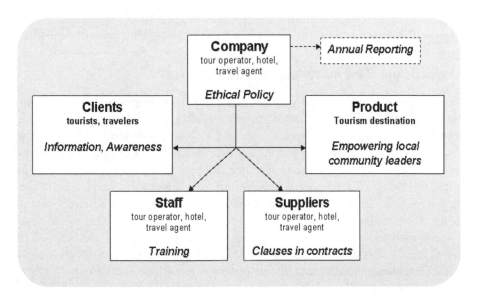

Figure 10.1. Operational framework

Under this operational framework, distinct competencies of various stakeholders are brought together to address a grave human rights issue in a coordinated manner. Implementation activities take place both in originating (tourism sending) countries, and in destination (receiving) countries (see Figure
10.2). Monitoring of the model is facilitated by a multi-stakeholder, coordinating body of international standing, which is supported by the leading IGOs
working on the child sex tourism issue.

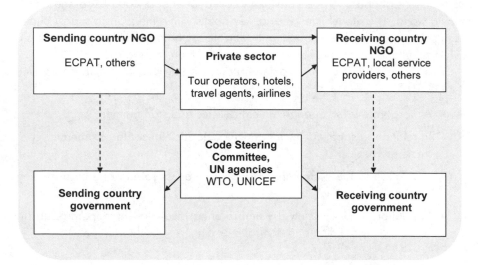

Figure 10.2. Institutional stakeholders playing a role in the implementation of the model

Development of the model and its current status

This system of public-private partnerships started with implementation in Scan-
dinavia, and expanded to other tourism-sending European countries during
2000 – 2004. The model was introduced in North America in 2004 and in
Japan in 2005, and there are ongoing actions for testing it in Eastern Europe
with the support of the Organisation for Security and Cooperation in Europe
(OSCE). Over 250 companies, including tour operators, hotels and travel
agencies from 21 countries are currently implementing this framework worldwide. Companies engaged in this process include both large, well-known
brands such as Accor, CarlsonWagonlit, Radisson, TUI, Kuoni, etc., as well as
small local hotels or travel agents. This expansion was possible through a process of knowledge transfer and dissemination that followed two different paths: a
corporate and an NGO path.

The corporate path focused mainly on transfer of knowledge intra-company,
across borders. Multinational companies that had positive experiences with the

implementation of the model in one country were able to transfer this know-how in other destinations. For instance, Accor Hotels Asia, starting from the pilot implementation of this model in its Accor Bangkok Hotel in Thailand, moved then to expand training and awareness to Accor staff in Laos, Vietnam, Sri Lanka, Dominican Republic, Mexico and French Guyana.

The NGO path focused mainly on capacity building in tourism destinations. Consultations, seminars, training sessions and visits, were carried out in destinations in the process of monitoring the implementation of the model. Experts from tourism-sending countries went to destinations in tourism-receiving countries in order to review the effectiveness and create local know-how. Often, when the suitable political and social factors were in place, awareness campaigns originating abroad were subsequently pursued independently in the receiving country by NGOs, local or national governments.

This model was internationally recognised as a successful approach to CSR in tourism, being awarded in 2003 with the British Airways Tourism for Tomorrow Award in the Large Scale Tourism category. More than 30 million tourists a year are using the services of a tour operator engaged with this model of preventing child sex tourism.

10.3 Application – the case of child sex tourism

Commercial sexual exploitation of children in tourism (SECT) also named child sex tourism, is a global phenomenon and an international crime, making it the object of extra-territorial legislation. An estimated 2 million children enter the multi-billion dollar commercial sex trade and are forced into commercial sexual practices every year according to the United Nations Children's Fund (UNICEF). This exploitation occurs in all countries, mainly in South-East Asia, Latin America, Africa and Eastern Europe. The Western world accounts for the greatest demand for child sex.

For political reasons and image concerns, and despite its visibility, SECT often occurs without governments' reaction in many developing countries. Furthermore, corruption, poverty and insufficient law enforcement undermine the capacity of governments to confront the problem. On the other hand, the tourism industry is represented in most of the world's cities, providing visitors, and, hence, potential child sex-tourists with access to its infrastructure, transport, accommodation and services. Even though statistics and anecdotal evidence indicate that the largest portion of the child sex trade caters to local clients, the incidence of tourists from industrialised countries travelling to developing countries for SECT is a very visible part of the problem.

SECT was defined at the first World Congress against Commercial Sexual Exploitation of Children in 1996 as the 'sexual exploitation of a child by a person or persons who engages in sexual activities with a child while travelling away from their own country or region'. An Agenda for Action was adopted, including the recommendation of 'mobilising the tourist industry and the business world so that their facilities and networks are not used for the child sex trade'. A number of tourism bodies responded to this recommendation by issuing statements and internal guidelines and other types of self-regulatory policies.

Case Study: A CSR model to prevent child sex tourism through an industry code of conduct

The framework created for the implementation of a CSR model addressing SECT was a voluntary code of conduct. The Code of Conduct for the Protection of Children from Sexual Exploitation in Travel and Tourism (the Code), was initiated in 1998 by the non-governmental organisation ECPAT with the support of the industry, the WTO and UNICEF. The Code implementation requires direct collaboration between the tourism private sector and national NGOs with children's rights expertise, with the support of the competent IGOs. The roles of the different participants in the Code model are:

The tourism industry

Building on the assumption that the tourism industry is directly interested in the long-term development of destinations, the sector is called to sign the Code, and accept its monitoring by an international supervisory body. Companies adopting the Code commit to: Establish corporate ethical policies against SECT; educate and train their personnel both in the country of origin and in destinations; introduce clauses in the contracts with their suppliers, stating a common repudiation of SECT, provide information to travellers by means of catalogues, brochures, posters, in-flight spots, ticket-slips, websites, etc., liaise with local 'key persons' such as community leaders and authorities in destinations; and report annually on the implementation of these criteria.

NGOs with children's rights expertise (ECPAT)

ECPAT was established in Asia in 1990 as a response of local social workers and activists to the child sex tourism phenomenon. The acronym initially meant 'End Child Prostitution in Asian Tourism', and stands now for 'End Child Prostitution, Child Pornography and Trafficking of Children for Sexual Purposes'. ECPAT is today a network represented in 65 countries. ECPAT groups or other NGOs currently provide children's rights training and assistance in implementing the Code by the tourism industry in their countries and abroad.

IGOs in the fields of tourism and children's rights (WTO and UNICEF)

The 'Tourism Bill of Rights and Tourism Code', adopted by the WTO General Assembly in 1985 contains directives specifically addressing SECT. Following the 1996 World Congress, WTO proceeded to create an international Task Force against commercial sexual exploitation of children. Since 1997 the Task Force was engaged in an international awareness campaign seeking to 'prevent, uncover, isolate and eradicate the exploitation of children in sex tourism'. UNICEF, the UN agency working to protect children's rights in the framework of the UN Convention on the Rights of the Child became a supporting organisation in 2004, following the launch of the Code in North America. In a ceremony held in the presence of HM Queen Silvia of Sweden and US government officials, the Carlson group, owner of the well known Radisson and Carlson Wagonlit brands, was the first North American company to adopt the Code. The tourism private sector together with ECPAT, UNICEF and the WTO form an international multi-stakeholder group, the Code Steering Committee. This body is funded by UNICEF and its task is the global monitoring of the Code development.

10.4 Dos and don'ts in the implementation of the model

The framework presented requires establishment of direct relationships between the tourism private sector, NGOs and IGOs. Factors such as insufficient funding, lack of knowledge, reciprocal suspicion, misconceptions, tremendous differences in work capacity, in work style and in the understanding of the problem, have often interfered negatively with the outcomes of the implementation. Clearly, all partners benefited from the experience by developing, or getting access to new knowledge. Lessons learned include both positive recommendations ('Dos') and negative ones ('Don'ts').

Dos

Engagement of IGOs at the highest level was a key component in determining national governments to approach a highly sensitive topic such as that of child sex tourism. The role of national NGOs was critical in initiating the process and in catalysing follow-up activities. However, a formalisation of the model especially in developing countries relied on the engagement of IGOs, leading subsequently to political support and resource allocation by the national governments.

Existent national – international affiliation relationships helped create a domino effect for the model dissemination. Individual countries are members of the WTO, UNICEF country offices respond to headquarters, and individual tourism companies are members of sector specific umbrella organisations. These relationships created effective leverage mechanisms for attracting more companies to join the model.

Working intensely with multi-nationals also maximised the international impact and the expansion of the model. The most influential tourism players are companies operating globally. Their activities in one country were easily replicable elsewhere through the mother-company management structures and central headquarters. Furthermore, as key players know each other well, they often have formal or informal regional operation agreements in place, leading again to coordinated action on implementing the model in specific destinations.

Pilot projects that started with one large industry partner attracted other local businesses more easily and built up momentum faster, as compared to projects that started by incorporating small or medium-sized individual businesses.

Proper understanding of the business by all model partners facilitates communication and agreement on common goals. While this may seem obvious, the experience with this model showed that often NGOs and the private sector don't have a good understanding of each other's roles and operations. Agreements commonly used in the industry – franchising, management contracts, brand rights, etc– require the modification of the model accordingly, and consequently a degree of flexibility and adaptability from all partners.

Don'ts

Deficiencies in the implementation of this model were mostly related to circumstances such as excessive reliance on a single partner (tour operator, hotel or NGO) in some destinations, and the dependence of the success of the implementation on the local political context.

Another major challenge at all times was the insufficient financial capacity for monitoring and evaluating the implementation in destinations.

10.5 Conclusion

This paper presented a CSR model of public-private partnerships created to advance a more comprehensive approach to protection of human rights issues in tourism. This framework allowed development of know-how that did not exist previously within the industry, and provided for the private sector reaction to an emerging issue transcending the usual sector boundaries. The challenge highlighted in the testing of the model was the need for balancing between flexibility in implementation at national level, and maintaining consistency of the international conceptual framework. The experience with its implementation until now shows that it is possible for the tourism private sector to effectively answer a real need of society in trying to curb the problem of child sex tourism, and in a wider context, to improve protection of children's rights in destinations. The key achievement of the model was the re-evaluation, and in some countries the re-shaping, of the relationships between the tourism industry and civil society. In this sense, this experience is also relevant and possibly replicable on other human rights issues within the UN Millennium Goals and UN Global Compact agenda.

References

World Tourism Organization (2001). *Protection of Children from Sexual Exploitation in Tourism. Tourism Training Module for Future Tourism Professionals*, Madrid: World Tourism Organization.

ECPAT International (2001). *The role and Involvement of the Private Sector. A Contribution of ECPAT International to the 2nd World Congress against Commercial Sexual Exploitation of Children*, Yokohama: Japan, 17-20 December 2001.

Tepelus, C. (ed.) (2004). *Code of Conduct to Protect Children from Sexual Exploitation in Travel and Tourism. Overview and Implementation Examples*, Madrid: World Tourism Organization.

Website

www.thecode.org

www.world-tourism.org/protect_children/index.htm

www.accor.com/gb/groupe/dev_durable/tourisme.asp

11 The Guangcai Model

GUO Peiyuan, YU Yongda, and DU Huixian (Fred Dubee)

Key words: The Guangcai Model, public private partnership, information symmetry, incentive, monitoring.

11.1 Introduction

Public private partnership

Public private partnership (PPP) is a cooperative approach between the public and private sectors. Such partnership mechanisms have been widely used around the world to promote the development of infrastructure, public utilities and services. In some cases such as 'Build-Operate-Transfer (BOT)' projects, a public private partnership can be seen as a socially responsible investment providing enterprises with an opportunity to both obtain a return on investment and contribute to society.

The Guangcai Model

The name of the model comes from a Chinese poverty alleviation programme, which promotes multi-sector cooperation between entrepreneurs, governments, non-governmental organisations and farmers to reduce poverty in rural areas. In essence, the Guangcai Model is a partnership between public and private sectors. In this partnership, each actor assumes a unique role. The company is pivotal in the Guangcai Model. Its contribution includes:

- Providing high quality materials such as seed, implements, etc. to farmers;
- Transferring practical know-how, technology and ensuring appropriate training;
- Purchasing farmers' products for a pre-agreed fixed price.

Farmers produce their goods using both their own resources (e.g. farmland) and implements (e.g. modern farming tools) provided by the company. Improved knowledge and skills provided by training help increase productivity and reduce losses caused by diseases and pests. After the harvest, the farmer has an assured market for his/her crops at a pre-agreed price. The government acts as a bridge builder and coordinator between the company and farmers. On the one hand, it is responsible for attracting and inviting entrepreneurs to invest in the project. On the other hand, it helps the company organise and manage the farmers in carrying out all aspects of the farming operations. Typically, it can also assist the company by providing and enabling environment and/or preferential conditions.

The non-governmental organisation (NGO) acts as a facilitator both promoting the creation of PPP projects and providing added value in their management. However, the major tasks and prime focus of the non-governmental organisation are in the areas of monitoring and mediation.

11.2 Essence of the model

Shared comparative advantages

The Guangcai Model provides a public private partnership that is well developed and functions effectively. The key success factor is that in the model, the comparative advantages of each participant are used and the overall responsibilities and risk allocation are optimally distributed between the public and private sectors. A cost-benefit analysis for each partner provides a useful illustration to better understand the model and its power (see Figure 11.1).

As participating in the Guangcai project does not significantly increase fixed costs, a company in the Guangcai Model is not only able to increase its profits but also gains additional benefits. These benefits include:

- Access to government support: subsidies, tax reduction, reduced interest rate loans and an appropriate infrastructure;
- Political recognition and an enhanced reputation which can reduce political and business risks;
- Decreased cost of information gathering and communication as a result of the support from the NGO.

Farmers gain income predictability and assurance, optimised profitability over the long term as well as reduced risk thanks to income guarantees and access to the broader market resulting from the company's support. Furthermore, farmers can get technical services and useful support which help increase their productivity. In the Guangcai Model the farmers only generally invest in labour and land.

For the government, the following benefits accrue. Through the Guangcai approach, the government not only achieves its objective which is to develop areas in need but can also leave the private sector to deal with market risks. The government eliminates or reduces a whole series of operational and management costs which it passes on to the company. Experience shows that business

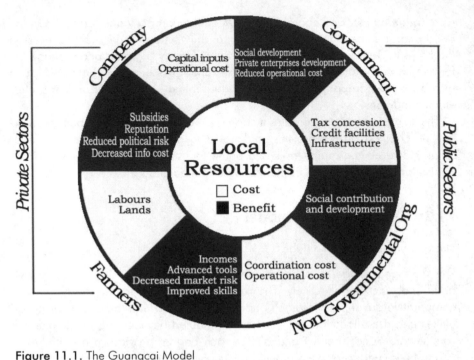

Figure 11.1. The Guangcai Model

is better able to manage market opportunities and risks than the government. In the Guangcai Model, the key responsibility of the government is to provide an enabling environment for the private sector through tax concession, favourable credit facilities and an adequate infrastructure.

As for the NGO, normal cost-benefit analysis is not applicable as its goals are established in terms of social contribution rather than profits. In the Guangcai Model, NGOs are working toward their appropriate goals and are making a definite contribution toward sustainable poverty alleviation. Its costs are mainly for communication, operation, pre-project assessment and post-evaluation. Compared to the value added of the entire project, these costs are not significant.

Key elements ensuring success

The model demonstrates a sound partnership arrangement between public and private sectors. To ensure success, three elements are necessary.

The first element is information symmetry. The poor in rural areas are often adequately endowed with natural resources and social capital but lack financial capital while capable urban business leaders may have significant financial assets but are often not aware of economically and socially sound projects where their funds could reap multi-dimensional returns. Around the world, this information gap is one of the prevalent reasons for poverty in rural areas. It is only when such a gap is overcome with an efficient and effective connection or bridge that the comparative advantages can be used to help regional development.

Who bridges the gap? In the Guangcai Model, the public sector, i.e. the government and the NGO assume that role. Both have nationwide networks which they can use to collect sufficient, high quality information. This enables them to understand the potential and limitations, the assets and needs of each partner. The results of their research can provide an effective platform for potential partners to meet and explore possible cooperation.

The second element is incentive. To ensure appropriate and responsible corporate behaviour an effective incentive mechanism is essential. Without appropriate incentives, it is difficult to see how the model can be successful. For instance, philanthropy or charitable donations are helpful in the alleviation of acute hardship, but they are by their very nature not sustainable and sometimes can even damage the fragile dignity of the recipient. The sad results of the billions of dollars poured into Africa in the form of aid published in the Millennium Development Goals reports are a clear indication of the fact that this approach neither ensures access to basic necessities nor provides the basis for sustainable economic, social and environmental development.

Therefore, it appears that appropriate incentives are an important if not essential factor in encouraging corporations to invest while at the same time guaranteeing the sustainability and effectiveness of investments by combining sound business goals with the objectives of poverty reduction. The Guangcai Model provides a clear demonstration that each participating partner can find its own incentive: the government and NGO achieve their goals in terms of social development; the company makes profits; farmers earn considerable income and all increase social capital. What is more, the farmers learn they can rid themselves of poverty through their own efforts and business learns that investments with a high social pay-back are also good business. These results and the derived learning not only motivate the partnership but provide examples for others to explore similar approaches.

The last element is monitoring. Monitoring and the feedback it provides to the partners is important not only to ensure that all participants adhere to the agreed rules but that they also identify potential problems and opportunities and use the information to find ways to improve the performance of the overall approach. For example, in the Guangcai Model, both the company and farmers face the risk of default by the other. A change in market prices for products could result in a company reneging on its purchase commitment to the farmers. Equally, the farmer might refuse to deliver the harvested crop to the company as contractually agreed. The involvement of the public sector can help ensure compliance and avoid default behaviour. As coordinators, the government and non-governmental organisation can use their information systems and market knowledge to warn of potentially dangerous situations. Their understanding of both the company and the farmers ensures that they can consistently and accurately monitor relevant developments and provide mechanisms and support measures to ensure compliance with the partnership agreements and if necessary to initiate timely corrective action. In addition, the NGO can play a vital role by monitoring the government authorities to prevent and deter any form of unfairness and/or corruption. In short, the Guangcai Model helps to reduce the overall business and legal risks and greatly increase the potential for smooth and profitable cooperation between the company and farmers.

11.3 Experiences

The Guangcai Model has evolved based on the successful Guangcai Programme created by ten Chinese entrepreneurs in 1994 aimed at reducing poverty in the poorest areas of China with socially oriented, profit-generating investments in sustainable enterprises in these regions. In 1995, the Guangcai Programme established its own organisational set-up under the name of the China Society for Promoting the Guangcai Programme (CSPGP). Various key stakeholders participate in the Guangcai Programme including the central and local government authorities, non-profit organisations, such as CSPGP, the All-China Federal Industry and Commerce (ACFIC), private enterprises, and farmers.

The Guangcai Programme has developed a unique framework for partnership between investors and beneficiaries which is usually referred to as the Guangcai Model. Within this framework, investors and beneficiaries create legally binding contracts which clearly define the roles, responsibilities, rights and obligations of each participant as well as the expected benefits and synergy. In addition, the participation of the Government and the CSPGP ensures that investors have access to various subsidies, less political risk, as well as lower costs for information gathering and dissemination.

The original work programme of the ten pioneer business leaders envisaged ten projects, with the development of ten different sources of funds and training for one hundred people every year. However, the achievement of the Guangcai Programme far surpassed this original plan. By 2003, over 10,000 Guangcai projects had been started and had helped to free approximately 4.5 million Chinese people from the constraints of poverty by providing opportunities for employment, personal development, better health care and dignity. By promoting investment in sustainable enterprises, job creation and infrastructure development in the poorer regions, the Guangcai Programme is also helping smooth regional disparity in China and is contributing significantly towards increasing the quality of life of people in the western parts of the country. The Guangcai Programme and its significant contributions have been well received by the Chinese Government, as well as by the international community. This fact was underlined in 2000 when the United Nations granted the CSPGP the consultative status at the Economic and Social Council of the United Nations.

11.4   Dos and don'ts

Development steps

Today, the Guangcai Programme in China is the product of a ten-year development and learning process. The programme cannot be replicated and the
model cannot be used without going through a series of developmental steps
and a learning process. A possible approach:

Gather and share information on the Guangcai programme and prepare reviews of a broad range of potential projects. These reviews should ideally be
carried out in the field so that all the programme participants gain a deep understanding of the programme as well as potential opportunities and challenges.

Once this has been done, define and implement pilot projects. Two or three
pilot projects should be enough to provide valid experience from which to build
a formal programme definition and operating approach.

Once the pilot projects have been completed and analysed by all the participants and the programme adjusted based on this analysis, it is possible to
consider additional projects with greater scope.

Involvement of public and private sectors

As the Guangcai Model is based on the concept of a Public private partnership
(PPP), the public as well as private sector must be involved in creating the
framework for cooperation otherwise the shared comparative advantages will
not be realised. In this model, the company and the government are the two
critical partners. The former brings in business thinking while the latter helps
reduce non-market risks. In some countries, government-organised or govern-
ment-related organisations sometimes assume the roles of the government.

Network

To achieve information symmetry, a comprehensive network is important.
Therefore, to replicate the Guangcai Model, it is necessary to ensure the development of a purposeful and heuristic network. One effective approach for consideration is cooperation with the government and utilisation of existing territo-
rial or functional networks. The function of the local agencies is to be an information and support hub, therefore they do not need to be very big or cumbersome.

Applicable fields

Basically, the Guangcai Model can be applied to resource-based or labour-
based industries and should support social development. That is because (1)

farmers' contribution would be more significant in such circumstances, (2) areas where such industries are located are usually less developed not only in economic terms but also in terms of entrepreneurial and business acumen, and (3) the government will be keen to support the project if it can promote regional development and through this make progress in poverty reduction. Consequently, the Guangcai Programme should serve as a model for development and not for duplication.

11.5 Conclusion

The Guangcai Programme provides a realistic model that demonstrates the potential of corporate social responsibility based on public private partnership. The essence of this model is a well-conceived and organised partnership that capitalises on shared comparative advantages as illustrated in Figure 11.1. Three key components are essential for success: information symmetry, appropriate incentives and effective monitoring. This model has been extensively tested in China and has made significant contributions to economic and social development which has in turn resulted in large scale poverty alleviation. The Guangcai Model is gaining in significance as it is fully integrated into China's overriding goal to build a 'Xiaokang society' which strives for economic, social and environmental wellbeing for all. Based on the results achieved in China, it is felt that the Guangcai Model can be used around the world as a basis for the development of public private partnerships that in the words of Kofi Annan: 'reconcile the creativity of business with the needs of the disadvantaged and the requirements of future generations'.

References

World Bank (2001). *China: Overcoming Rural Poverty*, World Bank.

Dreiblatt, D. et al. (2000). *Public-Private Partnership for Poverty Eradication and Local Development: Highlighting the Chinese Experience*, Regional Development Dialogue, 21(2): autumn , UN-CRD.

Lung, L.S. (2000). *The Guangcai Programme in China*, United Front Work in China. (9): pp. 27-30.

Guo, P. (2003). *The Guangcai Programme for Poverty Eradication (China): a study in engaged governance*, Newsletter of the DPADM, UNDESA, 2(107): p. 7.

Annan, K. (1999). *Speech at the World Economic Forum*, (www.unglobalcompact.org).

Website

www.cspgp.org.cn

12 Community Learning in the Indian Education Sector

Subhasis Ray

Key words: Primary education, rural, community, technology.

12.1 Introduction to the model

In India, the concept of CSR has been mostly confined to the realms of employee welfare. Industrial firms like the Tatas and the Birlas have played pioneering roles in taking care of their employees- building residential colonies, schools, hospitals and temples. This was in the early part of the twentieth century. The Tatas worked on community building (through integrated townships and self-employment schemes) while the Birlas focused on building educational institutions for primary and secondary schooling. However, the focus of the rest of the business community did not change much until the last decade. Liberalisation of the Indian economy in 1991 brought in a flood of multinationals. Concepts like CSR became more important. After 2000, CSR started making it to the covers of business magazines and an awareness of how CSR can be strategically important to companies started to grow. Part of the credit goes to extensive research carried out by NGOs, often funded by multilateral agencies like the UN. Going beyond random philanthropy, companies started to look at areas where they could contribute significantly to the social development process in a long-term and sustainable way. Various models have been adopted to link company business with existing programmes. The country's emerging IT giants are taking a lead in the effort. Infosys, Wipro, Tata Consultancy Services are some of the top IT players. All of them have focused on CSR and on education in particular. Being in the knowledge industry, education may have been their obvious choice. To understand the decision process underlying most of the strategic CSR initiatives, it may help to look at a typical model (see Figure 12.1).

12.2 The essence of the model

Companies first identify areas where they can contribute knowledge and expertise. This is a paradigm shift from earlier trends of allocating a percentage of total revenue to schools, hospitals or community development. Based on knowledge

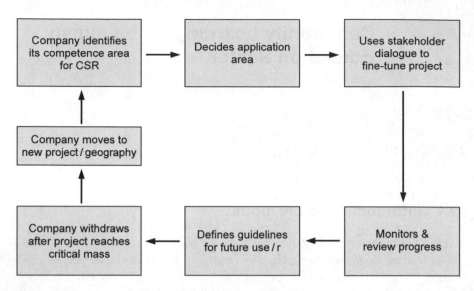

Figure 12.1. Process flow chart for the learning centre project

resources, companies are able to focus on areas where they have competence. Often these areas help to improve the competitive context of the
company. Dialogue with stakeholders identifies the methodology and review
mechanisms. Here communication plays a vital role to keep stakeholders
informed of the company's current activities and future plans. Done in isolation, CSR projects become the corporate showpieces with little long-term
value. The Indian experience shows many innovative initiatives that have
failed to take off to the next level. In this model, periodic review and defining
guidelines are of critical importance to give momentum to the project. However, it is the last step in the process that is the most challenging: how to
make the project stand on its own, i.e. can there be a viable revenue model?
Indian banks have often looked at bad debts from farmers as part of the social cost of operation. It took a Grameen bank in Bangladesh to change the
model and make micro-financing a viable business. In CSR project management, this is a big challenge. Once a CSR initiative starts generating
revenue for itself, companies need to delegate operations and look for the
next project. Maybe they can identify new areas (geographical or functional)
where their expertise and experience can add value.

Chevron is training Nigerian youth in technical skills relevant to the oil and petroleum industry. It is trying to achieve hundred percent indigenous procurement
for its oil projects in the Niger Delta. For the community, in the short term, this
means increased literacy rates leading to better jobs and better quality of life. In
the long term, technical competence also brings in more equitable regional de-

velopment. For Chevron, it is not only about social responsibility but also about finding low cost, closer-to-home suppliers. All community employment programmes are sustainable as long as the parent company continues operation. Once natural resources are depleted, retraining the community can be very tough. In its Kelian project in Indonesia, Rio Tinto is planning to retrain the community in fishing, agriculture and automobile repairs so that they can continue to enjoy the same quality of life long after the gold mine has closed down.

In India, companies like Ballarpur Industries and Patton are working with this approach to formulate policies or carry out specific projects. Some of them select a community, work out the primary area requiring focus and work on it. Others select a functional area (e.g. education, health) and then select the communities. Many of these programmes are also gender-specific e.g education for the girl child or male awareness about the risks of HIV transmission through multiple sexual partners. The IT major Wipro, has taken an innovative step in generating a sustainable model in the primary education sector.

Wipro has chosen education as its focal area. Elementary education is a key area of the Indian government, too. To achieve the status of a global super economy by 2020, the government has identified health and education as priority issues. It has been revising policies, investing funds and sponsoring computers in schools as a part of its literacy drive. However, there are no mechanisms to monitor effective administration of such programmes, just as there are no review mechanisms to understand the bottlenecks. Beyond literacy, there is a need to look at the quality of the learning and its delivery. Using its computers and its knowledge in software development, WIPRO is exploring ways to enhance the quality of learning at primary school level. Improving learning delivery and outcomes are the key result areas (KRA) of its efforts. In a 2002 survey of more than 100 companies, around 48 % mentioned 'nation building' (working in areas crucial for overall national development) as part of their corporate social responsibility.

The Azim Premji Foundation (APF) is headed by the Wipro chairman, Mr. Azim Premji. APF has set itself the task of effectively introducing technology in rural government schools. Apart from improving the quality of education delivered, one of the focal areas is to make elementary education more of a community effort rather than a traditional government project. The Community learning centre (CLC) is a tool for this purpose.

The concept has been tested on 10,000 children in 34 schools with encouraging results. It will not be a substitute for the existing process, but a well-researched supplement to it. Children are happy with this new tool and the academic performance has shown corresponding improvement. There are two broad themes here: the use of IT (mainly in the form of computers and software content) in the learning process and involvement of the community in the project.

The basic objectives of community learning centres are:

- Attracting school drop-outs back to the schools;
- Increasing the attendance rate of pupils;
- Improving the quality of learning for the children;
- Identifying and helping slow learners;
- Using IT to make learning fun.

The decision to start a community centre depends on the number of out-of-school children in an area (the higher the number the more suitable the solution), the school infrastructure and the enthusiasm of school authorities. The community as a whole should also be interested in this project. The village or community should also ensure that there are educated youths who could take charge of the learning centres. Stakeholders occasionally raise a pertinent question such as whether when schools are without blackboards or even permanent classrooms money should be spent on computers? While it is true that there are schools without a basic infrastructure, it is also true that, within schools having requisite infrastructure, there is a huge gap between expectation and performance, particularly when one considers the number of drop-outs and different levels of learning among the children in the same class. It is here that community centres are useful. They encourage children to return to school by arousing their interest in education. The sheer fun of working with computers (with their multimedia contents) is reason enough for many to come to school. (see Figure 12.2 for the stakeholder map of the model and the benefits accruing to them from the project.)

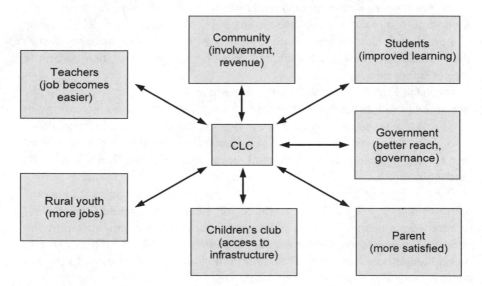

Figure 12.2. Stakeholder map of the community learning centre

Resource requirement

Generally one computer for every 40 children is found to be an effective ratio at the learning centres (One computer with an average configuration costs around Rs. 30,000; 1$= Rs 45 approximately). Therefore, for a school with 250 students, the norm is 6-7 computers. Additional hardware may include microphones, printers, an Internet modem, MS office and a web camera. The average class size is 36. Dividing the class into two batches of 18, allows a children-to-PC ratio of 3 to 1. The fixed costs of setting up a learning centre amounts to Rs. 200,000. The operation costs include salary, electricity, maintenance, insurance and other costs. The average total cost is Rs. 40,000 per year.

To make the community responsible for the project, youth from the local villages are selected to run the learning centres. To qualify for the post, they have to be educated to at least up to senior secondary level (sixteen years of education). Called Young India Fellows (YIF), they are trained in computers and rudimentary teaching. They learn to work both with the community and school authority. Since existing teachers are normally overloaded with the coursework, they are not considered for running the centres. Moreover, in many schools the teacher-student ratio is poor making it difficult for teachers to assume additional responsibilities. Identifying and training teachers during the initial stages of the project is often found to be difficult. As teachers are often transferred from one school to another, continuity is another problem. Under such circumstances, a local dedicated youth, who is likely to remain in the area and knows the community well is thought to be a is a better solution.

Role of the schools

Schools play a vital role in the scheme. They ensure that adequate space is provided for the project to run smoothly. Each class has a 'computer period' of its own in the regular schedule. The target group is children in grades 3-6 with provision for children from classes 1, 2 and 7. During term time, the school ensures that computers are used properly and are secure. During school holidays, the learning centres are used as computer clubs or to provide intensive courses in computer applications for local youth. The children's clubs consist of children from other schools. Special courses are designed for them.

Role of teachers

The head teacher plays a crucial role in determining the success of community-based learning centres. He introduces the changes in the timetable, allocating space for computers and making teachers available. Much of the staff motivation depends on the head teacher's approach to the project. The school's permission is also required to keep centres open beyond school hours. It acts as a bridge between the community and parents of the children. Parents appreciate the effort and feel encouraged to send their children back to school. In rural India and in poor families, parents often use the children for domestic labour or field labour. Particularly, when there are many children in a family some of them are encouraged to help in business or agriculture. The head teacher also helps in making the centres self-sufficient by generating revenue.

For the school teachers, these centres are a boon. Children are taught science, mathematics, social studies, and languages through multimedia CDs (available on request from APF). Teachers can effectively use multimedia to introduce new topics. The idea is that each topic will be introduced in the community learning centre after the teacher has initiated discussions on the same topic in regular class. Even basic computer skills are not taught separately; children pick up these skills on their own through interactive CDs. Interactive games make the learning process informal and fun. The local volunteers teach the children the basics of computer operation. These centres are not for IT education but rather IT for education. Therefore, the focus is on curriculum-related learning. Sometimes extra-curricular teaching is also available.

A group of villages are clubbed together as so-called 'blocks'. In each block coordinators monitor the activities of a group of learning centres. These coordinators are drawn from original groups of YIFs. They act as the nodal point for the centres, community and government. They attend the review meetings and are trained regularly.

12.3 Problems faced

Sometimes communities receive these projects with suspicion. There is an initial lack of involvement. This can be overcome in time with the help of good communication and community involvement in discussions. Generally, communities interested in the project will contribute to the payment of maintenance costs, electricity bills etc. They will also refurbish rooms and provide security for the hardware. There are cases where the community has even convinced individuals or companies to sponsor printers and other products. The centre can also be used for special information purposes such as meetings and training courses as well as for general communication to the community. A number of areas would be possible e.g. pulse polio eradication programmes, vaccinations, adult literacy programmes, continuing education, different rural development programmes etc. This area has not really been developed yet. Lack of continuous power supply makes it difficult to maintain a uninterruptible power supply (UPS). General hardware problems are sorted out by giving annual maintenance contracts to hardware vendors. The security of the hardware is also crucial, as cases of hard disc theft have been reported.

Many children (approximately 30%) do not develop basic reading writing skills even in standard/grade 3 (i.e almost 3 years after starting school). Due to the shortage of teachers in villages and the inadequate evaluation methods, it is impossible to provide these children with special coaching. Thus, when they move from one class to another, they are not able to cope with the increasing learning pressure and eventually drop out of school. There are few resources, beyond text books, in rural areas to support additional learning for the students.

Sources of revenue generation

APF's strategy is to create and deliver this model. After the model has been successfully implemented, APF exits the project and moves on to a new area. Communities need to be well-equipped to continue the project.

Most CSR programmes concentrate more on developing their social responsibility agenda and pay little attention to making such programmes self-sustaining. This community learning centre project is a noteworthy exception. The project has focused on the self-sufficiency of the centres from day one. The time beyond school hours is used for this purpose. Some of the innovative solutions that flow out of this model:

- Children's computer clubs: children from other schools use the facility to learn to understand computers. They use the infrastructure on a pay-and-use basis;

- With IT generating lots of jobs in Indian hinterland, these community-learning centres are poised to become very popular with the rural youth who can be trained in Windows and applications;

- Villagers require a lot of documents for their interaction with the government offices. There are plans to use the Internet to provide the village people with information about crop prices, weather reports or simply to communicate via e-mail;

- The government can also use these centres for e-governance programmes;

- Revenue is generated for all the above activities. Part of the revenue is used for proper maintenance of the hardware. More importantly, it creates great word-of-mouth publicity for the centre enabling the entire district to take up these projects in due course.

The model is independent of the type of schools, governments, geography and social settings and easily replicable all over the country. However, power (for UPS) and space for running the programme are prerequisites.

Content development

Besides providing the infrastructure, it is crucial to develop suitable content to ensure the success of the learning centres. Contents need to be sensitive to local needs and child friendly at the same time. Rural children have different learning needs than urban children. For example an urban child is under continuous pressure to excel. This pressure is created both by parents and peers. Irrespective of what is being taught, the urban child is forced to work hard and learn. The rural child has no such pressure. Consequently, the only thing that can enhance their quality of learning is superior content, which will make them interested in the topics. Here lies the challenge for the learning centres. Computers and particularly multimedia provide a stimulating experience. Such contents again has to be in the mother tongue of the children. It has been found that rural children particularly enjoy using software where the learning takes place without conscious knowledge or effort on the part of the child.

The content typically focuses on creating an individually paced, learning environment. Pacing is important particularly for slow learners. The content also tries to help teacher with additional questions and gives them tips as to how to improve their teaching methodology. Content, however, should:

- Be self-sufficient i.e. it can be used without the help of a teacher (the 'Fellow' takes care of administration);
- Be set in a rural context and linked to the Minimum Levels of learning (MLM) set by the government of India;
- Facilitate peer learning;
- Be properly graded in terms of difficulty so that students do not get frustrated;
- Be concentric i.e take a core concept like addition and slowly develop the skills required for higher mathematics;
- Include the same topics as those taught during regular class hours;
- Be such that assessment and evaluation are not routine;
- Include non-curriculum content, too.

To facilitate content development, using its expertise in software development, APF has created a development tool kit for would-be content developers. While developing content, long conversations, foreign characters and solitary games are generally avoided.

Developing and running a CSR model like this would involve a proper knowledge and constraints of the communities, a continuous feedback mechanism and the ability to create networks with the local government. The Community Learning Centre project has got it right till now.

12.4 Conclusion

Over time, the learning centre becomes an integral part of the school environment (with its headmasters, teachers, parents, and school development and management committee members), self-help group members, school inspectors, education officers, leaders and prominent local members. It helps the community and makes primary education management a co-operative and self-sustaining effort.

CSR models typically marry a company's core competence with local or national needs. In this case Wipro's expertise in IT has found a suitable application in improving primary education in India. APF's CSR model is unique in the Indian education field thanks to its community focus. The model is cost-effective, scalable, and even self-sustainable. Given the high unemployment rates in rural India the YIF scheme is a good starting point.

Most of India's IT revenue comes from business-process outsourcing projects. Reports suggest some of the IT companies have started moving bases towards the countryside for projects which are less demanding. In such cases, there will be an increased need for an IT trained work force in the villages. In future, community learning centres can double as training centres for the youth. With the infrastructure in place, CLCs can become new hubs of rural India.

Wipro is one of India's largest IT companies and this project is definitely benefiting its brand image. Thousands of children (future stakeholders) are getting to know the brand name, communities regard it favourably and governments welcome such initiatives with open arms. Wipro is getting to be a part of India that aspires to be a top global economy by 2020. While doing good, the model will ensure that Wipro also does well financially in the long run. The learning centre model highlights how social regeneration and corporate social responsibility go hand in hand. It is a win-win situation for the country and the company; rural communities get quality education and the company is able to create and improve its competitive position in the business environment.

Websites

www.azimpremjifoundation.org
www.eduinfoindia.net

13 Creating Space for CSR in Melbourne

David Teller and Trevor Goddard

Key words: Constructive corporate participation, Global Compact Cities Programme, Committee for Melbourne, leadership, learning, citizenship.

13.1 Introduction

In his Davos commitment to sustainable development, Kofi Annan warned that the private sector as a dominant engine of growth is also the 'principle creator of value, and that economic growth and opportunity must address equity and sustainability; otherwise social justice will remain a distant dream'. Partnerships between government, civil society and the corporate sector provide this, for while role separation amongst government, societal and corporate sectors has given professionals a sense of freedom and independence in operation, the results have often been fragmented and blinkered activity, with sectors regularly working against each other, blindly preventing common gain through ideological, structural or political differences.

What is the Committee for Melbourne?

The Committee for Melbourne (The Committee) is a private, not for profit and non political network of leaders drawn from senior levels of major corporations, institutions and organisations across Melbourne's business, scientific, academic community and government sectors. The Committee is governed by a 14 member Executive board that meets six times a year, thereby providing a neutral space for interactions between non traditional stakeholders. In addition, the Committee's Advisory board meets twice a year, and consists of Foundation members who maintain oversight of the executive board and the committee's operations. The Advisory board also has the role of championing the reputation, ideas, projects and objectives of the Committee, while providing guidance, feedback, ideas and opinions relating to the operations of the Committee within the context of Melbourne's economic and social development. By seeking to translate 'ideas into outcomes' the Committee moves beyond the traditional think tank model, seeking to facilitate creative ways of challenging conventional CSR methodologies. The Committee believes that a dynamic city is good for both business and the community, fusing the often cited business case and social case for corporate social responsibility.

Committee for Melbourne strategic priority areas

In order to ensure geographic focus and the most effective application of scarce resources, the Committee maintains five key strategic objectives. Taskforces, projects and initiatives are categorised and defined within these objectives:

- Ensuring global relevance as the first 'city' to engage the UN Global Compact. The Committee has developed the Melbourne Model methodology (see www.melbourne.org.au) to tackle economic, social and cultural impacts of urbanisation by combining and coordinating resources, ideas, experience and knowledge inherent in the corporate sector, government and civil society (see Figure 13.1);

- Fostering leadership and creativity to enhance the attractiveness of Melbourne as a magnet for creativity and knowledge;

- Encouraging an innovative business culture that rewards creativity and creates the space for innovative solutions to complex problems;

- Facilitating leading edge infrastructure as a base to support further innovation and collaborative activity;

- Enhancing liveability through corporate connection to social issues within the scope of influence for business that makes Melbourne an insightful city; acknowledging the fusion of business and social goals.

What makes it work?

Creating opportunities to network and catalyse existing work for identifiable outcomes (Teller, 2003) increases the flow of knowledge between sectors, thereby helping to remove the fragmentation of many genuine localised efforts. Partnering involves active city involvement across multiple industries (see Figure 13.1), responding to societal problems that cannot be based in one system alone, the complexity commanding a synthesis of multiple ideas and knowledge. The Committee strengthens community actions by enabling the city to set priorities, make decisions, plan strategies and take advantage of the 'neural networks' (Teller, 2003) corporations create through operations. Central to this process is the community empowerment bringing together partners to draft solutions. Drawing on human resources enhances self-help opportunities and social capacity, developing flexible systems and strengthening public participation. Through this think tank and action programme leadership function the Committee creates a sense of community. Corporations engaging in the process have a real sense of belonging and a social connection, enabling the collective power of corporations to work within the framework of social justice – making identifiable and valuable contributions through active and concrete participation.

13.2 The Constructive Corporate Participation (CCP) model

The Committee fuses the creative power of civil society, government and the corporate sector, enabling business to operate beyond the conventional and purely economic-driven perspective. Driven by corporate issue-based endeavours, the Committee enables a level of engagement within a common space that provides for: safe creative expression, the joint acknowledgment of social capital being a product of government, society and business, and the notion of citizenship that includes both rights and responsibilities within civil society. The uniqueness of the Committee is represented through the interactions and particularly the intersections presented in Figure 13.1 below.

The important characteristics are that projects undertaken by the Committee are issue driven, and entirely focused on achieving real outcomes (examples of successful projects are displayed through the web site www.melbourne.org.au). The common ground, where Committee members and stakeholders work together, is characterised by trust, leadership and common space, with each of these discussed below. It is not surprising that each of these makes a strong contribution to social cohesion within the community, reinforcing that the Committee

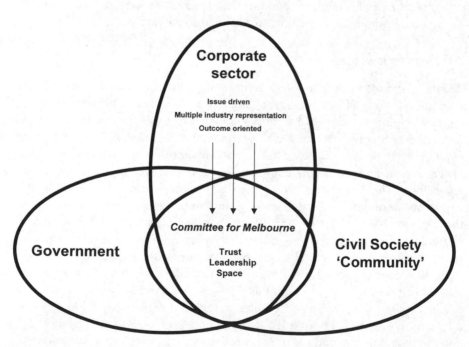

Figure 13.1. Committee for Melbourne – Constructive Corporate Participation (CCP) model (Teller, 2003; Goddard, 2004)

successfully intertwines social and economic development for the city, inspired through real business oriented activity.

Trust

Trust is essential to a city's social and economic wellbeing. Without community trust (commercially referred to as 'goodwill'), corporations retreat into bureaucracy, resulting in a slowdown or cessation of the creative process necessary for the creation of innovative solutions to complex issues. A retreat into bureaucracy is reflected in the awkward manner by which many corporations globally are seeking to address their corporate social responsibilities. Continual redefinitions of corporate roles within the community is a response to the reported absence of community trust in corporations and their leaders. The 2003 World Economic Forum in Davos conducted a survey of 36,000 people across 47 countries to rate trust in 17 institutions. Those deemed to be most trustworthy were armies, charities and schools with the lowest ranking going to parliaments and large companies.

Strengthening and maintaining 'goodwill' (trust corporations create with citizens) is an important objective for big business, embedding ultimate business success deeply within a humanitarian context, and one contextually difficult to define as corporations attempt to 'rebuild' global and local trust with community citizens. Trust remains the most elusive, yet important component of corporate success. 'Corporate social responsibility' (or Constructive Corporate Participation as we argue) perhaps presents the ideal opportunity for mature and insightful corporations to engage with communities in the creation of 'well being' for both individuals and corporations alike. This fusion of social capital within a community is a product of both individual and corporate interactions. The Committee enhances trust most effectively thought engagement of multiple corporations from the same industry who are able to put the greater good of Melbourne, or the city within which they operate, above individual corporate success.

Leadership

A PricewaterhouseCoopers (PwC) global survey (PricewaterhouseCoopers, 2003) identifies 'people of integrity' amongst factors contributing to public trust. Leaders appear less trusted than the institutions they lead; perhaps implying that declining public trust is as much about personal leadership as institutional leadership. The PwC survey sought opinions on trust from 1,000 CEOs across 43 countries, with 73 percent indicating public trust in their companies had not declined; yet stating that the corporate sector generally has suffered from a decline in public trust. In contrast an Environics International study of trust (Environics International, 2002), covering 15,000 people across 15 countries revealed that 'not doing what they say' is chosen by more than 40 percent of citizens as the factor that most leads to distrust of leaders, reinforcing the view that individual citizens look for leaders who are able to deliver on their promises. The action-orientated nature of the Committee is to translate ideas into action, assisting to bring CSR to life through community leadership. A previous Environics survey on CSR revealed that across 25,000 people in 25 countries, over eighty percent believed companies need to be involved in addressing social issues, ultimately contributing to societal well being. The Committee methodology seeks to avoid traditional and often expensive, inefficient and politically-driven processes by seeking to ensure that the 'best', as opposed to the 'usual', people are involved in the process of developing practical solutions.

Common space

Learning

Corporate memory, an important aspect of preventing the loss of valuable experience, ideas and information, is often subject to critique due to case study research often being dismissed as a non-rigorous research methodology. The Committee's work, however, provides real-life learning examples, experiencing phenomena first hand instead of only being content to learn about those practices that are open to public scrutiny. It is beyond the rules of public disclosure where 'truth' is found, often in the 'backstage' of social phenomena in a trusting environment. Case studies and narrative provide an efficient tool for policy intervention, bringing to life the reality of outcomes people experience in corporate life, rather than the perceptions of stale policy and procedure so rarely followed in practice. Rich case experiences provide 'truthful' meaning with the recording of corporate activity then becoming an essential part of building and maintaining trust in a corporate and community relationship.

Creativity

As developmental hubs, cities provide the 'energy' contributing to 'intellectual and creative capital'. Using a city as a defined point is beneficial as a city's future success lies in its sustainable economic and creative performance – bringing powerful people together as a catalyst for change and fresh ideas to be taken on by the government and the community. A competitive environment is often identified as a barrier to CSR activity with the inability of internal corporate structures to look beyond models of financial cost reduction and cost per unit production stifling a movement towards Constructive Corporate Participation (CCP). The systemic trans-disciplinary and future-based approach to decision-making alleviates this problem as corporations seek employees with leadership rather than managerial skills alone and those capable of integrating multiple business and societal functions rather than working in a restrictive ontological financial framework (Goddard, 2004).

As highly networked focal points of economic wealth, skilled labour, learning, government and infrastructure, urban centres are prolific incubators of new ideas, technologies and skills. However, owing to the 'silo mentality' and poor communication that often characterises relationships within and between organisations, such opportunities are often lost. The Committee, on the other hand, effectively captures and co-ordinates these outputs to provide solutions to otherwise intractable problems. The Melbourne Model (see www.melbourne.org.au), at the centre of the Global Compact Cities Programme, is a mechanism designed to identify, focus and facilitate the constructive capacity present in any given city—regardless of its economic, social or cultural structure. The Model puts the principles of the Global Compact (see www.unglobalcomapct.org) into practice by providing a framework within which business, government and civil society, in a city, combine their inherent resources, ideas, knowledge and experience in order to develop effective solutions to pressing local problems.

Citizenship

Citizenship goes beyond 'doing good things', corporations cannot remain neutral if something is wrong in the society their success is based on. Corporate citizenship requires corporate cultural change to embed values and objectives into corporations that are mindful of the community with whom they engage. Enlightened corporate members of the Committee focussing on 'moral ownership'; identifying stakeholders to whom they owe an allegiance, as they cannot discharge social responsibilities without determining exactly to whom they are owed and why. Companies engaged in citizenry activities then test ownership by assessing not with whom the board deals, but whom the board has no moral right not to deal with, supporting the models reach in needing to bring the 'right' people in to resolve the issue, irrespective of where they come from.

Social capital

Seeking to build social capital may appear risky in the traditional commercial model, however, it can allow corporations a means by which to tap into local knowledge, enhance their image, create goodwill and enhance social capital that cannot be 'bought' in the financial sense. It can become part of a risk management profile ensuring sustainability of the corporation in increasingly unpredictable environments. Social capital, according to the preferred OECD definition, refers to the very networks, shared norms, values and understandings that Teller (2003) describes as facilitating co-operation within and among groups. The Committee enables Melbourne to purse higher levels of mutual trust, reciprocity, unwritten and unspoken agreement about societal rules, and social cohesion.

13.3 Constructive Corporate Participation: A new paradigm

The Committee acts as an incubator for projects that are issue driven (for successful projects such as the Utility Debt Spiral Project see www.melbourne.org.au). The purpose for members to engage is clear, supporting the action-based nature of the organisation's philosophy to drive solution-based outcomes (see Figure 13.1), that deliver results strategically and enhance the social and economic vibrancy of the City of Melbourne. Corporate participation in partnerships includes ownership of the issue (contextually and interest driven). The Cities Programme provides a geographical definition of the ownership and scope of influence for all those involved. The clear geographical and cultural definition is an important component of allowing CSR to come to life.

This 'new economy' model of CCP, created by the Committee, requires: the integration of internal and external business and community drivers and, the creation of structures that move smoothly across corporate and community boundaries until the boundaries appear so permeable as to produce a new synthesis. Civil society as a driver of change will continue to influence companies, reinventing businesses that create identifiable opportunities for community-based partnerships (Goddard, 2004). CCP's are bred from economically successful cities that attract and retain creative people within industry, civil society and government activities, with the booming cities of the 21st century combining tolerance, talent and technology to resolve issues posed within their geographical boundaries.

Individual capacities are unleashed as the issues are larger than any of the individual organisations, with CCP representing the ability to harness the resources, ideas, skills and information inherent in the private sector for the creation of wider social value. Holistic corporate citizens interact with other parts of the community and function within a global system larger than themselves, interconnecting corporate and community activities, be they ecological, economic or social. This corporate capacity and willingness to make short-term sacrifices for long-term benefits moves Committee members towards holistic corporate citizenship. CCP relationships fostered within the Committee are more responsive to changes in the external political and social environments and enable change of context within which the relationships were formulated.

13.4 Corporate learning through constructive participation

Organisational learning can occur internally, alongside other corporate citizens, and through prospective learning; planning to learn before experiences take place. This cognitive function, undertaken by organisations, is a step towards the development of human-like qualities, or at least the ability to ac-knowledge their importance. The Committee is a collation of mature and in-sightful corporations searching for avenues to explore citizenship and espousing the Darwinian advice, '... it is not the strongest of the species that survive, nor the most intelligent. It is the most responsive to change'. As corporate citizens within the Committee structure, corporations appear better able to see them-selves as part of a larger public culture rather than the city's culture existing as something external to the company.

The CCP journey provides the answer to '... how does a company decide how to begin the seemingly overwhelming task of changing some deeply em-bedded practices and attitudes, and how can it develop the capacity to respond in such a way that turns effort into a business advantage not a business cost?'. The Committee takes corporate functioning out of the vacuum enabling active and anticipatory responses to community capacity issues. A discussion of multiple futures can be used in long range and multivariable planning to enable corpo-rations to be 'in the community' rather than simply responding to calls of the community.

13.5 Conclusion

The Committee fuses the unique characteristics of a think tank and incubator. Corporations engaging with this learning process enables CSR to become a 'practice what you preach' concept generating trust, a small step towards the resolution of complex community issues in which all citizens can take part. Ironically, in a corporate environment necessarily focused on the bottom line, trust is the only commodity once produced that grows exponentially with use, yet the one that cities and communities tend to least invest in, the Committee however is one such investment. With trust being the ultimate sustainable re-source and an active ingredient in citizenship, corporations engaging in CCP are those most mindful that 'a business that makes nothing but money is a poor business' (Henry Ford). The emotional competencies held by the Committee, and evident in its membership, allow this unique structure to successfully build CSR through CCP. These competencies include:

- Organising groups: formatting stakeholder representation across multiple sectors thereby assisting to break down the silo mentality;

- Negotiating: inviting partners to come together in a common space thereby assisting to create trust through openness created by common purpose over and above competition;

- Developing personal connections: networking across government, community and corporations to create 'neural' connections that may otherwise not have had the opportunity to develop;

- Social analysis: trans-disciplinary evaluations that fuse social and business measurements together to reinforce that social wellbeing and business wellbeing can be closely related.

References

Environics International (2002). *Corporate social responsibility monitor*. Retrieved 21st April 2002, 2002, (http://www.environicsinternational.com/default.asp?sp-csr.asp).

Goddard, T. (2004). Corporate Citizenship: Australian Corporate Attitudes Towards Stakeholder Engagement. *Journal of New Business Ideas and Trends* 2(2): pp. 12-28.

PricewaterhourseCoopers (2003). *6th Annual Global CEO Survey in conjunction with World Economic Forum*. London: PwC International.

Teller, D. (2003). The UN Global Compact Cities Programme The Melbourne Model: Solving Hard Urban Issues Together, *Journal of Corporate Citizenship* (11): pp. 133-142.

Websites

www.melbourne.org.au

www.ungobalcompact.org

Organising Identity

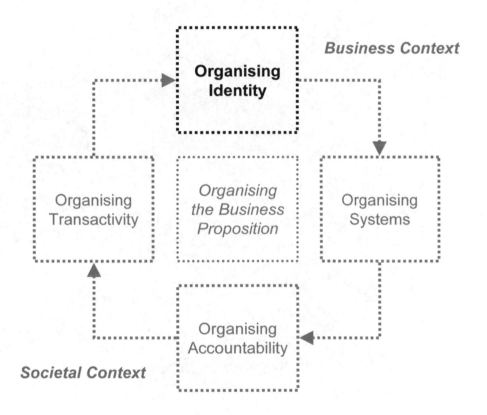

14 Integrating People, Planet and Profit

Fred Bergmans

Key words: Balancing people, planet, profit, decision-making, integrating CSR.

14.1 Introduction

The basic idea underlying Corporate Social Responsibility (CSR) is to find a proper balance between People, Planet and Profit. All companies have to face a major challenge when deciding on priorities in CSR. There is an increasing obligation to integrate CSR in business policies and daily activities. Turning it into a primary company process entails more than isolated projects linked to the company identity.

No simple techniques exist to help companies make the necessary choices which range from identifying and defining new CSR challenges to best fit the company to coordinating various initiatives and building up support for their implementation. The objective of developing the model was to provide an overview of the driving forces in creating added value for People, the Planet, and the Profit of a company. This overview is intended to serve as a guiding principle in setting priorities and strengthening links. This conceptual model is set out below. Two case studies show how the model can help generate insight and commitment.

The model

The balancing of People, Planet and Profit is often represented visually as a triangle within which added value is created. People stands for social well-being, Planet for ecological quality and Profit for economic prosperity. The triangle shape symbolises the idea that one P should not profit at the expense of another. Each company should define its own ambitions with respect to the three P's, thereby also taking into account the views of external stakeholders.

Balancing the three P's therefore means making choices and setting priorities. Since such decisions should be taken at the strategic level within the organisation, top management plays a crucial role. Their judgement about what to do is usually based not only on purely rational arguments. Gut feeling, and knowledge of what the company can handle, will also influence their views.

Managers respond with their intellect (head), feelings (heart) and knowledge about behavioural practices (hands).

These three perspectives (Head, Heart and Hands) can be visualised as a triangle; each side has its own meaning (See Figure 14.1):

- Head-Heart: Who are you? (the balance between rationality and feeling);
- Heart-Hand: How do you do it? (the mutual influence of feeling and action);
- Head-Hands: What is the impact? (the evaluation of whether it works as you want).

The integration of the PPP triangle and the HHH triangle leads to three other triangles that show in visual terms the decision-making process. This new triangle also includes the following corner segments:

- Operation: What are we going to do?
- Organisation: How are we going to do it?
- Origin: Why are we going to do it?

Within companies it is common practice to speak about 'What to do' and 'How to do it'. However, in order to be successful one should also talk about why

Figure 14.1. The basic model

one is doing something. The answer to the latter question creates clarity about the goal that it serves, how it fits into the larger whole, and therefore how important it is for the company.

Integrating People, Planet and Profit means bringing coherence to the three perspectives: origin, organisation, and operation. To successfully achieve this linking process it is important to understand the driving forces behind the three perspectives.

14.2   The essence: Three perspectives

Origin

The origin corner concerns the mentality, culture and behaviour of the company as well as the reasons for acting (the 'why'). It highlights the concern of people ('mission') and the spirit with which one works ('passion'). These driving forces together form the (shared) norms and values according to which people behave.

Mission

The mission of a company indicates how it views the world and which objectives it has set itself. The challenge is to formulate a mission statement which really touches the hearts of the people involved in the company. This makes people feel proud to belong to the company and leads to shared ambitions.

Passion

The mission is made alive through the devotion and commitment of the staff to their work. This 'positive energy' can also be called passion. Although this is an unusual word to use in a work environment, one instantly recognises a passionate manager or employee: someone who believes in what he does and is full of energy to make something out of it. Passion triggers others to join the effort.

Organisation

The organisation segment concerns the structure of the company and focuses on the manner in which the company works (the 'how'). It gives direction and definition to the role of people in the organisation by determining their responsibilities (People). It also guides the decision-making process about the amount of money to be made available by formulating the business strategy (Profit). It brings coherence to activities and people, so that it becomes possible to account for the way in which the company acts.

Responsibility

To be responsible means that one expresses what one wants to achieve; this gives direction to oneself and to others. It only makes sense to take responsibility when you are willing and able to do something. If one regards responsibility as a deliberate choice, the logical consequence is being accountable for the way one acts. Taking responsibility is a choice and also implies a first step towards action: the readiness to do something and to initiate actions from others.

Strategy

Strategy means making choices and focusing on achieving the goal. A characteristic of a good strategy is when one is able to reach the desired goal effectively with minimum effort. It creates synergy between the people involved and coherence in the activities to be carried out. This inspires people to take action.

Operation

The operation segment of the triangle concerns those activities and processes of a company which concern products and services (the 'what'). It is oriented towards what the company does ('execution') – and also the company steps to perform beyond current company limitations ('innovation'). The combination of both these aspects leads to 'best practice'.

Execution

Notwithstanding the kind of products or services which a company offers, the result should always meet two basic criteria in order to be effective: it should deliver both a financial and a material result. How one judges the quality of this result depends on the glasses one wears. In order to meet the expectations of the company itself but also those of external stakeholders it is wise to take into account more than one perspective.

Innovation

In principle, attention is directed here towards efficiency: how can the company reduce the dissipation of raw materials, energy and labour with improvement of processes and still reach its goal? Which measures can one take within the company itself and which within the product chain? Combining efficiency improvements both from an economic and ecological perspective is also known as the struggle for eco-efficiency. Such efforts can result in incremental improvements up to a certain point. Innovation, in terms of a technical re-engineering of the process, can move the company beyond the current restriction, thus leading to new products or processes with a higher added value.

14.3   Experiences with the model: The insights

In Figure 14.2 all dimensions of the model are brought together. On the basis of this complete model a deeper understanding is gained of how a company can decide on integrating People, Planet and Profit.

Figure 14.2. Complete Company FIT model

Bringing coherence to the driving forces achieves strong links between Values (Principles), Accountability (Processes) and Best Practises (Performance).

Values

Passion and mission form the basis of what is deemed important (the values) and the way in which people relate to each other (the norms). Norms and values motivate people to act and also function as the touchstone of corporate behaviour. They usually constitute the implicit rules of the organisation, firmly embedded in the culture or mentality. Increasingly, however, they are nowadays also expressed very explicitly in the form of codes of conduct.

Accountability

Accountability is based on the responsibility taken and the defined strategy. To be held accountable has a negative connotation for many people. This is due to the fact that it often implies a value judgement in terms of good and bad. However, it can also be viewed in a positive sense – as a way of evaluating the strengths and weaknesses of the company's efforts.

Best practice

Best practice is the optimal combination of quality execution and innovation viewed from the perspective of the three P's. It represents the best-in-class performance compared with peer companies in the sector, and has the lowest impact on the environment in a social and ecological sense.

14.4   Application of the model

The complete model pictured above in Figure 14.2 can be used in decision-making about balancing People, Planet and Profit. The model provides an overview of all the dimensions that should be taken into account. It makes clear that all dimensions relate to each other and therefore should be viewed in a mutually coherent way. The model also helps to assess where a company stands in terms of CSR. By analysing the situation from the perspectives mentioned in the model, a first impression can be provided of the current state of affairs. On the basis of this model companies can take action on those issues that are most relevant to them and need to be improved.

Actual experience: Two cases

The model was used in workshops to visualise the decision-making process and to better understand the context of CSR projects.

In the following two cases the application of the model is described, firstly in a profit organisation where it was used to align corporate and product strategy, and then in a non-profit organisation where it was used to stengthen the implementation of a CRS project.

Case 1: Profit organisation

The problem and the opportunity

The management team of an industrial paint manufacturer, based in the Netherlands, was strongly committed to providing high-quality water-based paint for professional purposes. In their product portfolio, they had only one brand delivering a natural, ecologically harmless paint. Though this brand has only a niche market share, it was felt to be the conceptual flagship of the company. The management team wanted to clarify how to improve on the People and Profit dimension, in order to reach a balanced PPP value creation.

The process

In a workshop with the management and senior staff the essence of the triangle's six driving forces were explored. In pairs of two, the meaning of the six words for the company and the brand were defined, and this was shared with all participants. As a group they discussed the difference in meaning for the company as a whole and the specific brand. This made it possible to explore similarities and deviations in the company and brand identity. After this first discussion on the separate meaning of all six words, the model was introduced to visualise the link between these various entities. Further elaboration on these links produced valuable insight regarding weak and inconsistent processes and practises, thereby creating an opportunity for improvement.

The outcome

The outcome showed that the strong passion of the company founders had driven product innovation to reach the highest ecological performance possible, but all efforts were exclusively focused on value creation on the Planet dimension for this specific brand.

The company mission was a less powerful driver. Lacking a formal written statement, team members had a broad interpretation of delivering quality products. However during the discussion the relevance of quality in customers and consumers terms was explicitly introduced. This triggered the team to start considering more ambitious goals and to redefine its responsibility towards changing industry practise in using paints. The strategy towards professional painters was adapted to intensify collaboration. First round table discussions with these users also revealed that the products could be improved in their application characteristics. This helped make the company realise that customers' demand for specific improvements could even make the brand gain more market share.

The management team decided to strengthen the People dimension by including customer and consumer statements in their mission and responsibility. This gave strong direction to a new communication and quality improvement strategy, thus opening the possibility for growth and more Profit.

Case 2: Non-profit organisation

The problem and the opportunity

A government project team was installed to implement a procedure for sustainable policy-making. The project team was uncertain as to whether the execution of the project fitted in with the organisational culture. Prior to the start there was a difference in opinion regarding the underlying question as to whether the project was a simple implementation of a procedure or whether an organisational change management perspective was needed to combat cultural resistance.

The process

The project team used its first meeting to explore the context of the project assignment.

The model helped identify the six driving forces and the relationship to the project. The essence was identified and expressed in key words in the model. During these discussions the differences of opinion were rather explored than debated.

The outcome

The discussion on the more abstract level regarding the context of the project brought the insight that an exclusive focus on the strategy and execution, (profit dimension) was the general attitude and culture in the non-profit organisation. However a true success factor was identified in the commitment of critical management layers. To get this commitment, it was necessary to consolidate the link between the project and the mission and responsibilities of the non-profit organisation (People dimension). The discussion also revealed the passion of the young employees for innovation – an opportunity that needed to be to capitalised on.

14.5 Dos and don'ts

A practical way to use the model is outside-in. Start by defining the six driving forces in the company: mission, passion, responsibility, strategy, execution and innovation.

Evaluate how the mission relates to responsibility, strategy to execution and passion to innovation. Finally strengthen the interaction of mission and passion to fuel values, the interaction of responsibility and strategy to fuel accountability, and the interaction of execution and innovation to fuel best practises.

Don't use the model for an individual paper-based exercise. It is far less effective than a team effort. Introducing the 'soul factor' is a discovery tour in decisions affecting the company's identity. Only when participants feel the meaning of the mission it is possible to achieve their full commitment.

Don't perceive the model for use by CSR professionals only. If you are facing internal resistance to CSR, the model can be used to help a team perceive the link between mission and action. This might help to open eyes to CSR responsiveness or opportunities.

14.6 Concluding remarks

The aim of the model is to support the decision-making process in integrating People, Planet and Profit. By defining six driving forces in three perspectives, management and staff can focus discussion on the essence of CSR for their company or projects. The visualisation of the triangles enhances the comprehension of links, revealing both weak and strong links. Identifying and improving these links strengthens the integration of People, Planet and Profit value creation in company policy and practises.

The use of the model in workshops appears to speed up group understanding of the complex concept of CSR and build up a shared commitment to change. The application of the model encourages employees to express their feelings as an integral part of the decision-making process. This explains why so much positive energy is released when individuals perceive their personal role in the implementation of CSR.

References

Cramer, J. (2004). *Learning about Corporate Social Responsibility: The Dutch Experience*, Amsterdam: IOS Press.

Website

www.freshbusiness.com

15 Reflexivity: Linking Individual and Organisational Values

Nick Osborne and Martin Redfern

Key words: Values, reflection, response-ability, reflexivity, effectiveness.

15.1 Introduction

The introduction to this book recognises that CSR policies and practices are frequently added on to existing organisational activities as afterthoughts. They are often ineffective because they are intended to modify embedded practices. Consequently they are commonly perceived as superficial, meaningless gestures. The challenge to proponents of CSR is to find ways of incorporating decisions compatible with social responsibility at all levels of organisational activity.

This article outlines a management development model which integrates CSR into organisational policy and practice by focussing on the role of values in decision-making processes. The model is based on the premise that it is a mistake to assign responsibility to organisations as if an organisation has a personality and so to speak of 'corporate decisions'. Decisions are not made by an organisation: people within the organisation make decisions. Personal values inform the perceptual filters which shape individual interpretations of organisational policy and decisions. Many people are unaware of the ways in which their values shape their interpretations and influence their decisions.

This model encourages individuals to be aware of their values and the role those values play in decision making. It also focuses on the relationship between individual values and organisational policy and practice. It is therefore a model which is particularly relevant to CSR as it suggests a relationship between individual and organisational values, while connecting them by improving managerial effectiveness. This results in better implementation of organisational policies in general and any CSR policies there may be in particular, which eventually improves performance and adds value all round!

This model has three components: personal reflection, group exploration and practical application. These components work together in repeated cycles of action and reflection:

Practical Application

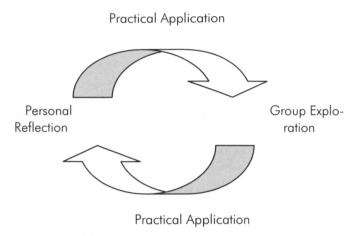

Personal
Reflection

Group Explo-
ration

Practical Application

Figure 15.1. Cycle of reflection and action

15.2   The essence of the model

The model is a programme of organisation wide management development. All managers could be involved, since CSR considerations are part of everyone's work. But to achieve effective and widespread organisational change the programme must involve senior decision makers, policy makers and budget holders.

Individuals can develop self-awareness independently by using personality profiling techniques as a form of self-assessment. There are many popular psychometric assessment and development tools available (e.g. Myers-Briggs Type Indicator, Personal Values Budget etc.). However, personal development is limited when attempted alone. People develop greater self awareness with the support of a professional practitioner in a structured programme.

Personal reflection

Through personal reflection the participant identifies a particular workplace problem. The practitioner then supports the participant in reflecting on their predispositions and exploring how these may be contributing to their experience of the situation. Links are made with a participant's general behavioural predispositions and patterns are identified, thus helping the participant see how these predispositions are limiting their repertoire of responses to the world in general and in the workplace in particular.

As their self-awareness is enhanced in this way, participants begin to see alternative ways of framing situations in which they become progressively more able to generate creative responses. They develop response-ability, the ability to respond to situations with self-awareness. The practitioner supports this development through repeated cycles of reflection on their reactions and consequent actions until the participant reaches adept reflexivity, at which point the practitioner is no longer needed.

Five steps to reflexivity through personal reflection

Reflexivity is self-awareness refined to the point where self-aware reflection and considered response take place in the same instant. Reflexivity is awareness of the way predispositions influence perceptions while they are being influenced and the simultaneous modification of responses.

Table 15.1. Five steps to reflexivity through personal reflection

Activity	Method	Result	Example
Identify learning goals	Reflect on how to improve performance	Personal reflection has direction and focus	I want to improve my communication with certain colleagues and sort out some conflicts with them
Focus on specific problem at work	Reflect on how personal predispositions contribute to the problem	Discovery of new responses to the problem	I see how my responses were rooted in unconscious beliefs which conflicted with those of my colleagues and so can accept their differing values without conflict
Reflect on personal predispositions	Identify patterns of responses and develop a personal and professional profile	Increased self-awareness leading to improved performance	I have a tendency to think I am right about certain issues and argue with those who disagree but can now see that my personal prejudice is at the root of such conflicts
Learn about learning	Reflect on how learning has occurred	Continuing development of self-awareness and improving performance	By identifying my unconscious belief in a particular value I saw how it contributed to conflicts and poor communication
Develop reflexivity	Practice modifying habitual response patterns before taking action	Ability to be reflexive	When I find myself getting into similar conflicts, I notice my habitual response pattern and remember that I need to listen to the other person before starting to argue with them

Group exploration

In group sessions participants explore organisational values and the relationship between individual decision-making and those values. They develop their individual understanding of how the values espoused by the organisation relate to its CSR policies and practices, and the combined role these values and their personal values play in the individual decisions that they make. They also learn from each other's experiences of seeking to implement organisational policy and consider the wider ramifications of such practice. They relate individual decisions with organisational policy and practice and look beyond to shareholders, other stakeholders, market forces and government regulations and thus develop a perspective which is responsible to all.

Practical application

After personal reflection participants go back to work to put new learning into practice. They then attend group sessions to share their emerging awareness about the role of values in making decisions and how this affects the implementation of policy on a day to day basis. They then go back to work to apply these new insights and then reflect again. Repeating this cycle provides the mixture of action, reflection and sharing experiences which are essential to change embedded individual and collective practices.

Rationale

The role of values in decision making in organisations is complex and often misunderstood. Personal values shape individual interpretations of organisational policy and decisions. Espoused organisational values often differ from values implicit in practice and the relationship between personal and organisational values is often obscure at best. So any values expressed in CSR policy may or may not be aligned with actual individual and organisational practice.

Individual worldviews are shaped by perceptual filters which colour experience according to predispositions inherited at birth and learnt during life. These predispositions are a complex of fundamental beliefs about the world, assumptions, conditioned responses, ideas about meaning and significance, habits and so on. An important group of such predispositions is personal values, which found many of the judgments people make about their worlds. Such values are often unconscious and yet play a significant role in informing our perceptions in the same way as a pair of glasses affects our vision even when their presence on our nose has long been forgotten.

In the workplace, individuals interpret organisational policy through just such perceptual filters and consequently make operational decisions according to personal beliefs. Not only do their values colour their choices, they also limit the options they perceive as available to them. Becoming aware of these subjective limitations enables individuals to see beyond them to discover new possibilities for interpretation and action. The more aware an individual becomes of how their personal values affect their interpretation of organisational policy the more effective their decisions will be.

   Enhanced self-awareness leads to a better understanding of organisational aims and a wider range of options for action. Managers with these attributes are better able to assess whether their intentions are in harmony with organisational policy and are better able to act effectively because they understand what they need to achieve. They are flexible, creative decision-makers who learn quickly, communicate clearly and create better working relationships with colleagues. When many managers behave in these ways, organisational effectiveness is increased and value is added in every way.

   Thus effectiveness is perceived as the link between individual and organisational values. A management development model which focuses on individual values is an ideal tool to use when working with organisational activity that is value-driven, such as CSR. All organisational goals are value-driven in the sense that they represent positive outcomes for the organisation. This method can be used to work with any goal-oriented activity. That CSR goals in particular are perceived to be value-driven makes this method an ideal way to achieve CSR while also developing all aspects of organisational performance.

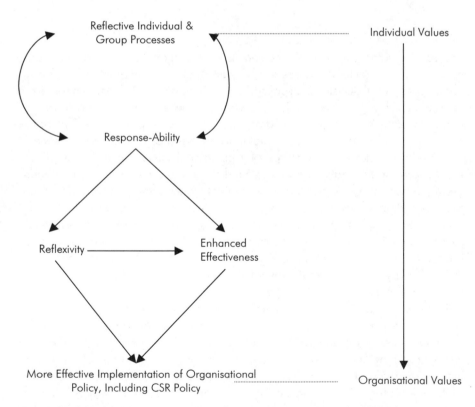

Figure 15.2. Linking individual and organisational values through reflexivity

Results: response-ability, reflexivity and effectiveness

As described above, the model develops reflexivity skills across an organisation. Reflexivity is self-awareness refined to the point where self-aware reflection and considered response take place in the same instant. Reflexivity is awareness of the way predispositions influence perceptions while they are being influenced and the simultaneous modification of responses. Reflexive managers are self-aware decision-makers who are able to effectively implement policy in practice with alacrity and consistency. If they disagree with policy they have the critical self-awareness to understand their disagreement and are able to communicate accurately and appropriately about it.

The development of response-ability in many managers leads to what appears to be organisational response-ability but is in fact the development of shared understanding of organisational values. Organisations are not personalities and so cannot be attributed with values. Rather, individuals in organisations make decisions according to values which create the impression of emergent personality characteristics in the same way as colourless molecules combine to create the appearance of surface colour. Furthermore, the way we are accustomed to speaking about organisations creates the appearance of character where there is none. We talk about them as if they were people, anthropomorphising them as if we were their creator in our own image!

It is because of this mistaken way of perceiving organisations that misguided projects intended to align individual and organisational values are proposed. This model of management development answers the need to address organisational values at individual decision-making levels without falling into the same trap. However, it also equips individuals with critical skills which they may use to seek alternatives to organisational policy where they feel the need to do so. A key feature of this model is that it acknowledges the mutual interdependence of individual and organisational values instead of assuming that one or another will prevail. Indeed, its focus on the interface between the two is what puts it at the cutting edge!

15.3 Experiences with this model in practice

A manager at the international headquarters of a multinational company was having trouble with community relations management at major projects with considerable local impact. Conflicts kept arising between her and one manager in particular which affected their working relationship. By exploring her responses to him she identified her belief that people are inherently good and saw how this belief prevented her accepting his perspective, thus causing conflict between them. As she became aware of how her belief shaped her response she also became able to find alternative ways to respond. Doing so improved her relationship with the manager enabling them to work more effectively together, as well as improving her relationships in general in the same way.

A team leader was struggling to motivate her team members. By exploring her responses to the situation she became aware that 'the way I had posed the initial challenge question was a direct reflection of my controlling tendencies'. Because of this realisation she said she was 'getting a better grip on my tendencies to be controlling and to think about how my shaper personality ... can bring the wrong result, or the right result with the wrong emotions or feelings'. One year later she felt she had become a more effective manager by making her leadership style more participative, an option that had not been available to her previously because she had not been aware of her habitual managerial style.

15.4   Some dos and don'ts

This model is rooted in the theory of social constructionism as described in the Complexity and Emergence in Organisations series of books by Ralph Stacey et al. Individual self-awareness develops in emergent and unpredictable ways, so practitioner intervention should be facilitative rather than directive. This allows insight to arise from experience, rooting behavioural change in personal learning.

The same applies to group sessions. New collective meanings and understandings are likely to emerge in collaborative explorations. Emergent understanding is the key. This approach is sometimes referred to as dialogue and is described in Dialogue and the Art of Thinking Together by William Isaacs.

Both individual and group sessions should iterate through cycles of action and reflection. Participants can reflect on their experience, finding alternative responses to ongoing problems which they can then evaluate for effectiveness. Repeating this cycle allows participants to consolidate their learning by embedding new behaviours through reconditioning. This recursion also supports the development of group understanding, thus enhancing organisational performance.

15.5   Wrapping up: Advice for application

Decision-makers at every level of organisation will benefit from this management development model. To be most effective, the model should be systematically implemented as a programme of management development across the whole organisation to involve key decision makers, policy makers and budget holders. Programme commissioners must decide who best to choose from a range of personnel including key CSR professionals, senior executives and other managers depending on the extent of an organisation's willingness to engage in such a programme. They must be clear about their reasons for this choice as it will critically affect the programme's effectiveness and outcome. In a situation where organisational management development resources are limited, judicious selection of personnel to represent diverse managerial responsibilities may be more effective than simply focussing on policy-makers. Where budgets are more flexible, inclusivity is the aim.

As a key attribute of this method is the perceived link between individual and organisational values, practitioners must identify CSR policy values as comparable with general policy values. As all organisational goals are inherently value-driven, CSR goals are no different to economic or strategic goals. Many managers may think otherwise because CSR goals are often externally imposed by regulatory or market forces whereas economic and strategic goals are usually internally generated by executives and profit-motivated shareholders. It is this misperception that creates misalignment of organisational culture and CSR policy. However, responsive adaptation to external pressures is a significant characteristic of evolutionary advantage and therefore economic profitability. Consequently, organisational investment in such adaptive skills will enhance effectiveness and CSR at the same time.

References

Isaacs, W. (1999). *Dialogue and the Art of Thinking Together*. New York: Doubleday.

Griffin D. and P. Shaw (2000). *Complexity & Emergence in Organisations*. London: Routledge.

Berger, P.L. and T. Luckmann (1966). *The Social Construction of Reality*. New York: Anchor Books.

Website

www.response-ability.org.uk

16 Self-Organising Leadership: Transparency and Trust

Richard N. Knowles

Key words: Self-organisation, Self-Organizing Leadership™, authenticity, transparency, ethical behaviour, trust.

16.1 Introduction to the model

Corporate social responsibility (CSR) must be authentic for it to be both sustainable and a prudent business investment. The leaders in the corporation need to behave in a way that is visible and consistently ethical, both internally and externally to the organisation. CSR begins at home by developing transparency, ethical behaviour and trust within the organisation, through comprehensive sharing of information among all the employees, through co-creating interdependent relationships in the ethical agreements among the corporation's people, and through helping everyone see the whole corporate picture and their identity within it.

Information needs to be shared about important issues like how investment decisions are made, how the personnel and pay systems work, how the pension and IRA funds are set up, managed and protected for all the people's future. People need to know about the rules of their work and understand why they are the way they are. All information except that, which is personal and protected by law, needs to be shared openly in their conversations.

Management needs to establish conditions in the working environment to foster open dialogue and support honest exchanges and questioning. Answers to questions need to be provided in a timely and full way with everyone having access to anyone they think may have the information they need to do their job well. These conversations will open up the corporation so that the rules, procedures and processes can be scrutinised and understanding developed. This high level of transparency will help everyone know what is going on and why. This will lead towards increasing trust.

Management needs to engage the employees in conversations to develop their agreements on how they will be together. For example, they need to agree to fully share information, up, down and across the organisation; to be open and honest; to respect and help each other; to tell the truth; to go to those who have the information that they need to get their job done well; mistakes will be seen as learning opportunities; they won't kill the messenger of bad news; no cover-ups or lying; treat customers honestly and respectfully; treat the members of the public honestly and respectfully; as a minimum, comply with all laws; fulfil all quality and safety standards; keep agreements; seek to understand, etc. These agreements apply to every one (from the top to the bottom of the organisation), and each person agrees to hold themselves and each other to be responsible in living up to them. Co-creating and living up to agreements like these builds high levels of authenticity, interdependence and trust in the organisation.

As information is being openly shared, strong, professional relationships build, trust and interdependence emerge. Trust is the invisible glue that holds the corporation together. It is also what makes communications with the outside world credible and meaningful.

Management needs to co-create the corporate vision and mission with the employees, so everyone can begin to see how they fit into the corporation's future. This begins to help them develop a sense of meaning in their work. They can be proud of their corporation developing a deep sense of satisfaction in what they are doing.

Sharing information, building interdependent relationships and helping people to see how they fit into the corporate picture are the basic conditions for the processes of healthy self-organisation. When these internal self-organising processes are robust and healthy, the employees of the corporation will become ambassadors for the corporation in its efforts of CSR. The outside world will see this support and be much more inclined to engage positively with the corporation's social responsibility efforts. Without this internal credibility check, the outside world will simply view the corporation's social responsibility efforts with cynicism and distain.

Management must become conscious of the process of self-organisation and the basic conditions that support it in order to build the internal and external credibility and coherence for authentic CSR. This requires a shift away from the more traditional top-down management process towards one that is more open and engaging of the people. This does not mean that management loses control of the corporation, but rather develops a stronger, more effective way to lead. This way of leading is called Self-Organizing Leadership™.

16.2   The model

This model relates to the use of Self-Organizing Leadership™ (Knowles, 2002). The model helps managers to see and pay attention to what is going on and to facilitate a shift to self-organising leadership processes. Traditionally, most managers use top-down, mechanical, linear processes to work on structure, pattern and process which are interconnected and visible things. These are il-lustrated in the upper part of Figure 16.1.

They work on structure which relates to things like buildings, manufacturing plants, training manuals, rules of work, etc. They develop and monitor work processes to be sure they will get the desired results and they pay attention to the patterns for the work being done to try to find the most efficient way of do-ing things. In thinking about structure, pattern and process it is helpful to think of a road map. The structure relates to the terrain shown on the map. The pat-tern relates to the way the roads are laid out, and the process relates to the way the traffic flows at different times.

There is the belief that cause-effect relationships can be established and that the organisation can be controlled from the top. Many managers have a pas-sionate desire for reliability, predictability, stability and control. Yet, most are not satisfied with the results they are getting.

The model is shown in Figure 16.1.

The model also helps managers see the self-organising leadership processes shown in the lower part of Figure 16.1 below the arrows indicating the transi-tion zone. These processes are like the roots of a tree; invisible yet vital to suc-cess and sustainability. The model helps them to pay attention to the need for sharing information, to building strong, interdependent relationships and to helping the people to see how they fit into the whole picture, thus allowing meaning to emerge.

These self-organising processes behave as if they are living. They are cyclical. They are emerging. The world is neither stable nor predictable at the surface level where most people have traditionally functioned. But at deeper levels

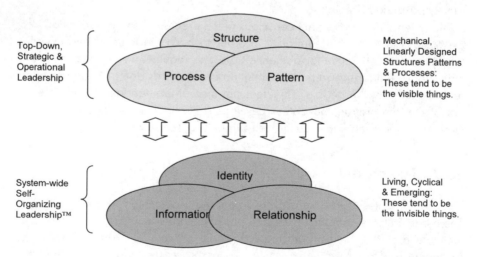

Figure 16.1. With Self-Organizing Leadership™ the changes are co-created

there are reliable and consistent patterns of behaviour which are very useful for being able to function successfully. In fully sharing information, building healthy, interdependent relationships and in developing a clear identity, managers can build a bowl which is the reliable, stable container (a deeper pattern) that provides a sense of direction and control for the corporation while at the same time opening a space where the people in the organisation can have the conversations they need to grow and develop.

Within the bowl, people do not need to be micromanaged; rather they know what needs to be done and work to achieve the best results they can. Meaning emerges; energy and creativity open up. This form of leading requires a willingness of the managers to be open, transparent and authentic. This way of leading builds the trust to the levels needed for the corporation to perform at the highest levels possible and to be credible to those working inside the corporation and with those working and living outside the corporation. This is Self-Organizing Leadership™ and is fundamental to CSR. People working in this way become great ambassadors for the corporation in their CSR efforts.

How to use the model: The process steps

The process begins with a clear statement from top management that they want to build a more credible and sustainable organisation. In order to do this they intend to share information more fully, build more trusting, interdependent relationships and to help everyone to see how they fit into the whole of the organisation.

A facilitator is then charged with organising the effort and in helping people to come together to have the serious conversations about issues that are of importance to the corporation and its people.

The conversations can be about things like the pay structure, the savings and investment plans, how the corporation calculates and reports its earnings, how investment decisions are made, how they communicate with the investment community, the basic values of the corporation, etc. The conversations may be brief or they can last over several sessions as needed. The intent is to have everyone understand how these systems work and to see that they are being used fairly. With this approach, management is building transparency into their systems.

Invitations are issued to all those who may be interested in a particular issue. These sessions need to include managers and others (not the facilitator) who are knowledgeable in how the systems work so that questions can be answered openly, authoritatively and clearly. Ground rules like those mentioned earlier in this paper need to be co-created with management and the other participants about how they are going to behave together. All levels in the organisation must support and live by these agreements. This is the process of building interdependent, ethical behaviour so it's critical that everyone behaves authentically.

In these sessions, suggestions for possible improvement in the systems may emerge. Management needs to be open to this possibility and be willing to have people form teams to explore and develop them more fully. The final decision as to whether or not adopt these changes rests with top management. They need to be open and honest in sharing the reasons for their decisions. Transparency and trust are being built here. These are basic building blocks for corporate sustainability and social responsibility. Summaries of these sessions need to be shared with everyone so that all can be as fully informed as possible.

As the transparency, ethical behaviour and trust build within the corporation, more and more people will become authentic spokes people on behalf of the corporation and effective ambassadors to the communities and governments around them.

16.3 Experiences

When the author was plant manager for The Du Pont Company in Belle, West Virginia, from 1987 to 1995 he developed and used the Self-Organising Leadership approach. Within the plant credibility, authenticity and trust grew. Injury frequency rates dropped by over 96%, productivity rose by 45%, chemical emissions to the environment dropped by 85% and earnings rose by 300%. With this strong base within the plant, the author helped to lead a community-wide effort in 1994, using Self-Organising Leadership, in which 13 chemical plants from 8 companies told a community of over 300,000 people 29 ways that we could hurt and kill them with a worst case scenario chemical release, and trust went up! Many of the people from the plant played key roles in the community to help this CSR effort to succeed. Without this credible, active support by the employees none of the community people would have believed anything we had to say, and our effort would have failed. When McNeil Consumer Products, a Subsidiary of Johnson & Johnson Company had the Fall of 1982 incident where someone had put poison into a Tylenol® container, they proactively shared information and took strong steps to recall their product to ensure its safety. They communicated openly and fully with the public about all that they were doing. Their people rose to the challenge because they were proud of their company and believed in their management. J & J had built high levels of trust within their corporation which paid off for them in this difficult incident. Their proactiveness and authenticity enabled their CSR effort to succeed. When an Ashland Oil storage tank ruptured in January, 1988, spilling oil into the Monongahela River in Pennsylvania, their CEO fully shared information with the public and assured everyone that they would take the responsibility for the clean-up. This proactive approach built strong credibility with the regulators and public; lawsuits were minimised. The credibility and trust within their company was the basis for this CSR effort to be successful.

16.4   Some dos and don'ts

Do take this approach to leading if you want to develop the conditions and credibility to reach high levels of performance. It'll take real work by everyone to learn to live and lead this way.

Don't take on this approach to leading unless you fully intend to be authentic and credible. People will see through any falsely based approaches and you will fail.

16.5   Wrapping up

Self-Organising Leadership enables the people to achieve high levels of performance. The organisation becomes more nimble and quick as it is able to quickly sense and respond to changes that will impact it. This approach builds credibility and trust, enabling the organisation to more successfully compete in this rapidly changing world. It also is the basis that is needed to have a sustainable CSR effort. This process begins with simple conversations about things that are of importance to the people in the organisation. There is no need for any new capital investment or big training programmes. The conversations grow like the circles made by a stone tossed into a pool of water.

References

Knowles, R.N. (2002). *The Leadership Dance, Pathways to Extraordinary Organisational Effectiveness*. Niagara Falls, New York: The Center for Self-Organizing Leadership.

Lewin, R. and B. Regine (2000). *The Soul at Work*. New York: Simon and Schuster.

Knight, J. (1982). *Tylenol's Maker Shows How to Respond to a Crisis*. The Washington Post, October 11.

Petzinger, T., Jr. (1999). *The New Pioneers*. New York: Simon and Schuster.

Websites

www.soliancegroup.com

www.centerforselforganizingleadership.com

17 The CSR Brand Positioning Grid

Bart Brüggenwirth

Keywords: Branding, marketing, positioning, external communication, advertising.

17.1 Introduction to the model

CSR provides an interesting way to build better brands. The challenge is to find the right balance between CSR and other brand values. The opportunities for integrating CSR in marketing have to be selected carefully. There are subtle differences that can be extremely decisive. The CSR Brand Positioning Grid is a tool that helps define the right balance and determines the importance or role of CSR in developing and building a brand. It offers a framework for deciding how explicitly or implicitly CSR should be expressed and what the relationship with other brand values should be. It can help companies to use CSR to differentiate their products or brands from those of their competitors.

Before developing the brand, its positioning and value proposition (e.g. lowest price, best product, customer intimacy, sustainability champion) need to be defined. This decision reveals the level or importance of CSR within the business strategy.

Most mainstream companies have no ambition to become a sustainability champion. They have chosen another value proposition and CSR is integrated within this strategy. CSR provides the environment within which the value proposition is delivered. This can be a result of different motives. Defensive: because stakeholders demand it and the company wants to avoid possible risks. In this case there is little room for using CSR in branding. Or offensive: CSR is an expression of its identity, it reinforces the business strategy. Only then can it offer opportunities to strengthen the brand and its market position.

In very green-oriented companies, which are often driven by their ideology, the focus on sustainability is the primary choice and could in itself be described as their value proposition. To start from this point influences the business model, the structure, the quality and price of their products etc., and thus the competitiveness of the value proposition they can deliver to their clients. They often operate in niche markets and CSR plays an important role in branding.

The model is derived from a marketing technique, called the means-end chain. This is a method which helps to ascertain the reasons underlying consumers' purchase decisions. It is common practice in advertising and campaign development. The chain consists of:

- Attributes: concrete, often physical or tangible aspects of a product or company: product features, competencies, systems;
- Consequences or benefits: the solutions the product or company offers;
- End values: values people live by, lifestyles.

Benefits and end values provide the answers to one of the most important marketing questions, namely: 'what's in it for me?'. Take Volvo for example; safety is the core of its brand positioning. A means-end chain for Volvo could be: 'a Volvo is equipped with a solid bumper (attributes), which offers me safety (benefit). This is important for me, because I care for my family (end value)'.

Branding has become more complex and subtle in recent years. It is not only about what we sell or about the benefits of our product. Customers also want brands that offer them inspiration. The consumer's choice for a brand is not only based on these three elements. The identity of the company behind the products or brands has become more important and creates preference with consumers. For this reason, the consultancy company b-open has added an element to develop the CSR Brand Positioning Grid: the inspiration that a product or company offers. Inspiration comes from inside. This reflects the 'softer', intangible aspects like philosophy, mission, principles, ideals and shared values.

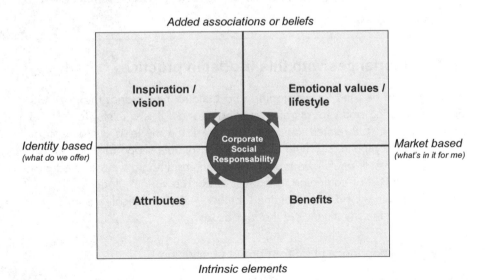

Figure 17.1. The CSR Brand Positioning Grid

17.2   The essence of the model

The four elements are integrated in a quadrant, consisting of two dimensions:

1. Identity based ('what do we offer?') – market based ('what's in it for me?');
2. Intrinsic elements – added associations or beliefs.

The result is four boxes appointed in Figure 17.1.

In positioning a brand clearly, one should focus on one of these boxes, although a brand becomes stronger and harder to compete with, when it is embedded in more than one box. The grid can be applied in the branding process on three levels, corresponding to three successive stages, as shown in the following chart.

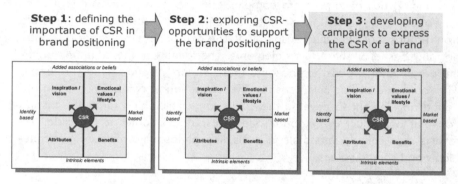

Figure 17.2. Applying the CSR Brand Positioning Grid

17.3   Experiences with this model in practice

The model can be used for developing and building new brands and for monitoring, evaluating and repositioning existing brands. It is a useful tool for exploring relevant CSR-related topics. Furthermore, the model is a practical tool for analysing competitors. It helps identify the available scope for communicating CSR in terms of one's own brand and offers insight into ways of creating a distinctive method or campaign to express CSR. The various stages of the CSR Brand Positioning Grid are explained below, using practical examples and elaborating on the significance of the four boxes.

Defining the importance of CSR in brand positioning

The first stage in using the model is the creation of a brand. The challenge is to choose the right focus for the brand positioning. The CSR Brand Positioning Grid offers a framework to explore the strengths and opportunities for a product or company. An inventory was drawn up for an organic food company that included various options:

- The company could simply concentrate on the characteristics of the product: it has an organic or natural composition and doesn't contain any artificial additives (position bottom left); or

- it could communicate its corporate identity and describe its philosophy or the nature of the production process: that the food is produced in a traditional way, by a family-owned company, where there is a clear focus on animal welfare and the environment (position top left); or

- the company could consider a more market-based perspective and concentrate on relevant consumer benefits, like quality, health or the good taste of the food (position bottom right); and finally

- the company could decide to create a lifestyle brand (position top right), targeting the product, for example, specifically at people with a environmentally-conscious lifestyle, a group which is involved with the well-being of our planet such as the group called the Cultural Creatives. An alternative would perhaps be mothers who care for their family and want food that has not been messed around with. Their lifestyle and values could also offer a valid perspective.

In each box an inventory of all the relevant possibilities should be made. There are only a few examples included above. After putting all relevant options in the four boxes a trade-off process takes place to select the brand positioning. The final choice will be based on criteria such as distinctiveness from competition, relevance and attractiveness for the target groups, authenticity and credibility of the claim. For the organic food company, positioning the brand based on its identity (left) may lack the relevance to attract a broader, mainstream audience. Healthy or tasty food may seem more attractive directions. The fact that it is organic would then support this claim. However, it would be of relatively minor importance in its brand positioning, where taste is the decisive factor.

One of the results of this trade-off process may be to promote CSR or related aspects of sustainability to become the core element of the brand positioning. This is only possible for green companies or products which can muster sufficient supporting evidence. As a consequence, the company knows it will attract mostly green consumers and will have to be satisfied with serving a niche market.

However a green company, that wants to attract a larger audience, can also choose personal benefits for the consumer, like quality, body care and health, or a lifestyle to position its brand. A brand that has made this shift is the Dutch fair trade brand Max Havelaar, that uses 'max genieten' (= maximum enjoyment) as an advertising theme.

Exploring CSR opportunities to support brand positioning

After defining the positioning and supporting values of the brand, the model can be used to explore relevant CSR aspects for building the brand. This is perhaps obvious for brands that choose a position based on CSR, mostly green-oriented companies, but it also applies to mainstream brands where other values or propositions such as innovation, taste, health, customer orientation, or price leadership are the focal issue.

This is the case for most companies. In this situation the CSR Brand Positioning Grid can be of great value, because it can inspire these companies to find existing or new CSR-related characteristics that support these claims. What is even more important for the implementation of CSR in these companies is that it offers interesting opportunities from a marketing perspective that stimulates the CSR process and really integrate CSR into the business. The Grid was used in a multinational pharmaceutical company that operates in a business-to-business market. The strategic focus was to increase loyalty. This was the starting point for investigating the opportunities. Moving through the four boxes with a CSR perspective an inventory was made of relevant CSR-related topics and issues (internal or external) to support the customer intimacy strategy. One appeared in the mission statement (top left). It included the company objective to enhance the quality of life of patients, an objective it was pursuing with its products. But why not enhance the positioning in other ways and encourage clients (mostly hospitals) to develop ideas to support this cause? The best ideas were then rewarded with a grant. The patients benefit, and at the same time the programme generates sympathy and builds up the loyalty of the hospitals towards their supplier.

Another example is of a telecom supplier whose brand positioning was to offer connectivity to as many people as possible. A CSR consideration inspired them to identify special target groups with social needs, like the disabled, and to develop solutions for them to increase their mobility and safety (market based: bottom right). This added a niche, but commercially interesting, market – and one that also strengthens the brand image.

Developing a campaign to express the CSR of the brand

The third way to use the model, is a more tactical one: to develop a campaign with which to build a sustainable brand. This may be an advertising campaign or an internal communications campaign. This applies particularly to brands with CSR as the core element, but is also valuable for brands that have defined another focus for their brand positioning, yet still see CSR as a relevant supporting or additional brand value.

The challenge is to translate CSR into an attractive and effective key message. The CSR Brand Positioning Grid helps to find the most relevant or distinctive angle (box and subjects in this box) for conveying CSR. This focus is the strategic starting point for the creative development process. Again, the other boxes can offer inspiration, supporting evidence or other relevant information for this angle.

For several years Shell has run corporate advertising campaigns to express its CSR. In the Netherlands they started with a print campaign that explained the dilemmas and philosophy of Shell. The pay off was 'Profit. Principles. Or both'. (identity based: top left). Now they run a corporate campaign which focuses on the sustainable solutions that Shell is exploring or offering on a product level (e.g. cleaner diesel, V-power). They use a testimonial concept, in which clients or other stakeholders give their opinion about these products. They moved in the Grid to a position on the bottom right.

This corporate campaign adds a (sustainable) value and sympathy to the brand and to the product claims in its marketing campaigns such as 'more power for your engine' for Shell V-Power. BP has a different approach. In its marketing campaign for BP Ultimate it has combined an environmental claim with a consumer benefit: 'more power, less pollution'.

17.4   Some dos and don'ts

Marketing is not selling ideology

Traditional CSR companies – i.e. involved in CSR because of the firm conviction of their founders, board members or employees – are often emotionally tied to their identity and principles. They want to sell their ideals. However, that is not the way to reach a mass market. Therefore it is necessary to combine these ideals with the relevant benefits for their clients. Conveying CSR implicitly is often more effective than obvious claims.

Don't hide

Mainstream companies that have achieved a great deal in the field of CSR may miss opportunities in the areas of branding or marketing if they fail to communicate these efforts. This model can help them to find the subtle and relevant perspective.

Co-ordinate corporate and marketing efforts

It is still business practice to treat corporate communications and marketing as two completely separate functions, especially within larger corporations. However, there is a mutual influence between marketing and corporate communications and branding on a product and corporate level. Integration is necessary.

Don't concentrate exclusively on the final consumers

A strong brand positioning is not only aimed at the needs of the customers, but also takes into account the needs of other stakeholders (e.g. employees, NGOs, local communities). Such a positioning is based on a overall brand value or theme that connects with all these groups and from which they can each derive their own value. It should also leave room to differentiate the explanation of the brand positioning to each group. A leading Dutch bank ABN-AMRO uses 'making more possible' as a slogan in their advertising campaign, but it is also the title of their sustainability report.

17.5 Concluding remarks

The CSR Brand Positioning Grid is not a box-ticking exercise. Applying the model requires analytical skills and the ability to collect the right information for the four boxes. The information should be provided by representatives and specialists inside or outside the company. It is also a creative process that requires the judgement, creativity and intuition of the people involved. A well-tried method to achieve this is to arrange working sessions and to discuss the options for defining the role of CSR in branding with management teams or representatives of different management disciplines relating to CSR (e.g. HRM, quality, marketing, buying, operations, sales).

Branding is more than advertising, especially when CSR is at stake. It is about building strong relationships which people value. This is achieved by the way a brand behaves: through its employees, its products, prices, community involvement and its communications. All these elements build the brand and contribute to a brand image. As values like sustainability and trust become more important, so CSR and branding gradually converge. For those companies that embrace CSR, the Brand Positioning Grid is a valuable tool in their objective to 'live their brand' and 'walk their talk'.

References

Fombrun, C.J. and C.B.M. van Riel (2004). *Fame & Fortune. How successful companies build winning reputations.* Upper Saddle River: Financial Times Prentice Hall

Hoijtink, J. (2004). *Van Geitenwollen sokken naar designjeans. Over duurzaamheid en marketing.* Amsterdam: Kluwer.

Ray, P.H. and S.R. Anderson (2000). *The Cultural Creatives. How 50 million people are changing the world,* New York: Three Rivers Press.

Organising Transactivity

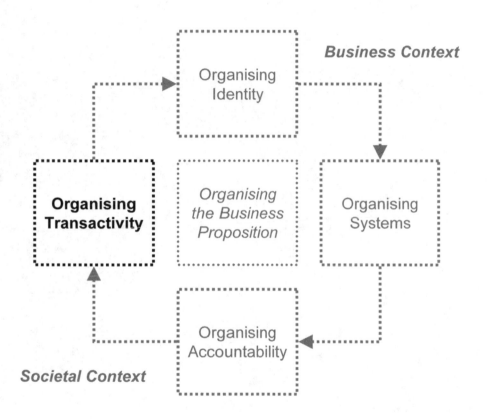

18 On Dialogue: A Self-Development Tool

Robert Beckett

Key words: Dialogue, self-management, open-thinking, communication ethics, citizenship.

18.1 Introduction

The underlying theory presented in this dialogue model is founded in communication ethics. This new practical discipline situates the human capacity to communicate in a close relationship with ethical reasoning; the human ability to live cooperatively as well as to understand and use moral principles and their underpinning values. Christians and Traber (1997) characterise dialogue in the following statement which indicates how human relationships, knowledge, wellbeing and 'talking together' are all fused through dialogue, a form of 'face-to-face' communication that remains an essential procedure to establish and balance ideas of human wellbeing in community. 'Communication is not the transference of knowledge but a dialogic encounter of subjects creating it together.' (Christians and Traber, 1997, p. 9).

The '5circle' used here is based on the hermeneutic circle, a concept in philosophy, suggesting that knowledge and interpretation are linked through an emergent 'understanding over time'.

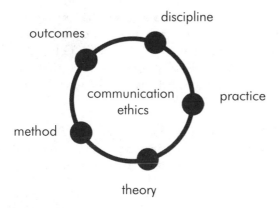

Figure 18.1. A disciplinary model for communication ethics

Discipline: The necessary human condition of always being in relationship with others establishes communication as human beings' most valuable skill. Ethical responsibility is to understand the effects of communication and its responses on the other and to privilege the personal, the human and the cultural over the imposed realm of technological, political, media and organisational ideologies, in Habermas's expression to 'privilege the lifeworld over the systemworld'. (Habermas 1984/7).

Practice: A practice of communication ethics offers all people, not just specialists, an opportunity to be involved in dialogue, through a) problem identification, b) examining deeper issues, c) offering hypotheses, d) establishing knowledge e) and building competencies.

Theory: Dialogue emphasises communication that is two-way, rather than one way, that is unrestricted by one of the partners and that emphasises human beings as specially privileged in being together. See the discourse ethics of Jurgen Habermas and the particular the notion of the 'public sphere', a theoretical realm protected from co-option by political and other systemworld attempts at control. (1984/7, 1990), thereby providing a space for the discussion and resolution of foundational ideas such as human rights, democracy, citizenship and self-governance.

Methods: This model uses the '5circle' to enable participants to identify their own issues, although the example below has been filled out with working models of communication ethics. Each circle is read from the top right in a clockwise fashion. If an issue becomes 'live' controversial etc, the group may then pursue their own thinking using their own hand-drawn '5circles' to describe the results of their dialogue. As a network model 5systems may also be used to join issues from other sources (see www.5systems.net).

Outcomes: Using this 'heuristic technique', to promote 'open thinking', concepts of various kinds can be examined, new ideas may be captured and alternatives discussed. The more conceptualisation the participants bring to the dialogue, the greater opportunity for shared knowledge formation and thereby, shared consideration for the implications of those actions the dialogue intends to affect.

This guide analysis is composed of questions that may be asked in dialogue, thereby to identify underlying assumptions and concepts important to the dialogue. Many further questions can be added to these as part of the dialogue.

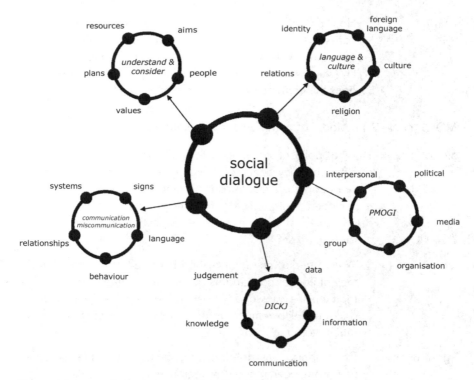

Figure 18.2. A self-development model for dialogue

Language and culture (circle 1)

Foreign language   Which language groups are represented? What assumptions lie behind these languages? What terms? What ruling ideas? What can we learn that informs the current discussion?

Culture   How do our different cultures affect dialogue? What cultural assumptions do we bring? Which are dominant cultural values? Which are subsumed cultural values? How can we use culture to improve lives?

Religion   Which religious groups are represented? How do their values differ? What critical values are important to the dialogue? How may these affect outcomes? What principles can we agree?

Relations   Which relationships do we all hold important? Who does not attend the event? Who is overly powerful? How might they influence the dialogue? What people should we take particular care of? How do we value our relationships?

Identity
How do individual notions of identity affect our interactions? What can we learn from individual viewpoints? How do we understand the link between relationships and identity? How are fragmented identities dealt with fairly? How does the community support the individual?

PMOGI (circle 2.) – Model of communicative relations[1]

Political
What political structures are involved? Who controls them? How can they benefit? How do they disturb the dialogue? Are people protected from outmoded forms of political association (i.e. are dialogue participants self-governing?) are principles of self-governance, or self-determination open for discussion?

Media
Which media may inform the dialogue? How can they affect dialogue participants positively or negatively? Is the medium the message? How can media be used to build dialogue? How much information is necessary and how much more required?

Organisation
Do organisations dominate the dialogue? Is the dialogue free from coercion or interference by organisations? Are organisation assumptions similar to participant assumptions? Are organisation structures outmoded in the network model of information? Are organisations able to deal with individual concerns without resort to 'disciplinary' behaviour?

Group
Can the group agree a clear process for managing its dialogue? Can it work with other groups? Are leaders necessary? Are followers able to affect leader decisions? Is an ethical process of group discussion established?

Interpersonal
Can individuals affect the dialogue? Are individual concerns met? Are solutions that are creative accepted in the dialogue? Does dialogue analysis value individuals? Do the other structures of the PMOGI model respond to individual concerns?

---

[1]   See www.communication-ethics.org.uk.

DICKJ (circle 3)

Data	How is data collected? By whom? What are the assumptions of its collection? Who is in involved in its capture and dissemination? How can new data capture techniques be employed to support dialogue?
Information	Where is the information from? Who controls it? In whose benefit does it work? When is information re-interpreted? Are information systems 100% transparent?
Communication	Is all communication open to changed assumptions? How is communication used to benefit people? Who controls communication? How can individuals and groups affect communication with political, media and organisation systems? How is communication ethical?
Knowledge	Who claims knowledge of a subject? What principles is the knowledge founded on? Have these been examined? What techniques have been used in knowledge formation? And how is new knowledge accounted for?
Judgement	Whose judgements prevail? Are these historical judgements? How can judgements be reversed even if benign? If the community decides new judgements are necessary, then how can old agreements be updated?

Communication – miscommunication (circle 4)

Signs	How does symbolic communication operate in the dialogue? What symbols are used? Who owns the symbols? Can they be used by the community? How can symbolic (graphic-visual-behavioural) communication be improved?
Language	What assumptions operate in the languages used in the dialogue? How do people use terms? What technical vocabularies are used? How can new language ideas/words be included in community learning? What terms control and/or reduce lifeworld concerns?
Behaviour	How do the actors and audiences involved in analysis behave? Are they open and honest? Able to change? Committed to their own path? And able to work with each other?
Relationships	Which are the key relationships for communication? How are they understood as significant? How can they be improved or changed? Which people are limiting the dialogue? Who is cared for, or not?

| Systems | Which powerful systems (technologies, media, operations, resources etc) reduce dialogue possibilities? How can they be affected? Who controls them? Are they open to 100% transparency? How are changes timed i.e. are the effects of technology used to slow or reduce change? |

Tactics for dialogue (Circle 5: short form for complete dialogue)

Aims	What are the aims of the dialogue? Are they fair? Are they balanced? Who do they privilege? Who is disempowered?
Roles	Who is involved in dialogue? Who is not? How are communities identified? How are people involved? What means are used to protect people, if necessary, from coercion?
Values	What values do people hold and why? How have these values been taken into account? Who protects values 'that cannot be measured'? What is the difference between facts and values?
Plans	What plans can be made to improve aims? Who carries them out? What alternatives are possible? Are all participants in agreement? If not why not?
Resources	What resources are necessary? And how do we measure success? Who provides the resources? Is this fair? Does resource management limit dialogue? How are further dialogues planned to oversee resource management?

18.2 Experience in practice

This model has been used successfully over a number of years by members of the Institute of Communication Ethics, a not-for-profit network of teachers in higher education. It has proven helpful to those studying and working in communication environments because of the model's innate flexibility. It does not tell participants what they should do, know, think or concede. It allows them to create their own models of what dialogue is and should be about, taking into account the foundational nature of communication and examined values (ethics) for living together. Theory is juxtaposed with the day-to-day needs of people working in dialogue, moving from the general to the particular and back again in the process.

The existing model has been left with its theory at quite a developed level, whereas for participants undertaking a typical community dialogue, they should only use theory where necessary, while being encouraged to create their own 'heuristic models' and to compare these against the theory, or other models developed by the group.

18.3   Some dos and don'ts

- Do let people work in groups to identify key issues;
- Do let them map out their own issues and present them using the model;
- Do look at each 'issue chart' and try and map them out collectively;
- Do spend time understanding all the issues; if it takes time, then that is what is required;
- Do enjoy the process of bringing collective thinking together.

- Do not delegate the important task of informing yourself to experts;
- Do not allow yourselves to be deflected from the task of ordering-evaluating information;
- Do not forget that thinking and revealing knowledge is a collective task;
- Do not take matters so seriously that you lose all sense of the outcomes;
- Do not forget that your human relationships are valuable and should not be damaged over personal disagreement, or temporary grievance.

18.4   Advice for application

Users can print out the '5graphics' as blanks and work with them to fill in their own detail. Or simply draw out a circle and put words around the circle to express an issue. The more dialogue is studied, the better participants will become at working with it, but don't forget this is knowledge that will be used again and again and is therefore of substantial value. This means knowledge should be carefully developed, explained and assessed before proceeding either to agree, or disagree.

Conclusions

The principle of dialogue is critical to notions of Western thought and to the Western model of democracy, which is specifically founded on communicative openness to change. If change cannot be made through dialogue, how then does democracy represent people? The aim of these dialogue techniques is to demonstrate how complex human communication is, quite naturally, and how simple graphic modelling techniques can show 'open-thinking' in a way that is available to all participants to see and understand. Ideas can be generated and discussed openly, allowing the evaluation of disagreement as well as the processes of moving beyond it. However, ideas that supersede historic privilege and pre-negotiated rights are not always welcome and this is where an evidential approach to dialogue is significant. The quicker key arguments are formed and understood through dialogue, the quicker historic injustice and misappropriation of society-community resources can be repaired. Shared and transparent information resources become important to understand issues and to evaluate alternative courses of action.

The '5dialogue' model can be adapted using a vast range of suitable concepts, – the number five is selected only as a guide to show how ideas often presented as simple, are in fact complex, and built on deeper assumptions that may themselves require reconsideration. Where an idea is simple and agreed, make sure this is clearly set out, not assumed.

Participants should contribute their own imaginative ideas and readings to the dialogue. Only when citizens can address their own unique issues in dialogue, unmediated by outside interference can they be free and able to determine their own futures. The responsibility for the community, however, is to manage their own dialogue(s) effectively and legitimately, a situation that can only be decided by the members themselves. 'Justice for all' might be the catchphrase for every dialogue. The final word goes to Thomas McCarthy, the communication theorist;

'The enlightenment of political will can become effective only within the communication of citizens. For the articulation of needs in accordance with technical knowledge can be ratified exclusively in the consciousness of the political actors themselves. Experts cannot delegate to themselves this act of confirmation from those who have to account with their life histories for the new interpretation of social needs and for accepted means of mastering problematic situations.' (Thomas McCarthy, 1997, p. 15)

References

Christians, C. and M. Traber (1997). *Communication Ethics and Universal Values*. California and London, Thousand Oaks: Sage Publications.

Habermas, J. (1984–1987). *The Theory of Communicative Action*. Vols. One & Two. Cambridge: Polity.

Habermas, J. (1990). *Moral Consciousness and Communicative Action*. Cambridge: Polity.

McCarthy, T. (1996). *The Critical Theory of Jürgen Habermas*. Cambridge: MIT Press.

Websites

www.5systems.net

www.communication-ethics.org.uk

19 Stakeholder Engagement: The Experience of Holcim

Anne Gambling

Key words: Cement, community involvement, engagement process model, needs assessment, stakeholder engagement.

19.1 Introduction

No longer can business say that it exists simply to generate shareholder profit. Business aspirations reach beyond the financial dimension to encompass contributions to a broader set of societal goals, including those focussed on environmental and social responsibility imperatives. One need only read a selection of organisational mission statements to draw this conclusion. Business decision-making and strategy development does not occur in a vacuum defined only by economic considerations. The contextual landscape is much wider, as wide as the world itself. To assess the impacts, opportunities and risks of its operations, products and services, therefore, a business must engage with, learn from, and understand the needs and expectations of its stakeholders.

For a global cement company such as Holcim, with operations in more than 70 countries, this is a very real challenge, not something that has come to the organisation's notice from the realms of academia. Perhaps in past decades there was no umbrella concept which described our methodology for negotiating relationships with different stakeholders. Nevertheless the practical experiences of our local operations were key to elaborating the process model of stakeholder engagement described in this paper.

The model is used by Holcim Group companies to assist in preparing, implementing and evaluating their local stakeholder engagement strategies; it details, step-by-step, the cyclical process of engaging with stakeholders. Each step contains basic principles, tools and mechanisms to apply. It delivers a consistent approach across our worldwide organisation, yet is born of hands-on practice in the field.

A guidebook explains the model and its tools to those directly involved in stakeholder processes. This is then supplemented by online support materials, such as templates, matrices and good practice examples, with in-person support available when required. A quick reference pocket guide is used to sensitise a broader internal audience to the value of stakeholder engagement as well as reinforce the need for a common approach.

19.2   The essence of the model

The checklist approach enables local management to proceed logically from step to step whilst applying the recommended tools which supplement the model at each stage of the process:

- Analyse situation: What is the current situation? From the company's perspective? From the stakeholders' perspective?

- Define objectives: What do you want to achieve? Are the objectives measurable?

- Outline internal roles and responsibilities: Who should do what? And why?

- Map stakeholders and assess their needs for information: Who are your stakeholders? What are their needs and expectations?

- Develop key messages on relevant topics to meet these needs: Has their understandability been tested with the chosen audience?

- Use the most appropriate engagement method for stakeholders: e.g. dialogue (group or one-to-one), community advisory panel, public hearing, focus group etc. Are you well prepared for the actual engagement 'event'?

- Evaluate engagement plan: Were the stated objectives achieved?

- Invest in corrective or preventive action: Will some stakeholder recommendations be acted upon? Will aspects of strategy be changed to better meet stakeholder needs?

The step-by-step and cyclical nature of the model is described in Figure 19.1.

19.3   Experiences with the model in practice

To illustrate how the model is used in practice, one must step back a moment to understand the nature of the cement industry. Reliant on heavy manufacturing plants, generally close to their raw material (extractive) source, the cement industry can have significant environmental, social and economic impacts on stakeholders – both positive and negative. Our licence to operate, therefore, comes very directly from the communities surrounding our facilities.

In this context, some of the dilemmas facing Holcim include:

- How can we ensure that we contribute to improving the quality of life of our stakeholders within our spheres of influence?

- How do we decrease CO_2 and other emissions, decrease impacts on biodiversity, and generally shrink our ecological footprint while at the same time meeting the increasing demand for cement and other related products from a rapidly growing population, particularly in the developing world?

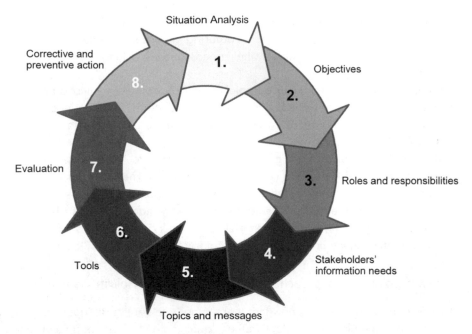

Figure 19.1. Engagement Process Cycle

- What is our responsibility for the environmental and social impacts of our products when, in most cases, we have little influence over construction methods and processes?

The model provides Holcim with a framework for engaging stakeholders on these and other issues in a continuous cycle of learning and improvement. Moving onward and upward enables the engagement to become richer, while delivering more and better outcomes. The relationships developed with one's stakeholders are stronger as a result and our licence to operate more secure.

However, it was not always like this. Prior to introduction of the model, Holcim had been haphazard in its attention to stakeholder needs. At some operations, stakeholder management practices were well-established, at others only in their infancy – a situation which the application of a global model clearly sought to address. Experience in the field has taught us that ongoing direct engagement with stakeholders is key to ensuring their active involvement during, for example, the lifecycle of a community project. In this way the priorities, skills and resources of Holcim are best matched with the community's needs.

Firstly, a formal stakeholder 'needs assessment' is undertaken to ensure that the right information is collected in the most efficient way – usually via document reviews, surveys, focus groups and interviews. As a stakeholder engagement tool, the needs assessment is a required component of Step 1 of the model. However, it also has the advantage of capturing knowledge needed for Step 4 of the model – where stakeholders, their needs and expectations are mapped and analysed.

Wherever possible, and when acceptable to stakeholders, facilitation of focus group discussions or individual interviews is undertaken by an independent, yet internal specialist from Holcim Group headquarters. There are several advantages to this approach:

The facilitator is able to bring professional expertise to the process, yet still be fully cognisant of the Group company's perspective. The facilitator can better manage stakeholder expectations about what is possible in terms of company support, compared to an external facilitator who may not have such requisite knowledge about boundaries, parameters or focus areas. There is still a high level of objectivity in the process as the facilitator is not perceived as 'local'.

A case in point – the approaches of Holcim Spain and Holcim Vietnam

Lessons learnt from the field show that there is no 'one size fits all' approach. In practice, for example, several steps in the planning stage of the model can occur concurrently. Application depends very much on the local stakeholder 'landscape'.

To illustrate, the Holcim operations in Spain and Vietnam represent two disparate locations with very different social, cultural, economic and political backgrounds, thus requiring different needs assessment approaches to analyse company/community relations. The objective, however, is the same throughout – to:

- Determine the company's primary and secondary stakeholders;
- Assess the current relationship with, and needs of, these stakeholders;
- Match these with the company's priorities, resources and expertise;
- Develop a relevant and responsive plan of community action.

The Carboneras cement plant of Holcim Spain is located on the Mediterranean coast. Taking account of the local socio-cultural landscape, the analysis comprised separate focus groups with plant management and plant workers (including union representatives), as well as individual interviews with a broad cross-section of external stakeholders – e.g. environmental groups, political leaders, community administration, education facilities, social clubs etc.

The focus group discussions provided a reflective space for company employees to consider their current relationship with the community (including an analysis of their history of engagement). It enabled the identification and prioritisation of issues where opportunities could be seen for adding value to both Holcim and the community. These inputs were then factored into the individual external stakeholder interviews for 'sounding'. An internal working group then took all findings and developed appropriate community actions to meet local needs.

The findings indicated that a previously agrarian seaside community had welcomed the industrialisation brought by various major firms to the region, which included developing infrastructure and education opportunities. However, in the latest wave of development, the port town had found itself at the centre of tourist promotion, and a large retiree and second homeowner population (principally non-Spanish) had evolved. Community actions therefore needed to take account of the potential for conflict between industry and tourism – and restorative environmental projects were the agreed net result.

By comparison, the needs assessment process at Holcim Vietnam sought to determine the company's impacts since commencement of the Hong Chong operation (a greenfields site in the primarily agrarian community of Binh An) five years previously. For this level of scrutiny, and to ensure a high degree of independence of findings, collaboration was undertaken with Ho Chi Minh City University for the external stakeholder consultations. Nevertheless, the Holcim needs assessment approach was followed by the university researchers in their stakeholder interviews and consultations. They questioned about the main events and developments of the community over time, the impacts of the company's arrival, the major issues facing the community, and their desired future life quality.

One major community need identified was clean water and sanitation in the community's schools, cross-cutting the various themes raised. The joint project team involved the People's Committee of the local commune, further embedding stakeholder engagement in the process. Also identified in the needs assessment was the critical importance of hygiene-awareness training to the long-term sustainability of the project, to ensure that the schools make best use of their new infrastructure.

19.4 Dos and don'ts

Based on the applied knowledge from the use of the model in the field, advice is provided to Holcim management about some fundamental keys to success – a case of 'the dos, not the don'ts[1]':

---

[1] This list is drawn from the work of the WBCSD's Capacity Building programme. The brochure 'Stakeholder Dialogue – the WBCSD's approach to engagement' is freely available for download from http://www.wbcsd.org.

- Have a clear, well-articulated objective;
- Be realistic – do not start what you cannot finish;
- Allow enough time for planning, planning and more planning;
- Be aware and manage expectations – both yours and your stakeholders';
- Start thinking about the longer term engagement process early, and consult your stakeholders on what they want in terms of continued communication;
- Focus on quality, not quantity – participants should be invited on the basis of their credibility and ability to be thought-provoking;
- Acknowledge genuine differences. Everyone should make an effort to share perspectives, listen and learn;
- Be prepared to be as open and transparent as possible;
- Aim to build joint ownership for actions toward change;
- Ask the right questions – be flexible and open to improvising based on stakeholder needs;
- Be ready for a messy, time-consuming process;
- Listen!

Guiding principles[2] are also elaborated to assist management in their engagement activities:

- Preparation – all parties need sufficient information and preparation;
- Openness – by all participants, without fear of restriction or discipline;
- Accountability – engagement should inform decision-making;
- Respect – acknowledge all opinions; be sensitive and facilitate fairly.

19.5 Conclusion

Holcim has found that the systematic planning of stakeholder engagement represents good risk management. It helps builds reputation and contributes to the achievement of business objectives, enabling us to:

- Stay on the same wavelength as our neighbours;
- Mitigate the negative effects of potentially 'hot issues';
- Spot opportunities and address stakeholder concerns proactively.

---

[2] These principles are derived from and extend the learnings received from the independent think-tank and strategy consultancy, SustainAbility Ltd (http://www.sustainability.com).

The Holcim experience shows that implementing local solutions according to a global methodology is a powerful tool. It enables us to engage with stakeholders covering a diverse spectrum of cultures, languages, and aspirations. One could expect that the model would have wide application across the business community, providing an opportunity to better understand and meet stakeholder needs in a spirit of openness and collaborative effort.

Websites

http://www.holcim.com/sustainable
http://www.wbcsdcement.org

20 Managing Expectations in Partnerships

André Nijhof and Michel van Pijkeren

Key words: Stakeholder dialogue, business-NGO partnerships, Servqual, web-based instrument.

20.1 Introduction to the model

In this paper the BNI-instrument (BNI stands for Business NGO Interaction) is presented. This is an on-line available tool for NGOs and companies engaging in CSR. The aim is to create explicit understanding between those parties by comparing issues of CSR in a systematic way based upon a practical approach to the field. For this, a web-based self-assessment tool is developed, shaped upon the Servqual methodology. The result of this tool is a gap analysis signifying differences in mutual expectations of the process of dialogue and collaboration. This analysis is mailed to every respondent in the form of an automatically generated report, and can be used to construct a structured agenda for interaction, to be used at the start of or during collaboration between the parties involved. Furthermore, through the use of the instrument the underlying database is filled with a gradually emerging data set, providing an overview of the different expectations around CSR. This article presents the conceptual background for modelling the interactions between companies and NGOs, the experiences with the web-based instrument, as well as the outcomes of the analysis of the differences in expectations.

The tool is developed within a research project that was carried out in 2003 and 2004 within the framework of the Dutch National Research Programme on CSR, financed by the Ministry of Economic Affairs in the Netherlands. The National Programme consists of a coordinated set of research projects on Corporate Social Responsibility, executed by a group of researchers from 7 Dutch Universities in close cooperation with businesses. The research project focusing on the development of the BNI-instrument was led by the University of Twente in cooperation with Radboud University Nijmegen and the Erasmus University of Rotterdam.

Collaborating for CSR

The BNI instrument is based on a notion of CSR starting with the observation that companies and NGOs are increasingly interacting on emerging CSR issues. This interaction is seen both as an opportunity and as a huge challenge. Both parties have complementary competencies and interests. NGOs seek the support of business, since liberal governments tend to leave the regulation of an increasing number of social issues to the market-mechanism. Businesses do of course play a significant role in the market. Furthermore, businesses see the advantage of engaging with NGOs through improving their image and employee motivation, and in decreasing the risk of running into unexpected anti-business campaigns. The challenge lies in overcoming the world of difference between the parties, since differences in values and culture can frustrate and even destroy collaborative attempts. For this reason, exploring and managing the mutual expectations in the early stages of an interaction delivers valuable information about the possibilities and risks for cooperation.

The conceptual model

The model used to explore these expectations is based on an adaptation of the Servqual Method originally developed by Zeithaml, Parasuraman and Berry (1990). This is a tested method for measuring the possible match – or mismatch – between expectations of customers and the way a business perceives and translates these expectations into products and services. In this project the Servqual methodology was adapted to the context of CSR. It was assumed that the expectations of customers and companies with regard to the delivered products would be comparable with the expectations of NGOs and companies with regard to possible collaboration in the face of emerging issues.

Measuring expectations

In order to start measuring these expectations in a systematic way, the relevant concepts were derived from a literature study with respect to stakeholder theory and partnerships (Bendell, 2000; Zadek, 2004) and from interviews with NGOs and companies. These concepts gave way to seven criteria that were further elaborated in a list of indicators which is presented below:

1. *Issue:* The first criterion concerns the issue around which the parties intend to engage. This criterion is operationalised into indicators such as the rationale of the parties to get involved with each other and the degree of shared recognition of the problem(s) at hand.

2. *Representativeness:* The second criterion focuses on the legitimacy and representation of actual persons that will exemplify the contact between the parties. The first indicator refers to the critical mass (in terms of com-

petencies, professionalism and organisational resources) necessary to be perceived as a relevant and potentially satisfactory partner. Other indicators are the complementarity and recognition of capabilities and resources and the personal authority of the contact persons to make decisions that imply commitment for the organisation as a whole.

3. *Values*: The third criterion addresses the underlying values of the parties involved. It is assumed that a basic level of trust at the start needs to be plain in order to be able to engage in a constructive and fruitful dialogue. During the actual process of collaboration around a specific issue, the level of trust needs to be developed in order to foster the relationship. Indicators that contribute to trust are long-term commitment and respect for different value systems and worldviews between the different parties.

4. *Collaboration*: A fourth element in the mutual expectations of NGOs and companies relates to the recognition of the rules of the game. Important indicators relate to operational co-ordination and sharing of risks. Furthermore, the awareness of and flexibility to respond to changing environmental demands, and past experiences of the parties involved in similar processes need to be taken into account.

5. *Independence*: Collaboration influences by definition the independent position of the parties involved. Therefore the fifth criterion focuses on the risks that can accompany close contacts between NGOs and business, showing the reverse-side of collaboration. Relevant indicators are the loss of legitimacy and credibility of the NGO if its support is derived from a critical stance towards business, misuse of information, and expectations about practices of NGOs to take action while being in dialogue with a company.

6. *Transparency*: The sixth criterion deals with the transparency of the future collaboration. Sharing relevant and useful information beforehand and during a project is a prerequisite for effective interaction. This will enhance trust building, and enable understanding of the often different worldviews. Indicators provided by literature are: the reliability of the exchanged information, the possibility for third-party or other forms of external verification, and the nature of the (joint) communication with other relevant actors.

7. *Impact*: The last criterion points at the impact that both parties aim for and what is actually achieved. Impact refers to possible direct and indirect results, and is as such crucial in the development of patterns of expectation. Indicators are: linkage of activities with the core business of the organisation, clarity of common understanding of goals and results at the start, demonstrable achievement of results, and mutual learning.

Each of these indicators and subsequent criteria has been translated into a concise questionnaire of 35 closed questions with a 7-point Likert answer scale. This questionnaire was then mirrored for both of the parties involved, trying to frame mutual expectations and experiences at the start of a possible collaboration. After a discussion of the questionnaire with several representatives of businesses and NGOs, a web-based tool was developed.

20.2   The essence of the BNI-instrument

The picture shows a schematic overview of the model on which the BNI-instrument is based.

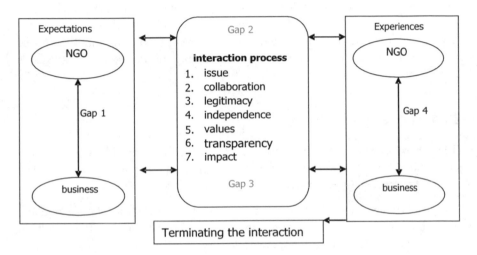

Figure 20.1. The BNI-model

20.3   Experiences with the BNI-instrument

In October 2004 the tool was released and disseminated through dedicated databases and an e-mail alert to approximately 20.000 people. In December 2004 we started with the analysis of the gaps identified in the questionnaires. By then we had 65 valid responses. This is too limited to draw any valid conclusions about the nature of the instrument and its functionality. Discussion of the results so far is therefore preliminary.

The goal throughout has been to support businesses and NGOs who have the intention to form some kind of a joint activity, maybe in the form of a partnership, and to provide them with practical means to create this collaboration in an explicit and transparent manner. The developed tool enables them to assess mutual needs and expectations at the start of this collaboration. Furthermore it enables them to identify the characteristics of the (desired) collaboration and to communicate about it. Some intermediate conclusions can be drawn, based on a brief qualitative and statistical analysis of the results.

The attitude of NGOs and organisations is above all determined by previous experiences. Pre-existing personal relations are a key point; initial doubts and perceptions on both sides turn out to be more positive once collaboration is established.

Different value orientations do not seem to be an important hurdle; investing time in developing common perspectives on the nature of the issues involved pays off; results on a short-term basis provide internal consciousness on both sides, leading to support and building trust.

In general, businesses are led by expectations of customers. A possible collaboration with an NGO needs to add concrete and short-term value in that respect; the often referred to reputation mechanism as an important driver for collaboration is not confirmed in the view of organisations, whereas NGOs indeed focus on this issue.

20.4 Lessons learned

Through questions on the instrument and the feedback on the reports, some suggestions have emerged for people interested in using the instrument. We formulated these suggestions as instructions on how to use the instrument:

- The identification of gaps is most relevant when both the NGO and the company involved in collaboration fill in the questionnaire. This results in an agenda for dialogue dedicated to these parties;

- However, most respondents filled in the instrument separately. In this case the results of the respondent are compared with the average scores of other users. Although the resulting report is not dedicated, it still can fulfil the function of reflecting on the possibilities and risks of the collaboration at hand;

- Filling in the instrument takes about 20 minutes. This results in an agenda for dialogue between an NGO and a company. The time needed to discuss the relevant gaps with each other depends to a large extent on the differences in the mutual expectations. When the parties focus on the most relevant gaps this discussion may take 1 to 1,5 hours;

- When a collaboration has developed for some time, the focus changes from expectations to experiences. Therefore the instrument has the opportunity to fill in the experiences at a certain point during or after the collaboration. The generated report compares whether the actual experiences match the expectations expressed beforehand. This results in important evaluation results about the added value and disappointments of evolving collaborations;

- The model with the seven criteria for the relevant expectations of NGOs and companies can also be used to select possible partners. It then serves as a checklist of success factors that foster successful collaboration. Making a conscious choice about what partners have the potential to deliver the preconditions for an effective collaboration is crucial, in order to prevent frustration during the collaboration;

- Although there is a large stream of literature on partnerships for CSR, many companies and NGOs have just begun to explore this. Until now most parties state that they underestimated the time needed to get started. Several cases even mention that it takes years to overcome the hurdles present at the beginning of a possible collaboration. This stresses once more the importance to take some time for a deliberate choice about the most promising partners.

20.5 Wrapping up

Collaboration between businesses and NGOs is a crucial element in the development of CSR. The instrument presented here is a first step in helping to identify important gaps that might frustrate the upcoming collaboration. Analysis of the results so far demonstrates that – once well debated up front – it paves the way for an effective collaboration. Common understanding and clear arrangements can diminish problems based on misunderstanding further down the process of collaboration. In this way effective interaction and dialogue has improved and real value added for those involved. Meanwhile a number of issues remain open for debate. Without any pretensions to be comprehensive we would like to stipulate the following:

(a) Implicitly, a rather mechanistic view is taken in this research project. Based upon explicit assumptions about collaboration it is still unable to capture the 'human chemistry' between people. Despite the fact that the use and outcome of the developed model can offer ample ground for a fruitful collaboration, it remains impossible to capture the emotion that is a fundamental prerequisite for collaboration. Unmistakably trust – as one of the criteria in the model – is a key component, yet does not cover the sentiments at stake.

(b) Although the presented list of criteria seems to represent rather accurately what is at stake when engaging in a possible collaboration, it is neither exhaustive nor can the interdependency between them be taken into account. The weight of these criteria will differ between the parties involved. In the Servqual methodology a weight is given by the respondents to their scores. Now that the first release is in full swing, it might become appropriate to add this methodological feature to the instrument. It will also differ depending on previous experiences, the business sector, the actual people engaged in the discourse, and so on.

(c) A final issue is how the stakeholders will perceive the usefulness of the instrument. Leaving aside issues of reliability, the core remains to create added value for the parties involved. This added value comes about in e.g. consensus concerning the issue at stake, the way it will be approached or the contributions of the parties involved. We assume that it is only in the actual testing and subsequent use that this practical added value can be demonstrated.

These hurdles, with respect to the present status of the BNI-instrument, point at possibilities for a further development of the instrument and underlying model. At the same time, the instrument available on the internet already contains a rather comprehensive tool for business-NGO interactions to make progress with regard to societal issues. In the coming years the instrument will be available on www.bni-instrument.org at no cost for NGOs and businesses. Furthermore, the involved researchers will make periodical reports on the relevant gaps based on an analysis of the expectations and experiences expressed, and make these reports available through the same website. Both the use of the instrument and the reports on the most important gaps may hopefully deliver valuable information for effective collaborations between businesses and NGOs.

References

Bendell, J. (2000). *Terms for Endearment, Business, NGOs and Sustainable Development*. Sheffield: Greenleaf Publishing.

Nijhof, A., J. Jonker and M. van Pijkeren (2005). Looking through the eyes of the other: Assessing mutual expectations and experiences in order to shape dialogue and collaboration between business and NGOs with respect to CSR. In: Jonker J. and J. Cramer (eds.) *Making a Difference, The Dutch National Research Programme on corporate social responsibility*. The Netherlands: Ministry of Economic Affairs.

Neelson, J. and S. Zadek (2000). *Partnership Alchemy: New social partnerships in Europe*. Copenhagen: The Copenhagen Centre Denmark.

Zeithaml, V., A. Parasuraman and L. Berry (1990). *Delivering Service Quality*. New York: Free Press.

Website

www.bni-instrument.org

21 A Stepwise Approach to Stakeholder Management

Céline Louche and Xavier Baeten

Key words: Stakeholder management, dialogue, corporate social responsibility.

21.1 Introduction

Corporations are embedded in networks of stakeholder relationships. These relationships can range from conflict to partnership. To operate within such a complex system of interests and influences, businesses need to carefully assess and evaluate these external forces as well as build up and foster their relationships with stakeholders. Effective stakeholder management is a critical requirement for the long-term success of any company. It provides a clear overview of societal expectations and a firm foundation for a stronger, customised and legitimate corporate social responsibility (CSR) strategy. However, managing stakeholder relationships is not an easy task and raises numerous questions. Although companies are aware of the importance of involving and managing their stakeholders, managers have a confused notion of how to actually implement the process.

The following model offers a clear trajectory from stakeholder analysis to strategy implementation, addressing the strategies a firm should take to best manage stakeholder challenges and opportunities. It concentrates on the practical side of stakeholder management and provides a systematic approach for managing relationships with stakeholders. The model is based on the assumption that CSR is a strategic aspect of a company's management and stakeholder management a necessary step to CSR operationalisation. The ultimate aim is to provide a guideline for managers in order to increase corporate performance.

The model: Trajectory framework for stakeholder management

Freeman (1984) defines stakeholders as 'any group or individual who can affect or is affected by the achievement of the organisation's objectives'. It includes a number of people and groups like non-governmental organisations, media, governmental organisations, employees, customers, shareholders, suppliers, communities and others, all of which may have conflicting expectations and interests. This list may differ according to each individual company and situation. As stakeholders are large in numbers and resources are rather scarce, a company will have to make choices and set priorities with regard to these stakeholders and their issues.

Note that opposing views do exist between the business world and civil society. The business world is mainly concerned with its direct stakeholders, whereas society as a whole is made up of a very heterogeneous set of stakeholders, all of whom have different expectations of corporate social responsibility. Business firms wishing to maintain a good dialogue with stakeholders need to develop a stakeholder process.

21.2   The essence of the model

The model offers a trajectory framework to guide managers in stakeholder management. It provides an innovative and long-term approach to corporate sustainability and successful entrepreneurship. The aim is to help companies work out a stakeholder audit, leading to concrete action plans that integrate an understanding of the stakeholders and their expectations, an estimation of their individual importance from a strategic point of view and a clear perception of

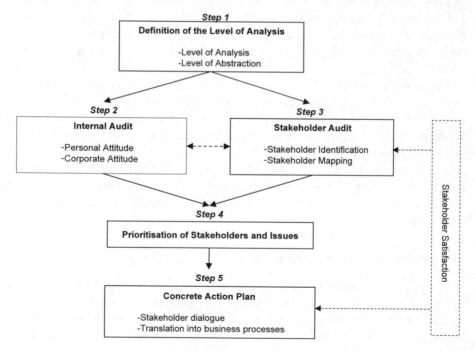

Figure 21.1. Stakeholder management trajectory

how satisfied the stakeholders are and what could be done to build sound mutual relationships. In this respect, the model can be regarded as part of the risk
management process.

Figure 21.1 shows the five steps of the trajectory: definition of the level of
analysis; internal attitude audit, stakeholder audit; prioritisation of stakeholders
and issues; and a concrete action plan. These steps are successive, however,
there should be room for feedback between the different steps. Each step leads
to a number of concrete questions.

Step 1: Defining the level of analysis

The first step consists of identifying and defining the level of analysis and the
level of abstraction.

The level of analysis refers to the level to which the stakeholder analysis will
apply, i.e. group level, national level (all companies in a certain country), com-
pany/site level, or business unit/department level. Also, the stakeholder audit
can be done for a specific project or problem. According to the level of analysis, outcomes may vary a lot.

The level of abstraction refers to the motives that underline the analysis. The
analysis may address a specific problem or project within the company or it
may be a general exercise aiming at integrating the stakeholder management
approach or CSR in the business. The level of abstraction needs to be clearly
identified as it will define the boundaries of the analysis.

Key questions

- What is the level of analysis: Group level? Country level? Company/site
  level? Or business unit/department level?

- What is the level of abstraction: Does the analysis address a specific problem or project within the company or the group? Or is it a general exercise aiming at integrating the stakeholder management approach or CSR
  in the business?

Step 2: Internal audit

The second step aims at exploring the internal position of the firm vis-à-vis the
specific problem/project, or CSR and stakeholder management in general
(according to the level of analysis and abstraction). In addition, the organisation's own definition of CSR is discussed.

The aim of this step is to obtain a clear idea of the company's attitude towards its stakeholders. An internal reflection and analysis is necessary in order
to assess the current position of the company and a clearer understanding of
the current actions and reactions of company stakeholders. This will make it

easier later to draw up an optimal, customised and realistic action plan. This step should be addressed at the corporate/company/unit level as well as at the individual level (e.g. attitude of senior management towards stakeholders).

Key questions

- How does the organisation define CSR? What is its attitude towards CSR?
- What is the position of the company and its managers regarding CSR or the issue in question?
- What are the main internal drivers and barriers for stakeholder management and CSR?
- Why do we, as a company, need to tackle this issue/problem/project (e.g. reputation, public relations, advertising, trust building, performance, vision, innovation, management, employees)?
- What is the actual state of affairs with regard to stakeholder management (e.g. mission statement, stakeholder approach, ethical code)?
- What are the previous experiences related to CSR or in dealing with the specific problem/project?

Step 3: Stakeholder audit

The stakeholder audit consists of the identification and mapping of stakeholders. It deals with questions related to who the stakeholders are and how important they are with regard to the company or problem/project.

A stakeholder audit starts with a clear definition of the stakeholders. Relevant stakeholders should be listed (the list should be as complete as possible even if some of them may be deleted later on) with a short description of: who the stakeholders are, what they do, what their position is regarding the company or specific problem/project, what their means of action are.

From this description, it is possible to draw a power/interest matrix[1] (see Figure 21.2). The matrix is a useful tool for evaluating the expectations and the impact of particular stakeholders. It helps to assess the degree of interest of each stakeholder group, the extent to which their expectations affect the organisa-

---

[1] Power is the mechanism by which expectations are able to influence strategies. There are four dimensions of power: status (e.g. position within hierarchy), resources claim (size, in all meanings), representation in powerful organisations, and potential to damage. There are several ways to exert such power, for instance by direct authority, lobbying or exerting a dominant market position. The power of stakeholders can be based on various sources such as hierarchy, influence, resources, knowledge. Power gives an idea about the company's dependence on the stakeholder. Interest refers to the stakeholder's willingness to communicate his experiences with regard to the company's strategy.

tion's decisions and the means and power they have to exercise their influence. The outcome of the matrix provides the basis for developing stakeholder strategies (e.g. how to communicate). It can also indicate whether certain decisions will receive support or resistance and provide guidelines as to which groups have to be included in the decision process.

The matrix provides a classification of the stakeholders into four distinct categories:

- Group A: the most important group of stakeholders with a high level of interest and power. They are the key players. Their support is strategic to the success of the company or project. They should be carefully managed and involved in all relevant developments;

- Group B: this group has a high level of interest in the company and its activities but has limited means to influence decisions or actions. However, this group may contain potential allies, therefore they should be kept informed;

- Group C: this group can present some difficulties. Although they behave passively they can have an enormous impact on the company or project. It is therefore crucial to keep them satisfied, and identify their potential intentions and reactions, engage in a dialogue in order to learn more about their discontent and involve them according to their interest;

- Group D: this group is less important and requires minimal effort. It consists of secondary stakeholders who do not have high interest in the company and no power to affect it directly. However, it is important to be aware of these stakeholders and their views. They should still be given the necessary and minimum amount of information.

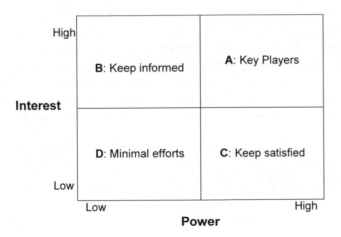

Figure 21.2. Interest/Power Matrix (Johnson & Scholes, 1999)

This matrix is a 'living' matrix. Some stakeholders will be key players when dealing with specific topics and they will be less important or interested when dealing with other issues. Also, stakeholder interest and importance can change over time, e.g. because of media exposure[2].

When carrying out this step, the present quality of the relationship from the point of view of the stakeholder, i.e. stakeholder satisfaction, should be considered. For each stakeholder, it should include: the most important satisfaction measures, the existence of open and structured communication, comments on the satisfaction levels and an overall satisfaction score. Such considerations are useful at a later stage of the stakeholder management trajectory in order to track the improvement in stakeholder satisfaction. Satisfaction measures may include for example the existence, frequency and type of communication and/or meetings between the company and the stakeholder, historical events, capital flows, existence of a personal relationship with the stakeholder and opposite interests. Neely et al. (2002) provide some example of stakeholder-specific potential measures.

Key questions

- Who are the relevant stakeholders?
- What power do they exert on the company?
- What interest do they have in the company or company's project/problem?
- What is the actual quality of the relationship of each of the stakeholders identified with the company (stakeholder satisfaction)?

Step 4: Prioritisation

In the previous steps, we have identified the organisation's drivers and stance with regard to stakeholder management/CSR and the relevant stakeholders.

Now, it is time for action. As dealing with all stakeholders at the same time is impossible, it is essential to prioritise stakeholders as well as issues. This focus is very important in order not to develop a programme that is too ambitious. The aim of this step is to synthesise the most important results and blind spots that have been discovered in the previous steps. It will help to identify potential areas of risk.

Building on the information collected during the internal and stakeholder audit, the aim is to identify the stakeholder(s), the issues, the activities, business units, and departments to be focused on, including the geographical focus.

---

[2] Therefore, the media are seen by some authors as a 'bridging stakeholder'.

Key questions

- What stakeholders should be focused on?
- What issues should be focused on?
- What activities, business units, departments should be focused on?
- What geographical area(s) should be focused on?
- What are the objectives with regard to the stakeholders?

Step 5: Action plan

The last step consists of the action plan. Based on the priority list, it should provide substance to the analysis by defining the objectives and strategies for the next years or months and setting out a timetable of measures as well as the financial implications necessary for achieving these objectives. The action plan should include stakeholder dialogue (incorporating stakeholder satisfaction) and translation into business processes.

Key questions

- What concrete actions need to be carried out and with which stakeholder or group of stakeholders?
- How will the stakeholder dialogue be organised, what are the dialogue techniques that will be used and what will be the content of the dialogue?
- When does each action need to be carried out (start and end date)?
- What resources does it involve (capital, human, goods, technological, etc)?
- What are the expected outcomes of each of the actions?
- What are the expectations of the overall action plan?
- What impact has the action plan had on stakeholder satisfaction?

21.3 Experience with the model

The model was first tested during an internal training for senior management in a multinational corporation which led to some changes and adaptations. It was used as a reference tool in a Belgian training programme for managers on sustainable development called Trivisi and is currently taught in Vlerick's Masters and MBA programmes. The use of this model in training programmes has been met with great approval by the participants, both managers and students, who praise its pragmatism and direct applicability. The trajectory framework offers a useful guide for managers navigating through the stakeholder process.

21.4   Some dos and don'ts

Our model offers a framework for developing the stakeholder management capability. This trajectory model helps to make clear which stakeholders should be prioritised and what actions need to be undertaken.

Our experience reveals that stakeholder management is very complex in practice and requires individual qualities but also collaboration and partnership. The model we propose necessitates in-depth discussions that involve representatives of the entire organisation. It is a significant added value to bring together managers from several departments. Another key aspect of the model is stakeholder dialogue. It helps to provide a clear concept of the expectations of the stakeholders and of these satisfaction determinants. This dialogue gives input for building and maintaining long-term relationships. Finally, the organisation should report to its stakeholders to what extent it has met its own objectives and the objectives of the different stakeholders. Measures will need to be developed and structured in a value scorecard.

21.5   Concluding remarks regarding the application of the model

The trajectory framework presented in this paper is intended to provide guidance and to help managers design the most appropriate stakeholder approach. It clearly maps the different steps that managers need to take in order to identify and understand the organisation's stakeholders, to define the opportunities and challenges stakeholders present and finally to draw up an action plan.

The model should be used as a strategic management tool and should be regarded as part of the company's long-term objective to understand and align its strategy with societal expectations. However, it may be inappropriate to use this model in a crisis, when tension is high and immediate action necessary, and could lead to manipulating rather than understanding stakeholders.

Applying such a model requires time and commitment in order to obtain the long-term involvement and trust of the stakeholders. Therefore timing is an important factor in the implementation. When used at the right time, the model can help managers to overcome opposition, build coalitions, and channel information and resources to promote and sustain the firm. Since stakeholders and their positions may change over time, stakeholder management needs to remain an ongoing process allowing for strategy design to adjust. Ultimately, the model is a critical tool in optimising the firm's environment and can help identify those parties that should be incorporated in decision-making processes. The successful implementation results in increased employee commitment and buy-in.

Ideally, it is best to carry out this stakeholder management process in the organisation every two years. A working group should be put together representing different hierarchical levels from throughout the organisation. This ensures the best results.

References

Freeman, R. (1984). *Strategic management: A stakeholder perspective*. Englewood Cliffs: Prentice-Hall.

Johnson, G. and K. Scholes (1999). *Exploring Corporate Strategy*, Hemel Hempstead: Prentice Hall Europe.

Neely, A., C. Adams, et al. (2002). *The Performance Prism: The Scorecard for Measuring and Managing Business Success*. London: Financial Times Prentice Hall.

Post, J.E., L.E. Preston, et al. (2002). Managing the Extended Enterprise: The New Stakeholder View. *California Management Review* 45(1): 6-28.

Wood, D. and R.E. Jones (1995). Stakeholder mismatching: A theoretical problem in empirical research on corporate social performance. *International Journal of Organisational Analysis* 3: 229-267.

Website

www.trivisi.be

22 Fair Labour Association Model

Jacques Igalens and Martine Combemale

Key words: Audit, supplier, brand, NGO, compliance.

22.1 Introduction

Suppliers of brand-name companies, especially in labour intensive sectors like clothing and footwear, are usually located in countries where labour regulations and their legal enforcement are less stringent than those in west European countries. Organisations of civil society have stepped in to promote improvements in such areas as human and labour rights and use a variety of strategies to try and ensure responsibility, accountability and transparency. Their demands are directed at both public and private bodies, but while public bodies have been slow to react, the private bodies, mainly multinational enterprises, started introducing private CSR initiatives in the 90s.

The approach to CSR in global supply chains puts the emphasis on monitoring the suppliers to compensate for the lack of an official labour inspection body. Among the more than 300 different CSR initiatives listed by the International Labour Organisation (ILO), the Fair Labour Association (FLA) is one of the most demanding. The FLA model, unlike other models, does not rely solely on one-off certifications but requires the total commitment of the brand-name companies to a programme of code implementation, internal monitoring and unannounced independent external monitoring. Under the FLA system, the brand is held responsible for the labour standards of their suppliers. Since experience has shown that CSR initiatives which concentrate solely on auditing fail to identify and cure the root causes of non-compliance, the FLA model integrates a system of monitoring, corrective action, third party complaints, and public reporting. The FLA Code of Conduct is based on the core labour standards of the ILO.

The FLA was formed in 1999 to promote respect for labour rights around the world. The FLA represents a multi-stakeholder coalition of companies, universities and NGOs. There are currently 16 brand-name companies participating fully in the FLA, including Adidas, Liz Claiborne, Nordstrom, Nike, Patagonia, Puma and Reebok and around 1000 university licensees who have included only their university production. With their membership in the FLA, these companies show their commitment to a rigorous programme of corporate social responsibility along their entire supply chain. 4000 facilities in over 80 countries are covered by the FLA programme, including 850 factories in China.

22.2 The essence of the FLA Model

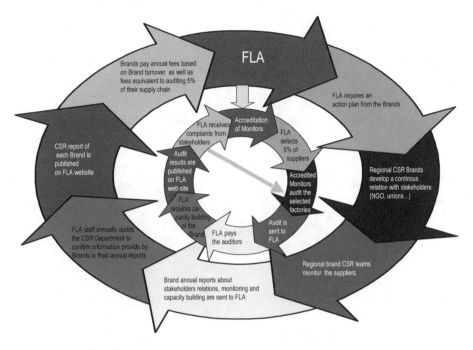

Figure 22.1. The FLA model

The first model is shown in the form of two rings to illustrate the fact that the FLA compliance programme is not a single but continuous process and, at the same time, that auditing is just one part of the CSR model. Even when the participating company programme has been accredited by the FLA (as in the case of the Reebok programme), the monitoring, corrective actions and public reporting continues. The first model shows the cycle of responsibility the FLA requires from the brand-name companies. The second model gives some details of the FLA monitoring system.

For the companies that join the programme, the FLA Model essentially involves:

- Implementation of the FLA principles (referred to here as the 'Code') in the factories that manufacture its products. This requires designating a person or division in the company responsible for promoting Code compliance at all levels of the supply chain and ensuring that factory management and workers are aware of the standards;

- Conducting internal monitoring and then correcting any non-compliances;

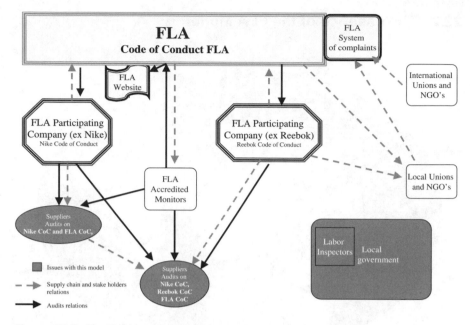

Figure 22.2. The FLA monitoring mechanism

- Submitting to independent external audits conducted by FLA-accredited auditors of a random sample of 5 % of suppliers. The results are published on the FLA website after the company has been given a chance to implement its corrective action plan;
- Reporting to the public on the various activities.

There are a number of additional activities that are used to support the FLA programme, but we shall concentrate here on the key steps making up the FLA programme: how the FLA collects compliance information, remediate the compliance issues identified, checks that remediation, and reports the results to the public.

Collecting compliance information

The external monitoring work is done by independent accredited monitors contracted and paid by the FLA. In order to be accredited, the auditors have to demonstrate their knowledge in audit work, in human rights and in the culture and language of the country they want to work in. They have to conduct a trial audit so that FLA staff can check their ability to conduct an audit according to FLA standards. The FLA works with international commercial audit companies but is increasingly encouraging local audit companies or NGOs to apply for accreditation. Two NGOs – Coverco and GMIES in Central America – for instance, have been accredited by the FLA.

The FLA provides the auditors with a short training course, tools and audit instruments which help them to consult knowledgeable local sources, conduct worker and management interviews, review wage and hour records and inspect the facility to identify problems of non-compliance like health and safety issues. What makes them different from other CSR programmes is that the monitoring work is regarded as a measurement tool and not as a pass or fail assessment. FLA-accredited auditors report on the problems that they find with a view to identifying areas for improvement and making the participating companies accountable for ensuring long-term and sustainable progress in their factories. The auditors' reports are sent to the FLA which ensures they meet the required quality before sending it to the participating company so that they can use it as a basis for the remediation process. The FLA staff can accompany any auditor to check the quality of the audit.

Remediation is the heart of the FLA programme. Companies are required to work with their factories to correct and prevent any instances of non-compliance identified by internal or FLA-accredited independent external monitors. Companies report to the FLA on the status of their remediation plans for factories that have been subject to audit and the FLA updates this information on its website on an ongoing basis. The companies are urged to continue production at factories that are found not to comply with the standards and to work with them to improve conditions and protect the rights of the workers responsible for manufacturing their products. It is only in cases where the supplier factory is unwilling or unable to meet the requirements of the FLA that the participating company may terminate its contract with the supplier.

In order to receive accreditation for its programme after the implementation period, a company participating in the FLA programme has to demonstrate to the staff that it meets ten requirements of the FLA Charter.

The FLA staff also makes the field visits to observe the work of the participating company's local compliance staff and assess factory conditions. In order to be closer to the factories and the local compliance staff of the participating companies, the FLA opened regional offices in Asia and South America. This also allows the FLA to be in contact with the stakeholders. By consulting and working closely with local groups around the world, the FLA has participated in the formation of a global network dedicated to improving labour rights.

Transparency is one of the most important aspects of the FLA model. This is a quality that is rare enough in CSR models to merit particular mention. The FLA issues a public report for each participating company. In order to verify, evaluate and publicly account for the compliance programme of a participating company staff members of the FLA conduct an internal audit of the compliance programme of the participating company on an annual basis as well as an external audit of their suppliers. The FLA publishes both a report on the company's compliance programme and the results of the external audits on their website.

Any third party (for example an NGO or trade union) is able to file a complaint regarding alleged non-compliance at a supplier of an FLA affiliate. The participating company then has up to 45 days either to investigate the alleged non-compliance internally and demonstrate that it has been remedied, or to request that the process be assessed by the FLA. The FLA will prepare a summary report of the complaint and its progress to date and provide that report to the complainant, the company and the FLA Board of Directors.

The costs (the affiliation fees, the cost for the FLA external audits which are paid once a year and the administrative fees) are paid by the participating companies and university licensees. The accredited monitors are selected and paid by the FLA for each audit.

22.3   Experiences with the model in practice

The FLA has often mediated in disputes between workers and management in companies participating in the FLA programme. In Guatemala, the Dominican Republic, Sri Lanka and Thailand the FLA responded to complaints from workers that their freedom of association rights were being violated and through mediation was able to secure recognition for the unions. In two of the cases collective agreements have also been negotiated.

There are ten charter requirements that a participating company must meet to have its programme accredited by the FLA. These range from establishing clear standards, creating an informed workplace, developing an information database, establishing a programme to train company monitors, conducting periodic visits and audits, providing employees with the opportunity to report non-compliance, establishing relationships with labour, human rights, religious or other local groups and establishing means of remediation for their factories. In April 2004, the FLA accredited the monitoring plan for Reebok footwear (41 suppliers) which was implemented over a period of two years, and in April 2005 a further six company compliance programmes were accredited. Even if the accreditation by the board means that the programme has been fulfilled, all the performance requirements remain the same and the FLA stresses the need for continued improvement at the level of the factory and the company. The FLA revaluates the accreditation every two years and may retract it.

22.4   Dos and don'ts

Does this model lead to an improvement in the well-being of the workers? Does it help to put in place free representation in the factories and freedom of association and collective bargaining? Does it help to build social dialogue between workers and employers? Do monitoring strategies increase the capacity of factories to comply?

As we saw with the example of Reebok, by pushing the participating companies to work with a global approach, the FLA helped to create positive competitive pressure for suppliers engaged in business with the FLA participating companies. This position is important to ensure that all workers in the supply chains, regardless of their country, experience the benefits of improved labour rights.

In spite of the positive aspects, the FLA model needs some improvement. The FLA is aware of the necessary improvements and has already introduced steps to remediate them.

One of the issues is that FLA doesn't require the auditors to have human resources management knowledge – which limits the quality of the result of the audit. The problem is common in CSR audits., Comparative analysis[1] of the reports and methodologies of CSR audits in general showed that auditors, whether they are from NGOs or private firms, simply list problems and do not conduct acceptable social audits (Combemale and Igalens, 2005).

The quality and methodology of compliance audits limit the information available to the public.

Audits and code of conducts are too numerous and generate confusion and frustration mostly for manufacturers and suppliers. The participating companies audit the factories based on their own code of conduct even when they share factories with other participating companies. What is more, the FLA code of conduct is very confusing for the suppliers; it is not unusual for the supplier to undergo several audits, carried out by different participating companies, in the same month. Therefore the remedial responses of each company may duplicate the efforts of others and the results can even contradict each other. The FLA is beginning to share or combine remedial initiatives to reduce duplication, achieve some economies of scale and maximise the leverage and impact.

Ultimately, as for the other CSR models, suppliers are the recipients of imposed standards. This tends to generate rejection of the latter instead of appropriation because it doesn't improve their management system. The FLA CSR Model as the other CSR organisation in general places the factory manager in a double bind situation. He is caught between an injunction where the capacity of making a high quality product and demanding speed production are directly opposed to the implementation of a multinational code of conduct. He is put in a deadlock situation that obliged to turn to defensive strategies with negative impacts as cheating on social issues.

---

[1] Codes of Conduct Implementation and Monitoring in the Garment Industry Supply Chain- Summary Evaluation of the Field at the 10-year Mark – Fondation des droits de l'Homme au travail (infos@fdht.org), February 2005.

22.5 Concluding remarks regarding the application of the model

The FLA model shows the complexity of CSR issues and remediation programmes; it demonstrates that an inspection alone does not improve the life of the workers in a sustainable way. An 'audit' provides only the action list and would have to identify root causes if the remedial action is to have any chance of success. The FLA is emphasising the need for the root causes to be addressed through training and other capacity building programmes.

The involvement of suppliers in the process is essential. Suppliers are usually the recipients of imposed standards. This tends to generate rejection of the latter instead of appropriation. Some suppliers would like to establish partnerships with companies and invest the money spent in audits in improving their management system. Some multinationals are aware of their shortcomings and the conflict they create through their drive to lower costs and shorten lead times which can have perverse effects on working conditions in their supply chain. The FLA has therefore started to recruit suppliers into the FLA.

Considering the points mentioned above, it is imperative that social auditors competencies and practices improve to match the higher standards of the FLA and the participating companies. It is important to evaluate efforts and not only results. As we saw with the FLA model, improvement needs time and it is an ongoing process, the audit will never improve the lives of the workers by itself. In short, the FLA model is a model that results in capacity building because it does not concentrate solely on auditing.

References

Adam C., F. Beaujolin and M. Combemale (2005). *Codes of Conduct Implementation and Monitoring in the Garment Industry Supply Chain- Summary Evaluation of the Field at the 10-year Mark* – Fondation des droits de l'Homme au travail (infos@fdht.org).

Baddache, F. (2004). *Entreprises et ONG face au séveloppement durable: l'innovation par la coopération*, L'Harmattam.

Combemale, M. and J. Igalens (2005). *Audit social, Que Sais Je*, PUF.

Interview with Auret Van Heerden, President of FLA (2003/4). *FLA Public Reports*.

Le Roy, F. and M. Marchesnay (2005). *La responsabilité sociale de l'entreprise*, Mélanges en l'honneur du professeur Roland Pérez, EMS.

Servais, J.M. (2004). *Normes Internationales du travail*, LGDJ.

Website

www. fairlabor.org

23 A Stakeholder Model for Emerging Technologies

Gael M. McDonald and Deborah Rolland

Key words: Corporate social responsibility, stakeholder analysis model, emerging technologies, impact assessment, ethical values and principles.

23.1 Introduction

In keeping with the central dimensions of corporate social responsibility (CSR) and building on the experience of a chemical modified bio-based new product development project, the intention of this paper is to provide a stakeholder analysis model for use in organisations intent on demonstrating CSR specifically in relation to new and emerging technologies. This focus on new and emerging technologies is particularly important given the growth in, for example, environmental management, engineering, information technologies and biotechnology, and the desire to balance ethical, social and cultural impacts with sustainability as well as commercial factors.

For organisations active in the development and commercialisation of new technologies, the full pursuit of CSR has a number of challenges as these organisations grapple with the identification, evaluation and harmonising of stakeholder interests in relation to brand new areas of knowledge and their unique applications. All of this is frequently entirely new, both to the organisation and their relevant stakeholders, those known and yet to be identified. Specifically, with a wealth of issues commonly associated with new technological developments, mechanisms are being sought as to how environmental, ethical and cultural concerns can be effectively identified in order to assess benefits and risks appropriately for accurate evaluation, continuation or discontinuation of new technology developments.

Lee (2003) has suggested that the way to evaluate highly uncertain risks is to employ risk assessment as a scientific process within an explicit decision framework that directly addresses stakeholder values, trade-offs, and the uncertainty on decisions. The term 'requisite model' refers to a policy model that contains questions essential for informing the issue at hand. Questions that may be asked to develop such a model include:

- Who are the legitimate stakeholders?
- Who bears the consequences of the decision?

- Who is responsible for making/implementing/enforcing the decision?
- What do the stakeholders care about?
- What are the preferences for different outcomes?
- What trade-offs are they willing to make among different consequent dimensions, e.g., cost versus safety?
- What are the competing decision options to be evaluated?
- What information do the stakeholders need to make well-informed decisions/what questions are they asking?
- What information is immediately available about the probable consequences of different decisions?
- What data gaps and uncertainties exist, and what means exist to reduce uncertainties?
- What analytical tools and experts are available?
- What are the resource and time constraints on making the decision?

With this information in hand, analytical frameworks such as multi-attribute utility theory (MAUT) and multi-criteria decision-making (MCDM) can be employed, although these frameworks have, in the past, not been commonly used for biotechnology analysis.

Private entities, research bodies and governments who are directly investing in scientific discovery can face extreme scepticism and caution from the general public in relation to the introduction and acceptance of new technology products resulting from scientific endeavours. The increasing number of technologies becoming available is likely to result in a large number of people voicing their concern in regard to the potential impacts of these technologies. Investment in this research is considerable, as is the desire to obtain some return on this investment. Therefore, means are being sought in a number of different domains to ensure appropriate recognition and evaluation of social, cultural, ethical and environmental impacts, as well as an effective information dissemination process following appropriate assessment of these impacts.

23.2   The essence of the model

The stakeholder analysis model for emerging technologies is made up of a number of key dimensions, such as perceived benefits and threats, perceived societal impacts, guiding values and principles, ethical decision-making guidelines and stakeholder information needs. These dimensions inter-relate toward the ultimate evaluation of the impact of an emerging technology by a specific stakeholder (see Figure 23.1). The model begins its process of analysis by presenting a new technology scenario to a stakeholder in which the stakeholder can identify what they foresee as general potential benefits of the technology as well as the general threats and potentially negative impacts. In doing so, the stakeholder begins the decision-making process by initially scanning their own internal perceptions in order to communicate perceived benefits and threats that might not previously have been identified by the technology developers. It is important that this step is undertaken before leading the stakeholder on to a more in-depth analysis of potential impacts.

The impact assessment section of the model allows the perceived impacts of the new technology to be examined in more detail. In addition to a generic 'other issues' category, there are seven specific impact areas:

- Health impact – the impact of the new technology on health, fitness and well-being;

- Social impact – the impact on social issues, i.e. privacy, security, safety and freedom;

- Economic and financial impact – the impact on general economic and financial conditions, i.e. earning power, financial profitability, financial security, economic development and competitiveness;

- Technology impact – the impact on the development of new technology, i.e. further development of new knowledge, products or processes;

- Political and legal impact – the impact on political legal conditions, i.e. need for political involvement, intervention, legislation;

- Environmental impact – climate and atmospheric impacts;

- Cultural impact – the impact on cultural and sub-cultural factors, i.e. cultural values.

In the questionnaire instrument that accompanies this model the impact assessment is undertaken in relation to the stakeholders themselves and their family, their immediate community or organisation, and future generations nationally and internationally.

Having assessed the perceived benefits and threats and undertaken a more detailed assessment of the likely impacts of a new technology, the model turns to the values used in evaluating a new technology. Here the stakeholder is able to indicate what guiding values and principles they believe are relevant to the technology scenario in question, and what values are being enhanced or eroded, such as recognition of rights, promotion of human welfare, respect for persons, etc. In the questionnaire accompanying the model, a list is provided to the stakeholder from which they can select relevant guiding values and principles.

With the establishment of the values and principles that impact on the relevant technology, the model then moves to identify the underlying ethical decision

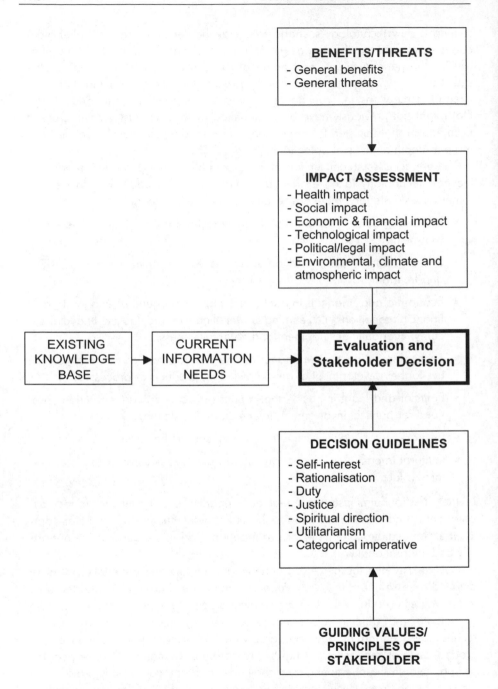

Figure 23.1. Stakeholder analysis model for emerging technologies

frameworks, i.e. what are the cognitive frameworks used by stakeholders when considering technologies which potentially contain ethical conflicts. Seven decision guidelines appear in the model:

- Self-interest – based on teleological/consequential theory, self-interest dictates that during the evaluation process the principal guideline used by the stakeholder in evaluating risks and benefits is the ultimate achievement of self-interest, i.e. what's best for the stakeholder;

- Rationalisation – a stakeholder utilising a rationalisation approach will have the ability to perceive both positive and negative impacts but will rationalise the negative impacts in favour of the positive outcomes of the new technology;

- Duty – the essence of the deontological school, here a stakeholder would be guided in their evaluation by what they perceive as being their duty or obligation despite the outcomes of the technology;

- Justice – here the stakeholder questions the ultimate fairness inherent in the evaluation of the decision perspectives;

- Spiritual direction – involves the utilisation of religious or spiritual frameworks in the evaluation process;

- Utilitarianism – the stakeholder would approach the evaluation of the new technology by balancing costs and benefits in an effort to maximise utility, i.e. to produce the greatest ratio of good over bad for everyone;

- Categorical imperative – drawn from deontological normative theory, the stakeholder would evaluate whether a technology would be appropriate or inappropriate regardless of the consequences. Consideration would be given to whether 'we would be willing to have others act in this way' and whether individuals or animals are being treated as an ends or a means, i.e. respected and in possession of rights, or are they being utilised purely for the sole achievement of a specific objective.

As emerging technologies are often dealing with new and complex areas of life, it is also important to assess the existing knowledge base of stakeholders. Those who are more informed on an issue, e.g. genetic engineering, may be deemed to be more insightful and their perceptions to have greater validity. The model establishes the stakeholder's existing knowledge base. Similarly, it is important to assess what new information would be useful to the stakeholder for further consideration of each of the impact areas, i.e. health, social, environmental as they may not be in possession of, or have considered, all the relevant information necessary to make a decision in regard to the new technology.

The ultimate outcome of the model, having examined the above dimensions, is the resulting consideration by the stakeholder in regard to the social, cultural and environmental impacts of a new technology, with a number of decision options being available. In the questionnaire accompanying the model, the stakeholder has the choice of:

- Making the technology available with no restrictions;
- Making the technology available with legal restrictions;
- Further consideration via a national referendum;
- Delaying availability pending further scientific study;
- Delaying availability pending further public discussion;
- Delaying availability pending further development of improved safeguards;
- Banning the technology;
- Fence-sitting – inability to make an informed decision.

23.3   The model in practice

The model was prepared in support of a New Zealand Foundation for Research, Science and Technology-funded project administered by New Zealand Forest Research in conjunction with the authors. The intended outcome of the project is to develop an 'acceptability threshold position' model for biomaterials-based technologies, which incorporates environmental, social and ethical concerns impacting on the design and development of next generation products and technologies. In doing so, the research is designed to provide mechanisms for informed dialogue and decision-making on new technologies, particularly relating to biomaterial opportunities and, in this instance, in relation to new technologies in the wood industry.

In the wood industry, recent restrictions on the use of the wood preservative chromate copper-arsenate (CCA), have redirected technological developments in the wood protection arena, with a subsequent search for alternatives to CCA. In his review of emerging technologies in wood protection, Evans (2003) has indicated that emerging technologies promise competitive advantage, reductions in the environmental impact of treated wood products, and solutions to problems such as the treatment of refractory timbers. Forest Research has been developing these new technologies and wishes to examine the environmental, social and ethical issues pertaining to existing and transitional biomaterial technologies with relevant stakeholders within the context of New Zealand. Within the research project, three decking materials with three different types and degrees of chemical modification are being evaluated: CCA treated pine (existing technology base), acetylate pine, and thermawood (transitional technologies currently under development). Following preliminary development through the use of focus groups (N=25) in two geographic locations in New Zealand, the model has since been fleshed out in the form of a written questionnaire (subject to modification) to be administered to a diverse range of stakeholders.

It should be noted that in relation to this model and of particular concern to the developers and to the New Zealand government, is the issue of cultural impacts of new technology. When examining cultural issues that impact on new technology, one usually refers to the dominant culture in evidence. However, in the New Zealand environment that would be inappropriate given legislative commitment to bi-culturalism and the vocal concerns of native Maori. Recent government commentary has indicated that there is heightened awareness among Maori regarding cultural and intellectual property rights, particularly the patenting of inventions concerning human, animal and plant life. The current concerns appear to be in regard to genetically altering indigenous flora and fauna, which is considered culturally and spiritually unacceptable to Maori, and the granting of exclusive rights over the genetically altered indigenous flora and fauna (Ministry of Economic Development, 2004, Maori Concerns about Patenting Biotechnology).

23.4 Implications and conclusions

While the primary focus of the research project relates to chemical modification of bio-based products leading to the design of new and innovative green technologies in the forestry industry, the model is not constrained by wood as the sole raw material. It has a generic application to emerging technologies, where there is an underlying theme of balancing sustainability, social and ethical influences with market factors. Clearly, there are numerous other arenas in which organisations are also grappling with investigating the social, ethical and environmental impacts of existing and emerging technologies.

To conclude, and as a cautionary note, there is a concern that stakeholder analysis provides an excellent codification of current hot-buttons but that it does not help in rationalising or resolving existing stakeholder differences. Stakeholder analysis may give the appearance of decision-making but it is, in fact, only part of the process. Stakeholder analysis is the fact-gathering and analysis component while resolution is still awaited. 'In many bitter political conflicts involving environmental issues, environmentalists cast business people as greedy and uncaring, while the business people portray environmentalists as ideological zealots' (Cordano, 1996, p. 347). A stakeholder analysis in these circumstances may only serve to reinforce existing prejudices and opinions. More investigation is needed if we aim at developing a sustainable development framework for bio-technology innovation and to tackle resolving differences among stakeholders.

References

Cordano, M. (1996). The Attitudinal Bases of Stakeholder Conflict: An Examination of Business-Environmental Stakeholders. *Academy of Management Proceedings '96*, pp. 347-351.

Evans, P. (2003). Emerging Technologies in Wood Protection. *Forest Products Journal*, 53(1): pp. 14-22.

Lee, R.C. (2003). *Risky Genomics: The Roles of Risk/Benefit Assessment and Rational Decision Frameworks*. ISB News Report, May. (www.isb.vt.edu).

New Zealand Ministry of Economic Development (2004). *Maori Concerns about Patenting Biotechnology*. (www.med.govt.nz/buslt/int_prop/biotech/patentbiotech).

New Zealand Ministry of Research, Science & Technology (2003). *New Zealand Biotechnology Strategy*. (www.morst.govt.nz).

Organising Systems

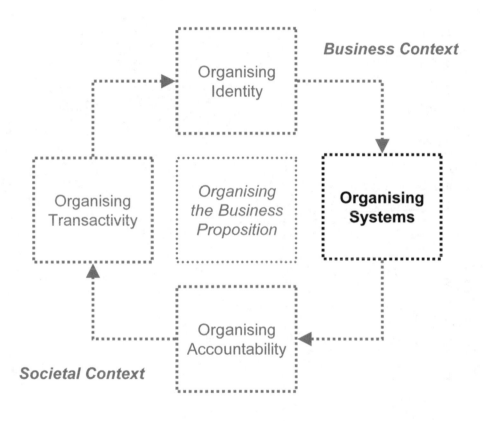

24 Product Stewardship for CSR

Helen Lewis

Key words: Product stewardship, life cycle management, packaging.

24.1 Introduction

The term 'product stewardship' is generally used to mean a product-oriented approach to environmental management. It is one of the many issues being addressed by companies under the broader umbrella of CSR. It is being driven by a global trend to make companies more responsible for the environmental impacts of products that they make or sell. The two key principles behind product stewardship are 'life cycle thinking' – the need to consider impacts over the total life cycle of the product – and the 'shared responsibility' of different stakeholders for managing these impacts. One of the problems however, is that specific responsibilities of companies are often not defined. This chapter provides a framework for product stewardship which translates a broad concept – product stewardship – into a series of performance indicators that can be used by practitioners in the field.

Introduction to the model

The approach used for this study was to analyse product stewardship within a CSR framework originally developed by Carroll (1979), which had 3 dimensions:

- Types of responsibilities: the range of obligations that companies have to society;
- Social issues or topics that companies must address;
- The strategy behind corporate responses to social responsibility (responsiveness).

Labatt (1991) took this further by developing a system for assessing discretionary corporate responses to environmental issues. A set of indicators and a measurement scale was developed for each indicator. Quantitative scores were used to measure performance against each indicator along a CSR scale, from 'defensive' to 'proactive'. The following model builds on this earlier work by exploring product stewardship as one of the CSR issues being addressed by companies, and by developing a series of indicators and a measurement scale for different aspects of product stewardship.

24.2 Description of the model

The model provides 17 product stewardship indicators. These are allocated according to that part of the business which is most likely to have responsibility for a particular activity, i.e. management, product development, production, marketing or external relations, and to the relevant business activity. Each business function has a direct influence on environmental impacts at particular points in the product's life cycle (Figure 24.1), although decisions made by management and product development functions are likely to influence all aspects of the life cycle.

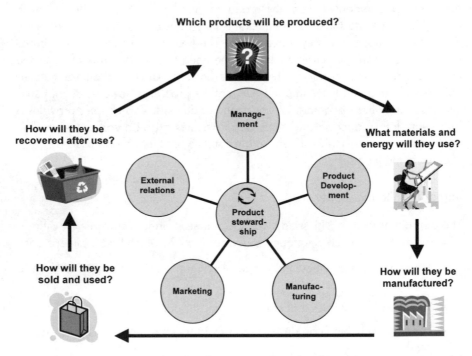

Figure 24.1. Links between business functions and product life cycle impacts

Company performance against each indicator is scored from 0 to 3, from 'defensive' to 'proactive' (Table 24.1). Labatt's category for 'appeasement' (the minimum required to maintain a good public image) is interpreted for this purpose as legal compliance.

Table 24.1. Responsiveness score (based on Labatt 1991, p.165)

Score	Description
0	Defensive: do nothing or denial
1	Compliant: do the minimum required to maintain a good public image
2	Progressive: issues approached with desire to improve social conditions
3	Proactive: anticipatory; being a leader among all industries in advancing social conditions

Performance indicators

Each of the indicators is briefly introduced below.

Product stewardship policy and objectives

A company's product stewardship objectives and strategies may be outlined in a stand-alone document or integrated into a broader Environmental Policy.

Resource allocation

Building an internal capability to implement product stewardship requires allocation of appropriate resources, assignment of responsibilities to staff members and building internal expertise.

Product-oriented Environment Management System (POEMS)

This has been described as an EMS with a special focus on the continuous improvement of product eco-efficiency through the systematic integration of eco-design in the company's strategies and practices (Rocha and Brezet, 1999).

Product-based accounting

Environmental accounting systems can support planning, monitoring and reporting of product stewardship. Measures may include the mass of products which is produced, recycled and disposed to landfill.

Product stewardship reporting

In recent years there has been growing pressure on companies to report on environmental and social performance. A product stewardship report could be a separate document, or included in a Sustainability Report, Annual Report or corporate web site.

Environmental assessment of products

Environmental assessment will help to identify priorities for environmental design of products. This involves assessment of environmental impacts throughout the product life cycle, for example through use of life cycle assessment (LCA) tools.

Research and development

An ongoing research and development programme will help to identify opportunities for new product development linked to innovation in materials, technologies or markets.

Design for environment (DFE)

DFE involves integration of environmental requirements in the product development process to ensure that lifecycle impacts are minimised.

Supply chain management

DFE also requires a certain level of engagement and cooperation with other organisations in the supply chain, particularly with suppliers and customers. Sometimes companies need to work with organisations beyond their traditional supply chain, for example with recyclers.

Cleaner production

Cleaner production involves redesign of manufacturing processes to eliminate or reduce wastes and emissions.

Recycling of solid production waste

Cleaner production tries to eliminate waste at source, but any waste which is generated during manufacturing and which cannot be reused in another process should be recycled.

Environmental marketing strategies

Environmental marketing is normally interpreted as strategies aimed at increasing sales of products to environmentally aware or concerned consumers, but it can also include marketing of corporate policies or initiatives.

Product labelling

An important element of any marketing campaign is the communication of essential information to consumers on the product label, including information on the environmental attributes of the product.

Product recovery

Product stewardship has always been politically driven by the problem of increasing waste, and the desire to improve recycling or reuse of products at end-
of-life.

Litter management

Litter management is another important aspect of product stewardship for companies involved in packaging or other single-use products consumed out of
doors.

Regulatory compliance

There are an increasing number of product stewardship regulations worldwide,
such as the European Packaging Directive. Participation in voluntary environmental programmes is perhaps an even better indicator of CSR, as this involves
going 'beyond compliance'.

Consultation and education

Some companies undertake surveys or use other methods to gather the views of
stakeholders about product stewardship (and other CSR) issues. Education
strategies may also be used to inform stakeholders about product stewardship
programmes.

24.3   Experiences with the model

The author has worked for many years at the Centre for Design at RMIT University, Melbourne, Australia. The Centre is internationally recognised for its programme of research and consulting with industry on environmental assessment
of products, eco-design and product stewardship. This work has informed the
development of the product stewardship model, which is currently being tested
through a study of the Australian packaging industry's responsiveness to product stewardship.

The study used secondary data from annual company reports to the National
Packaging Covenant (NPC) Council, as well as other publicly available information such as annual reports, EHS or sustainability reports and corporate web
sites. This information was used to score each company against the 17 indicators contained in the model. Guidelines were developed to provide a consistent
basis for scoring companies in the Australian packaging industry, e.g. with specific reference to the requirements of the NPC for the 'compliance' score. These
guidelines are presented in Table 24.2.

Table 24.2. Guidelines for a product stewardship (PS) evaluation in the Australian packaging industry

	Defensive (0)	Compliant (1)	Progressive (2)	Proactive (3)
Management				
PS policy, objectives and targets	No policy in place	The company has a stated commitment to PS	The product policy identifies PS objectives, strategies & quantified targets	The product policy includes ambitious PS targets, e.g. 100 % recyclability, sustainability
Resource allocation	No indication of any resources allocated to PS	Financial contribution to NPC Transitional Fund	Financial & human resources allocated to PS activities	Responsibility for PS allocated across all aspects of the business with significant budget
Product-oriented EMS	No comprehensive management system in place to manage PS	Environment policies, objectives & monitoring system in place	Certified EMS in place for some sites (e.g. high risk sites)	Product-oriented EMS in place
Product-based accounting	No system in place to measure product flows or performance against objectives	A monitoring system in place to measure performance against objectives	A product database tracks product flows and achievements against NPC objectives & KPIs	The product database is also being used for strategic analysis and DFE
PS reporting	No public reporting on PS activities	PS commitments & achievements published in annual reports to the NPC Council	An environment or sustainability report produced with information on broader company impacts and initiatives, including PS	The company publishes an environment or sustainability report according to the GRI or AA1000 Standard
Product development				
Environmental assessment of products	Environmental assessment is not undertaken	Some research is being undertaken on the environmental impacts of products, e.g. process in place to review packaging over time	Policy & procedures in place to ensure an environmental assessment is undertaken for all product development (qualitative or semi-quantitative)	Policy & procedures in place to ensure LCA is undertaken for all product development

Table 24.2. (continued)

Product development (continued)				
Research & development	No expenditure on environmental R&D	Some expenditure on environmental R&D to achieve waste reduction	Some expenditure on environmental R&D to reduce environmental impacts of product life cycles	Significant R&D effort is focused on developing new technologies or products to position the company as a leader in environmentally-improved products
Design for Environment (DFE)	Environmental issues are not considered within the design process	The company has a stated commitment to DFE, uses the environmental code of practice for packaging (ECoPP) & there is some evidence of environmental improvement	The company has a written DFE policy and the ECoPP is integrated within the product development process	There is a DFE policy and procedures, and evidence of effectiveness of DFE process (i.e. products with reduced environmental impact)
Supply chain management	There is no process in place to involve suppliers in PS	Suppliers have started to be engaged in PS, e.g. involved in joint projects or encouraged to reduce impacts of products	An environmental purchasing policy is in place and environmental information is collected from all suppliers. Other product chain partners are also consulted about PS initiatives	Suppliers are selected on the basis of their environmental performance, i.e. the questionnaire is used in selecting suppliers
Production				
Cleaner production	No cleaner production initiatives	At least one cleaner production initiative has been implemented	There is a stated commitment to cleaner production & several initiatives have been implemented	Company has a zero waste goal & processes are in place to treat and recover all wastes in-house
Recycling of solid production waste	No recycling of solid wastes apart from in-house reprocessing of clean plastics	Recycling of some waste streams by external organisations, e.g. cardboard, pallets	Recycling of more difficult waste streams, e.g. stretch film, organic wastes	All solid wastes are recycled

Table 24.2 (continued)

Marketing				
Environmental marketing strategies	No environmental marketing undertaken	Some limited environmental marketing, e.g. environmental claims and labels	Marketing being used to sell the company's products as environmentally responsible	Marketing being used to sell the company as a leader in PS and CSR
Product labelling	The company does not use any environmental claims or labels, or makes meaningless or incorrect claims	Programmes underway to include logos on products to promote recyclability, recycled content or anti-litter	Programmes underway to include clear and detailed statements about environmental impact	Environmental benefits of products are certified by a third-party organisation
External relations				
Product recovery	Company does not take any action to ensure products are recovered at end-of-life	The company contributes to the NPC Transitional Fund which supports recovery. Products may display a recycling logo	The company is actively involved in an industry programme to reprocess its own products, or is undertaking R&D to find markets for its own recycled materials	The company is directly involved in collection of at least some of its own products for reuse or recycling
Litter management	The company does not take any action to minimise the impacts of its products in the litter stream	Products include an anti-litter logo	The company considers litter impacts during the design process and contributes funding to anti-litter programmes	The company can demonstrate that it has redesigned its products to reduce impacts in the litter stream
Regulatory compliance	Not a signatory to the NPC	Signatory to the NPC and submitted at least one Action Plan	An early signatory to the NPC (first Action Plan published in 2001 or earlier)	Also involved in other voluntary environmental programmes
Consultation and education	No communication with stakeholders about PS	Education provided for employees & contractors (e.g. NPC obligations)	Education provided for suppliers and/or customers	Other stakeholders are consulted about PS programmes, e.g. community, government

The preliminary evaluation found a significant gap between the strong perform-ance of a small number of industry leaders and the mediocre performance of most of the Australian and multinational companies assessed for the project. Very few companies are going beyond compliance in their product stewardship activities, highlighting the importance of regulation in achieving change.

For some companies, publicly available information on product stewardship activities was limited, which meant that they received low (or zero) scores for some indicators. While this may not reflect their actual level of activity, a 'non-compliant' score is justified because public reporting is an essential element of the NPC.

24.4 Some dos and don'ts

With some adaptation the model could be used for different applications and purposes (see 'dos and don'ts' in Table 24.3). For example, it could be used to identify areas of CSR performance which need to be improved, or to assist a company to decide where it wishes to be positioned in relation to its peers. Any company that intends to remain competitive in the longer term would not wish to be anything less than compliant. Whether a company wishes to be posi-tioned as 'progressive' or 'proactive' would depend on its core values, vision and corporate identity.

Table 24.3. Guidelines for use

Do	Use the model for strategic planning, gap analysis or benchmarking; Adapt the model for the specific regulatory requirements of the relevant product sector / country; Update the model over time for changes to regulations & best practice standards; Develop clear guidelines to assist in the evaluation (to facilitate consis-tency and transparency); Pilot test and refine the model before undertaking the study.
Don't	Expect the model to provide all the answers – a complete evaluation would require additional data, for example interviews with company rep-resentatives (e.g. to include initiatives which are not covered in public documents).

24.5 Conclusions

The model is a useful tool for evaluating the responsiveness of companies to one aspect of CSR, i.e. product stewardship. It was originally developed for an Australian study of responsiveness within the packaging industry, and therefore specific indicators (e.g. litter) were chosen to reflect community and government expectations of industry. It could very easily be adapted to other sectors or products by adding additional indicators or eliminating unnecessary ones, or by amending the guidelines.

References

Carroll, A. (1979). A three-dimensional conceptual model of corporate performance. *Academy of Management Review* 4(4): pp. 497-505.

Labatt, S. (1991). A framework for assessing discretionary corporate performance towards the environment. *Environmental Management* 15(2): pp. 163-178.

Rocha, C. and H. Brezet (1999). Product-oriented environmental management systems: a case study. *Journal of Sustainable Product Product Design* (10): pp. 30-42.

Websites

http://www.deh.gov.au/industry/waste/covenant
http://www.cfd.rmit.edu.au
http://www.sustainablepack.org

25 Sabento Model: Social Assessment of Biotechnological Production

Justus von Geibler, Holger Wallbaum, Christa Liedtke in support with Frederik Lippert

Key words: Technology assessment, biotechnology, sustainability assessment, social aspects of sustainability.

25.1 Introduction to the model

Currently technological developments, e.g. in ICT, biotechnology and nano-technology, pick up momentum to an increasing degree, emerge in a number of markets and enter the scientific and public discussions. There are a number of arguments for the promotion of those technologies, such as job creation potential, economic growth or contributions to sustainable development (e.g. OECD, 1998). However, there is a growing body of evidence that they do not automatically contribute to a sustainable development (see e.g. Kuhndt et al. 2003). Therefore, innovative concepts and practical tools are needed to evaluate technology development according to the implications of sustainability. Especially in early stages of technology design a large share of costs as well as environmental and social effects are determined, while at the same time information on sustainability implications is still limited (Von Geibler and Wallbaum, 2005).

Although the assessment of sustainability implications for different industry sectors has evolved and entered scientific debate, there is a lack of broad consensus on adequate indicators or a consistent method of their identification. Whereas in the environmental or economic area more or less widely-accepted indicators have been developed, a consensus on indicators evaluating the social side to sustainability is still to be developed, in particular for specific industrial sectors (Global Reporting Initiative, 2002).

The Research Group 'Sustainable Production and Consumption' at the Wuppertal Institute has realised the relevance of evolving technologies for sustainable development. Regarding biotechnology the research group is conducting the project 'BioBeN – Assessing social sustainability of biotech products', funded by the German Ministry for Research and Education. The aim is to elaborate a methodology for the social assessment of processes in the biotechnology sector and make it available for practical application through a software tool. This software, called 'sabento', can be used by corporations for assessing and steering potential sustainability risks of biotechnological production. (for further information visit www.sabento.com)

In order to identify relevant social aspects and to compile a set of indicators, four basic perspectives on technology assessment have been taken into consideration, drawing on the methodology approach of concept specification developed in social science. On a macroscopic scale the political relevance of the issue has been dealt with by regard of single political initiatives. On a more systemic level the relevance of stakeholders of the biotech sector has been addressed through an analysis of the outlook of both regional and global actors involved. The entrepreneurial and product relevance has been considered through a survey of biotech companies and the consideration of the information demands from rating agencies of the financial market as well as international sustainability reporting demands from the Global Reporting Initiative (GRI).

Taking into account the results gained from this multi-perspective approach on technology assessment (including the implications of an international stakeholder survey), it has been possible to identify eight aspects that are notably significant for the social assessment of biotechnological operations: health and safety, quality of working conditions, impact on employment policy, education and advanced training, knowledge management, innovative potential, customer acceptance, and societal dialogue.

Within the software-based evaluation, eight questions are posed for each of the eight aspects. This allows the transfer of the set of indicators to a more practical and applicable level. For the evaluation two layers of evaluation are distinguished: (1) The layer of the technology development and (2) its application. This distinction has been made since the social context of the biotechnological processes varies between developing and applicative stage. As far as e.g. the acceptance of a genetically engineered product is concerned, it does imply quite a difference whether a biotechnological process is implemented in a secluded laboratory under controllable conditions; or whether it is carried out on an agricultural area that is per se integrated into a compound and rather unascertainable ecosystem. The set of questions has been specifically developed for each layer. Within the software the answers to these questions given by the user are then transferred into a grading system. For each question a maximum of three points are given. Subsequently the achieved points will be accumulated and can also be presented graphically. A verbal summary of the evaluation is given at the end of the evaluation.

25.2   The essence

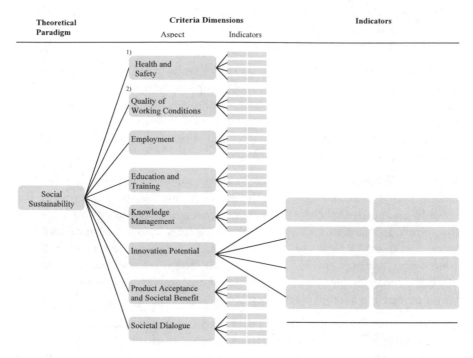

Figure 25.1. Indicator set for the evaluation of social sustainability of biotechnological processes (source: Wuppertal Institute)

25.3   Experiences with this model in practice

Due to the complexity of the biotech-sector and its sustainability implications, the integration of both the companies' and the stakeholders' perspectives has been regarded as a valuable approach. The two surveys among companies and stakeholders highlight a broad awareness of CSR and Sustainable Corporate Governance with most of the participants. However, an overriding experience drawn from the dialogue with the attendees shows the necessity to assist corporations in the assessment of social impacts arising from the technology. The eight aspects mentioned above are relevant to the actors of the biotech sector as outlined below:

Health and Safety. The term 'health and safety' refers to all measures to improve the employees' safety and well being at work – such as the prevention of working accidents, occupational diseases or work-caused dangers to health. In the context of biotechnological production, improved health and safety can lead to a higher motivation of the employees, reduced risk of damage to public image of the enterprise as well as cost reduction. Health and safety management is well advised to surpass compulsory legal measures to improve the conditions of work. Some aspects of health and safety, such as the use of hazardous substances, are subject to national regulation.

Quality of Working Conditions. The quality of working conditions is a competitive factor of growing importance. Quality implies aspects such as labour time arrangements, operational regulations of remuneration, social benefits or the elevation of the employees' psychological strain. In the personal-intensive biotech sector, positive working conditions can result in better work satisfaction, motivation and efficiency of the employees.

Impact on Employment. Due to its innovative potential and key-technology character, the biotechnology sector offers opportunities for employment. This leads to an improved societal and political acceptance and positively influences the granting of public support. Substitution effects in other sectors might yet lead to an overall loss of jobs. Besides the sheer number of jobs created, it is of overriding relevance, how long and in which region jobs are secured and created. Correspondingly, sustainable production requires a differentiated long-term approach to internal employment policies.

Education and Training. In the biotechnology sector, the qualification of the employees is an important factor, since academic research and development form a key activity of the companies. The qualification includes e.g. the consistency of advanced training, a frequent check-up of the demand of basic, advanced training by the executive management level, or the consideration of the employees' demands. Offering apprenticeships or taking voluntary measures to optimise an enterprise's training management likewise defines the quality of internal education and training.

Knowledge Management. Knowledge is an important factor of biotechnological production. Strategic knowledge management is to be pursued in order to achieve entrepreneurial goals. Knowledge management aims at the deliberate and systematic handling of knowledge, covering the creation, collection, distribution, advancement, and application of knowledge. Knowledge management addresses the quality of experience and information exchange, the check-up of this exchange's efficiency, the integration of EDP-based information systems, or the employees' participation in processes of company-internal decision-making.

Innovative Potential. Biotechnology offers a wide array of new development and application opportunities. For biotech companies the innovative potential is especially relevant, because it determines future income. This innovative potential is especially shaped by questions of national and international patenting, which become more and more important for issues of commercialisation prospects.

Customer Acceptance and Societal Product Benefit. The acceptance of products by customers is significantly influenced through product characteristics and information as well as production conditions. Regarding biotechnological production, the utilisation of methods of genetic engineering or the compliance with social standards play a key role. From a sustainable point of view, products should also have a societal use and help securing and increasing everyone's quality of life. A higher value for society can be ascribed e.g. to products that combat malaria or HIV/AIDS, rather than to the development of a new artificial sweetener that does not bear an extensive societal use or financial advantage.

Societal Dialogue. The most recent development in the area of biosciences, particularly regarding work with genetically modified organisms (GMOs), has attracted public attention and initiated an intense debate. Sustainability demands a sincere dialogue, which includes all societal segments. This societal dialogue can also optimise a company's competitive ability, e.g. when it is applied in the field of marketing strategies.

A software-based assessment tool turned out to be practical for companies to internally evaluate biotechnological production. In order to advance the application of the software in different entrepreneurial structures, including small and medium sized enterprises, and to improve the understanding and motivation of the operator, the tool is clearly and simply structured. Step-by-step the user is led through the assessment by the dynamic assistant concept, which conveniently leads into the assessment; for each question various development- and application-focused responsive options exist. In addition, concise background information is given to each criterion of evaluation of the biotechnological process. This allows an uncomplicated handling of the tool as no specific or complex knowledge of the subject is required. Eventually the assistant automatically generates a summary of the results.

The resulting evaluation of the biotechnological process outlines the strengths and improvement potential of the company with regard to the social dimensions of sustainability. The results are given both graphically and verbally, which assists the integration of the sabento software into existing entrepreneurial assessment concepts. The report can be used for the internal and external communication, especially sustainability reporting, and thereby be supportive to the promotion of the relevance of sustainability-based CSR activities.

The prototype of the social part of the software has been tested in actual biotechnological research and development environment by two pilot partners of the project. Interviews have been conducted to assess the practicability, relevance and benefits of the software. The interviews highlighted the high practicability of the software tool, as well as the completeness of the aspects covered. The interviews confirmed increased awareness towards aspects that were previously not regarded as being part of the company's influence and responsibility.

The analysis showed that the neglected aspects would have had a great potential of being negatively perceived by stakeholder groups with potentially harmful consequences for the company. The results were considered to be beneficial for internal and external communication, specifically in the area of financing and marketing.

25.4   Some dos and don'ts

Do take into account, that the assessment of the early product design phase is of major importance since it influences more than 80 % of the cost spent for a product (i.e. production costs, maintenance costs and end-of-life costs). Similarly, the environmental and social effects are also determined in early stages of process development. Meaningful assessment of biotechnology and other evolving technologies therefore has to cover early phases of technology development and take the implications of the Triple-Bottom-Line of sustainability into consideration.

Do perceive assessing social aspect of biotechnological production as depicted by the model as a starting point for continuous evaluation. Accordingly the launch of the software tool initiates a phase of verification of its user-friendliness and practical suitability. Hence only through a long-term approach to sustainability assessment CSR can enter internal management circles and have wide-range impact on operational production patterns.

Do be aware that the model has been specifically developed for the biotech sector and should not be applied to emerging technologies in other industries such as the ICT or nanotechnology. However, the methodological approach used can well be transferred to other industries. This is particularly appropriate as far as the identification of adequate indicators and their systemic arrangement is concerned.

Don't think that the application of a singular assessment tool alone will further sustainable development in the biotech sector. Along with internal evaluation and reporting tools it is necessary to develop a responsibly-minded culture of organisational learning (Hartmann et al., 2005). A culture that enables companies to actively and productively harmonise their economic objectives and (social) sustainability requirements.

Don't neglect the importance of stakeholders' integration into existing management and reporting systems. Stakeholders have substantially provided contribution to the identification of relevant evaluation aspects during the development of the sabento software. Equally significant is their consideration in companies' sustainability assessment procedures. Sabento as a software-based assessment tool can aid companies to optimise their communication with stakeholders.

25.5 Wrapping up

The sabento-assessment model highlights social indicators for the early-stage sustainability assessment of biotechnological production, which have been transferred into a software-based evaluation tool, tailor-made for SME of the biotech sector. Key companies' and stakeholders' perspectives have been addressed – granting the model a sector based approach and fostering a compound dialogue on potential sustainability impacts of new technologies that includes a wide array of actors. This dialogue on the potential of sustainability assessment vitally contributes to the promotion of CSR in the biotechnology sector.

References

von Geibler, J. and H. Wallbaum. Sustainability Assessment of emerging technologies: Social Aspects of biotechnological production, in: Heinzle, E., Cooney, C., Biewer, A. (ed.). *Development of Sustainable Bioprocesses: Modeling and Assessment.* (forthcoming)

Global Reporting Initiative (2002). *Sustainability Reporting Guidelines 2002.* Boston.

Hartmann, D., H. Brentel and H. Rohn (2005). Lern- und Innovationsfähigkeit von Organisationen und Unternehmen. Kriterien und Indikatoren zur Bewertung, [Learning and innovative ability of organisations and enterprises. Evaluation Criteria and indicators], In: von Geibler, J. et al. (2005). *Soziale Bewertung der Nachhaltigkeit biotechnologischer Produktion: Schlussbericht zum gleichnamigen Projekt im Förderschwerpunkt ,Nachhaltige Bioproduktion' des Ministeriums für Bildung und Forschung, Teil des Verbundprojektes ,Simulationsgestützte Bewertung der Nachhaltigkeit biotechnologischer Produktion'* Wuppertal Paper, Wuppertal. (forthcoming)

Kuhndt, M., J. von Geibler, V. Türk, S. Moll, K.O. Schallaböck and S. Steger (2003). *Digital Europe: Virtual dematerialisation: e-business and factor X.* Report to the European Community. Wuppertal Institute.

OECD (ed.) (1998). *Biotechnology for clean industrial products and processes. Towards industrial sustainability*, Paris.

Websites

http://www.bioproduction.de
http://www.sabento.de
http://www.wupperinst.org

26 The Branding of CSR Excellence

John Luff

Key words: Marketing, communications, brand.

26.1 Introduction

Being corporately socially responsible is a desirable thing in and of its self. But doing the right thing does not of itself build reputation, brand and therefore equity for shareholders or any other stakeholders. CSR needs to be built into marketing and brand: CSR and the future of brand are one and the same. The essence of brand in the 21st century is sustainable marketing from a place of integrity.

Getting and sustaining better results these days is about building and nurturing relationships. And every relationship – commercial or otherwise – is dependant on good communications. In the commercial world this is widely accepted as the key differentiator. Meeting the needs and demands of stakeholders is a critical success factor with regard to CSR. Stakeholders demand information. Not filtered, sporadic information, but regular, meaningful and sustained communication. CSR based on sustainability and responsibility without communication is virtually meaningless. More positively, CSR credentials, when communicated well, bring about self-perpetuating and self sustainable marketing. So key marketing/brand issues for any organisation should include how to (a) identify and (b) communicate CSR excellence.

26.2 A model for communicating CSR

The CSR driven contribution to the business proposition needs to be viewed in three interconnected but different contexts:

- Law: the legal duties of an organisation;
- Value Add: the value add for stakeholders;
- Core Values: the impact of core corporate values.

Within organisations these three elements of the business proposition are typically owned by different teams/units. These different organisational units have different cultures, languages, objectives and perspectives. As a consequence, 'front line troops' are confronted with CSR policies and strategies from divergent sources of information and different internal channels with different priorities and levels of emphasis: At best, confused and overloaded team members will make their own choices, at worst, they will ignore CSR imperatives altogether. To help overcome this challenge I have created the model shown as Figure 26.1 to address the issues outlined above in a practical, easy to apply manner.

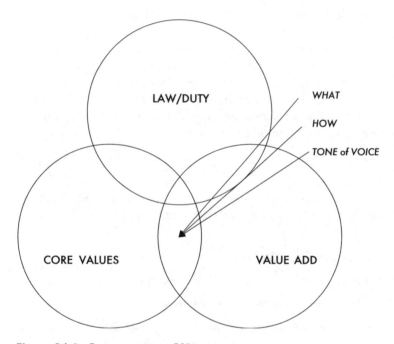

Figure 26.1. Communicating CSR

The model's aims are to:

- Structure CSR content information in a way which makes stakeholder (especially customer) contact more commercially successful, by identifying, organising and promoting CSR credentials;
- Tailor this information to specific stakeholder audiences;
- Facilitate joint planning, working and communication by establishing a common language and approach (model) for joint use by CSR specialists and non-CSR specialists, especially Sales and Marketing. And in so doing, improve the working relationships between CSR experts and front line operations;

- Help organisations identify value and equity for their stakeholders;
- The model takes as a core premise the fact that stakeholder groups require a different balance or focus of information. However, in my experience the information required falls in most cases into broadly three categories.

Here are more detailed definitions of these categories:

Law and duty

Law in this context refers to the laws of the countries the organisation operates in, including local by-laws. But it also refers to international agreements to which it is a signatory and the rules of professional organisations – procurement for example. These are things organisations do because it is the law, they reflect professional standards and / or they protect human rights at all levels. Compliance because organisations have to – it's the law – but also because it is the right thing to do. Stakeholders need to trust organisations to do what is right. A brand without trust is living on borrowed time.

Value add

These are things organisations do in the context of CSR because they increase revenue and / or drive down costs for themselves and customers and/or make life better for:

- Their clients (business and consumer);
- Their people (employees, contractors, associates etc);
- The societies they impact directly and indirectly.

When applying this model it is very important to remember that value add in this context may be measured in non-monetary, societal and environmental terms. However measured the critical aspect of value add is that what ever is being described will actually be delivered. Stakeholders need to know that organisations will deliver for them. CSR without delivery is just words. An organisation's brand is its promise. And in my experience the thing which all stakeholders, worldwide will forgive least is an unfulfilled or broken promise.

Core corporate values

These are the things organisations do because they passionately believe that they are the right things to do. This means having heart and standing up for what the organisation believes in. In many cases these may not have a quantifiable measure. Or the measure might be inapplicable. For example, consider racism. It is quite possible to make a strong business case to show that diversity adds to the bottom line. But an organisation that has 'zero tolerance' for racism is likely to value diversity irrespective of its final contribution to the bottom line. It follows that communications based on core corporate values only works when there is a clear statement of 'The way we work' or something similar in the organisation. Otherwise, everyone engaged in communicating is free to create their own interpretation of what they believe the organisation stands for and will/will not tolerate.

26.3 Using this model: Guidance based on experience

In the space available in this chapter it is very difficult to give detailed sector, geographic or other stakeholder specific guidance. But there are core principles which in my experience are applicable across most situations. At its simplest building and creating content for this model follows the following steps:

Information content owners (the CSR specialists) decide what they have that is appropriate in each of the circles. Choices have to be made in terms of priorities, verification, security etc. Simply providing every bit of unedited information will not help.

Users and providers decide on the preferred methods of sharing, maintaining, building, editing etc. the model. Prescriptive guidance here is impossible as every organisation will have its preferred method of internal communications. But in a large organisation this will probably be by intranet or something similar. Obviously this ongoing activity will not apply for a one off use of the model.

Users make choices with regard to the needs of their particular audiences. Audiences vary with regard to what type of information they require (facts or case studies for example), how they prefer to receive information (on line or paper or face-to-face) and the preferred tone of voice they like to hear (authoritative, guide or equal partner for example).

When applying these three steps in all the organisations I have worked with one important principle stands out. The needs of the front line user (usually in Sales and Marketing) should dominate. Something designed by a central administrative function in isolation is likely to remain unused. When using this model to balance and focus communication three questions regarding the needs and preferences of the target audience are important: dominance, sequence and dynamics.

Dominance

Consider an audience where one topic area is so all important that attention to it dominates.

So ,for example, 'Value Add' might dominate for a particular audience. An example might be SMEs. Virtually all SMEs will be pre occupied with the issues of how can what the organisation offers lower their costs, drive up revenue and/or make their lives easier. This is where communication with this audience will normally focus. For this audience over focusing on 'law' is inappropriate. They expect and trust CSR motivated organisations to lead in this area. Focusing on 'core values' may well come across as preaching. With all audiences it is important to remember that nothing is set in concrete. Irrespective of the audience if a scandal in the Enron mode were to occur then the areas of 'law' and 'core values' will temporarily dominate even with audiences for whom 'value add' is normally dominant.

Sequence

Consider an audience for whom core, corporate values are all important. An example might be a business customer such as the Body Shop or Co-op Bank. In this case the sequence of communication is important. Leading straight away with financial examples of 'value add' will probably be less appropriate than establishing common ground with regard to 'core values', backing this up with proof positive examples of compliance and leadership with regard to the 'law' and professional standards before moving onto the area of 'value add'. Clearly the appropriate sequence varies with the audience. To take another example, when dealing with financial analysts the areas of 'value add' and 'law' have to be addressed simultaneously ('we add value with appropriate corporate governance' being the message). Then it may be appropriate to discuss 'core values'.

Dynamics

Consider an audience with changing priorities. An example might be financially well-off consumers. All things being equal they will be interested in 'core values' (brand) messages about how well an organisation is doing with regard to building a better society and environment and 'value add' messages re how the organisation is making their lives easier. But when stories of corporate malpractice or other scandals hit the headlines their priorities switch to the 'Law' and compliance.

Summary

The core message is that every audience is different and their needs change with time and circumstances. The above examples are just 3 illustrations of dominance, sequence and dynamics. Users of this model need to think about these three things in order to customise the most appropriate information for their audience, to stimulate thinking and aid planning. Dynamics needs especial attention. The impact of global communications technology is such that the focus and balance of audiences' communications needs can change on a daily basis. The model is an aid to thinking. Intelligent interpretation and a flexible approach by users are essential.

26.4 Dos and don'ts

The model deliberately uses simply, international English. This is not just to facilitate cross cultural working in the sense of across geographies. It is also aimed at demystifying the languages used by CSR specialists so that they can communicate with others e.g. Sales and Marketing who often find the current terminology of CSR as at best difficult and at worst a huge turn off. So avoid CSR jargon. 'Triple Bottom Line reporting', for example, is not a phrase much used by Sales and Marketing.

I have found that those whose job it is to communicate find examples and illustrations especially useful with regard to using the model in the context of specific audiences. So using target audience specific examples helps. These of course are particularly helpful when developed on an organisation by organisation level. With regard to content, users of the model especially in Sales and Marketing have very clear preferences. Across all sectors and geographies, in particular they value facts and figures, case studies and links/further help.

Collaborative use of this model by CSR specialists and sales and marketing enables the creation of powerful materials for collateral, press interviews, online content, bid documents – all kinds of media. Building these CSR essentials into the day-to-day currency means organisations stay ahead – proactively – and it will ultimately determine whether they still have their stakeholders' permission to stay in business. When such collaborative work produces such useful outcomes, do ensure that this is noted, internally communicated and celebrated within the organisation. This helps build greater understanding of the contribution of CSR to the organisation's success.

Facilitating and encouraging usage of the model fundamentally depends on four things; simplicity, consistency, access and flexibility. Users want simple language free from jargon and they plead for consistency. Users get extremely frustrated when a model is introduced and then frequently altered or not used.

When these basics are satisfied, users then ask for ease of access. If, for example, they are used to using one intranet site, that is where they want to find the model. They are much less likely to go to a separate CSR specialist site.

Finally, when using this model flexibility is key. Customers don't come and their needs don't come in neat circles. The needs of stakeholder are blurring in a world where the roles, and needs, of governments, NGOs and markets are converging. Therefore common sense is needed when using the model. For most people, the analysis of the CSR activities is not a science. An organisation's judgments can be called into question by anyone with access to communications infrastructure. And as any marketer will tell you, they will base their opinion on emotional and common sense reactions more than on logical analysis. This model is an aid to structuring and communicating information, not a means for imposing artificial constructs on the needs of stakeholders.

26.5 Wrapping up

Progress re more effective communication and marketing of CSR is needed urgently. The World Wide Web, satellite channels, SMS and the rest of today's technological paraphernalia mean that transparency in business happens at the speed of light. Geography is history. In the future of brand, neutral is not an option. Put these things together and communicating CSR is inseparable from any organisations business proposition.

Using the model described in this chapter creates a virtuous circle where better communication leads to greater trust between CSR specialists and front line employees which leads to better communications which creates opportunities for adding value.

There are other uses of the model yet to be explored. I have, for example, had interesting conversations with government experts re its use for predictive strategic modelling. Another topic for exploration is the cross cultural differences with regard to Law, Values and Value Add. There has been some excellent work recently on cross cultural differences in marketing (Trompenaars and Wooliams, 2004). There is much less to date by way of research specifically in the field of cultural differences in marketing driven by CSR. Some more formal research to supplement practical experience would help.

All stakeholder relationships are CSR dependant and better relationships – inside and out – mean better business. Getting and, more importantly, sustaining better results is about building and nurturing better relationships with all stakeholders. The needs and demands of regulators, customers, pressure groups, shareholders etc. are converging. And stakeholders are becoming increasingly informed and demanding with regard to their communications needs. In this environment the only sustainable marketing is visible, well communicated ethical marketing. Communicating CSR is not an option for any organisation. Better communications means better relationships, means better business and government. And ultimately that means a better world.

For me this is the link between CSR and marketing. Good brands outlive products, offers, fads and fashions. The best marketers know that their brands cannot survive without attention to CSR. My hope is that those whose concern is CSR, sustainability or related areas pay more attention to the power of brand and communications. And in this process I hope this model will help.

References

Trompenaars, F. and P. Woolliams (2004). *Marketing Across Cultures (Culture for Business)*. Chichester, England: Capstone Publishing.

Website

www.sustainablemarketing.co.uk

27 The Four Dimensions of Responsible Purchasing

Osbert Lancaster and Kyla Brand

Key words: Fit for purpose, aspirational, collaborative design, sustainable, scope.

27.1 Introduction

The Centre for Human Ecology model describes a process for implementing environmentally and socially responsible procurement within an organisation. It is based on working with the champions within the organisation to:

- Agree, and communicate, clear definitions of the scope, breadth and depth of responsible purchasing that are relevant to the organisation;

- Agree where, in relation to responsible purchasing, the organisation is now; and where they would like to see the organisation in the future;

- Identify and understand the influence of the main players within the organisation;

- Identify and understand key external influences on the organisation with respect to responsible purchasing;

- Develop an initial objective for implementing responsible purchasing in terms of scope, breadth and depth;

- Develop and implement an action plan towards the initial objective;

- Prepare to review and agree development objectives and action plans.

Central features of the model are the three dimensions of responsible purchasing:

- Scope: the range of issues that will be addressed by the organisation's responsible purchasing policies and procedures;

- Breadth: the extent to which each of this issues will be addressed, along a spectrum from legislative compliance to the expectations of society that are still emerging and perhaps contested;

- Depth: the distance down the supply chain that the issues will be pursued.

In defining scope, breadth and depth a number of factors are relevant including, but not restricted to: Justifiability: how can the decision to adopt an approach to social responsibility in purchasing be justified? Importance: to what extent are the issues recognised by key opinion formers in the organisation, as being important? Relevance: to what extent are the issues relevant to the goods and services purchased by the organisation? Risk: what is the risk of not addressing particular issues? Practicality: do practical means to address the issue exist, or can they be developed? To what extent can existing procedures be used or adapted to address these objectives? Legality: can the objectives adopted be pursued without breaching WTO, EU and UK procurement regulations? Verifiability: to what extent is it possible to demonstrate any policies adopted are being followed and objectives being achieved?

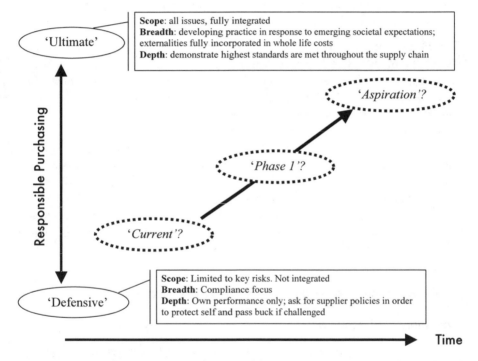

Figure 27.1. The Four Dimensions of Responsible Purchasing: Scope, Breadth, Depth and Time

The figure highlights the key features of the model, and introduces the fourth dimension – time.

Firstly, Responsible Purchasing is presented as a spectrum from 'Defensive' to 'Ultimate' responsible purchasing. It is important to note that 'defensive' responsible purchasing is not laissez-faire purchasing – there are clear policies and procedures in place, but the scope, breadth and depth are very narrowly defined, essentially the organisation is taking the minimum amount of responsibility consistent with legality. 'Ultimate' responsible purchasing represents the full potential for the organisation to completely integrate responsible principles into all its procedures and practice with the greatest possible scope, breadth and depth.

Secondly, the organisation places their current and future desired performance – defined in terms of scope, breadth and depth – on the spectrum by:

- Agreeing their responsible purchasing aspiration – where they would like to see the organisation in the future;
- Clarifying their current position in relation to responsible purchasing;
- Establishing an achievable objective for phase 1 of a programme of work towards the aspiration.

This model was developed by the Centre for Human Ecology in work for with the Procurement Office of the Scottish Parliament. The Scottish Parliament is a devolved, single chamber legislature within the United Kingdom, established by the Scotland Act 1998, with 129 elected members, over 400 staff and a multi-million pound annual procurement budget.

The Procurement Team already had high quality procedures for procurement with specific policies taking account of equalities and environmental issues. There was keen interest in the project among the procurement professionals leading to the following shared objectives: to create an overarching approach to guide treatment of other ethical and social considerations such as fair trade, employment practices and local supply, to promote compliance with current and possible future regulation, and to improve results though more complete risk management in supplier relationships.

27.2   Key stages in implementing the model

Workshops and interviews

Group discussions and one-to-one interviews were held with a broad cross section of procurement staff and contract managers (internal clients of the procurement staff). The intention was to ensure that all concerned had a genuine sense of ownership of the developments and did not have cause to react negatively or defensively to the eventual new conditions or procedures. It was also a mechanism for transferring knowledge and building the internal capacity of the team for tackling social responsibility issues with confidence, and it enabled the professionals to explore the concepts of social responsibility and to relate them to their individual areas of expertise. Genuine differences of opinion and of emphasis were expressed which clarified the challenge of defining common aspirations for responsible purchasing.

Consideration of good practice

Little directly comparable practice existed in similar institutions at the time of the project, but there was a strong element of learning from other initiatives where possible. A balance had to be struck between creating approaches that were fit for purpose in the Scottish Parliament, and demonstrating recognisable links with other practice, which were significant in building confidence. Most relevant practice was in the private sector and/or had a strongly environmental bias so innovation was necessary. Where recognised standards such as EMAS, ISO, SA8000 could be referenced, there was much higher confidence to include issues within the scope of the procedures. Where it would be necessary to create relevant standards of performance, there was justifiable hesitation to be pioneers.

Limits to opportunity

The team initially perceived tight constraints on what might legally be achieved in relation to responsible purchasing. The EU Directives were frequently quoted as limiting. The commitment to strict legal compliance inhibited exploration of the envelope of opportunity. In this context, the evidence of other successful developing practice, although limited, was very important. The subsequent development of public policy towards sustainable purchasing and growing practice in other public institutions appears to support growing confidence to address areas of opportunity.

Analysis of the dimensions of social responsibility

The analysis of scope, breadth and depth as defined above proved to be a valuable framework to describe the full potential framework of issues – as in the familiar grouping of typical social responsibility issues within marketplace, workplace, community and environment and governance.

Discussion also highlighted the seat of 'responsibility', which is an attribute of organisations or persons: a product or service itself cannot be 'responsible' – 'responsibility' relates to how the product or service is produced and used. So the analysis proceeded with consideration of the responsibility both of the purchaser (their ethics, fairness and consistency) and of the supplier (their practical observation of standards for example on working conditions, equalities, environmental impact). In the case of the Scottish Parliament this led to recognising three distinct sets of issues within the scope of responsible purchasing: professionalism and ethics, environment and sustainability, equalities and social justice.

The dimensions of socially responsible purchasing were agreed, firstly for the Scottish Parliament's aspirations (i.e. eventual goal) and secondly for Phase 1 of the work programme towards those aspirations (see Table 27.1).

Table 27.1. The Scottish Parliament's dimensions of responsible purchasing

	Phase 1	Aspiration
Scope	Widely defined to include all issues which have an impact on people and the environment in the present and the future. Integrated in principle, but not yet in practice.	Widely defined and integrated to include all issues which have an impact on people and the environment in the present and the future.
Breadth	In all priority areas: achieving, or clearly working towards, good practice, reflecting government policy, anticipating emerging legislation, and contributing to the achievement of international commitments.	In all areas: achieving good practice, reflecting government policy, anticipating emerging legislation, and contributing to the achievement of international commitments. In selected areas: At the cutting edge of developing emerging practice in response to social expectations.
Depth	Addressing own performance. First tier suppliers: active engagement to take account of, and seek to improve, performance of most first tier suppliers. Second tier and beyond: Processes in place to identify, and respond to, high risk issues right down the supply chain.	Addressing own performance. First tier suppliers: actively taking account of, and seeking to improve, the performance of all first tier suppliers. Second tier and beyond: Encouraging first tier suppliers to take account of, and improve, performance down the supply chain. Actively taking account of identified high risk issues right down the supply chain.

Definition and acceptance of responsible purchasing policy

From the exploration of the concepts, and matching these with the practical experience of current contracts, the procurement team identified the priority issues for attention. They also attributed value to social responsibility or responsible purchasing as an overarching concept, recognising that a patchwork approach to issues such as equalities, environment, and fair trade made it much more likely that important issues would slip between the cracks. The eventual definition was captured in a statement of principles (see Table 27.2), reflecting both the underlying values of the organisation and a commonly recognised articulation of sustainable development.

This statement of principles has in turn been used as the basis for integrating responsible purchasing considerations into procurement policies and procedures; in accordance with a risk management approach, all contracts will in due course be reviewed and re-let under the new policies and procedures.

Table 27.2. The Scottish Parliament's statement of principles on responsible purchasing

'The Scottish Parliament is committed to purchasing responsibly in ways which build on the Parliament's strategic priorities and contribute to sustainable development. Purchasing responsibly means:

- Effectively meeting the needs of the Scottish Parliament for goods, services and minor works;

- Taking account of the impact of today's decisions on people and the environment both now and in the future;

- Acting ethically at all times in our dealings with colleagues, customers, actual and potential suppliers;

- Having the necessary skills and knowledge to evaluate and respond to conflicting demands;

- Complying with regulations and taking reasonable steps to ensure that others act in compliance'.

Communicating to suppliers

Throughout the development of this approach to responsible purchasing, attention was given to the interests of, and impact on, suppliers. It was recognised that commitment by the Scottish Parliament needed to translate into opportunities rather than burdens for suppliers. While information had to be sought, and validated, this needed to be proportionate and relevant. And it was important that the burden was not discriminatory, for example against smaller suppliers. The approach to suppliers was very transparent, distributing a leaflet on the Scottish Parliament's approach to responsible purchasing, and including discussion of the issues in 'meet the buyer' events. The emphasis was on joint development and a collaborative approach towards best practice.

Incorporation in procedures

Work in hand to embed the responsible purchasing approach across procurement includes insertion of detailed conditions in procedures. Active internal communication continues to include internal clients and contract managers as well as the immediate procurement team. In particular, it is recognised that the impact of responsible purchasing is not limited to the stages of prequalification or contract specification – the principles must have effect throughout the management of the contract; furthermore, any lessons from specific contracts must be taken account of for the continual improvement of procedures.

Communication

It was recognised that management of expectations was a critical factor in success. Strategic management of external communication was particularly important in such a high profile and accountable organisation. The model of responsible purchasing was therefore implemented in a low key manner, but with strong internal communication.

27.3   Lessons from experience with this model

Engage staff at all levels and include contract owners. The purpose of the model is to facilitate the development of approaches and procedures that are appropriate and sustainable for an individual organisation. It is not a strait jacket into which different organisations must fit. It is therefore critical from the outset to stimulate thinking about the issues of social responsibility and to work for collective ownership of the conclusions. Staff interviews and workshops, including strategic professionals, implementing officers and contract owners, provide for effective engagement.

Recognise the importance of major players in the organisation and their potential to advance or hold back the process. Any organisation is political. Many have distinctive reputation pressures. Linking the definition and scope of responsible purchasing issues to the priorities of the core business is important to ensure that other leaders in the organisation support the process. Working with an elected body, a range of pressures were explicit including cost effectiveness, social justice, local and smaller business engagement.

Recognise both the starting position and the higher aspirations, to allow for managed progression. The framework approach enables an organisation to set the direction of their journey and determine how far and how fast they wish, or can afford, to travel towards their 'aspirational' responsible purchasing. Setting grand ambitions that may be beyond the needs of a particular organisation at a particular point in time is unlikely to command continuing support.

Maintain momentum, while being sensitive to external pressures. Realistic assessment of the resources required to implement new approaches to purchasing is critical. There will always be other pressures (particularly issues of cost and staff time) which threaten new initiatives that may be considered 'nice to have' rather than essential. Reaching for goals attainable in the short to medium term is prudent so that resource allocation can be assured. Even where, as in the case of the project under discussion, it was necessary to put development on hold for several months and then to absorb new lead players, the agreed development path and the embedded project partnership provided the necessary grounding to regain the pace of development.

27.4 Concluding thoughts

The authors believe significant change by individuals and organisations is essential and urgent to promote ecological sustainability and social justice, and public procurement is potentially a vital force for such change. However, for the widespread growth of good practice a more positive framework of policy and incentive is required – locally, nationally and internationally. Despite constraints, where there is enthusiasm and interest among professionals, much can be achieved, and the CHE Model provides a safe and supportive environment to bring together personal values with professional practice on a journey towards potentially fundamental change in procurement practice.

At the time of writing, the Scottish Parliament Procurement Office is making good progress towards its Phase 1 objectives: having reviewed selected contracts, staff are now finalising new policies, procedures and key performance indicators to embed responsible purchasing firmly within every stage of the procurement cycle, while also engaging with existing and potential suppliers to raise their awareness of the Parliament's commitment to responsible purchasing.

Lynn Garvie, Head of Procurement, explains 'the Centre for Human Ecology has been sensitive to the practical difficulties of addressing environmental and social issues in procurement. Throughout, their approach has been to build on the Parliament and the Procurement Office's existing commitments and to gain support from staff and other key players. We plan to continue making progress towards the aspirational objectives we have adopted.'

References

A practical manual by Forum for the Future and Higher Education Partnership for Sustainability, (www.forumforthefuture.org.uk/uploadstore/purchasing.pdf).

Chartered Institute of Purchasing and Supply (2005). *Ethical Business Practices in Purchasing and Supply*, (www.napm.org/ConfPastandOnlineDaily/Files/ May02/DI-LilesEthics.pdf).

Selling to BT. (www.bt.com/selling2bt).

International Council for Local Environmental Initiatives (2005). *Green Purchasing – A good Practice Guide*, (www.iclei.org/europe/ecoprocura/info/good_ prac.htm).

Impactt (2002): *East meets West: Managing the collision between trade and development*, (www.impacttlimited.com/site/5thanniversaryreport.pdf).

Websites

www.idea.gov.uk/procurement

www.sustainable-development.gov.uk

www.scottish.parliament.uk/procurement

28 The Hurdles Analysis: A Way to Greener Public Procurement

Lilly Scheibe and Edeltraud Günther

Key words: green public procurement, identification of hurdles, assessment of hurdles, strategy development.

> This is not a complicated method! It's a simple self-evaluation tool for the identification and analysis of hurdles to green procurement, which can help organisations to easily identify the strengths and weaknesses of their current green procurement practices and also support them in making improvements.

28.1 Introduction to the method

To enhance corporate social responsibility (CSR), the management of procurement processes can help to improve the environmental and social performance of the whole value chain because of the gatekeeper position of procurement. Procurement can be seen as the link to most of the other steps of the lifecycle of products and services, because the characteristics and the resulting environmental impacts of these are determined in this phase. Therefore greening procurement can be seen as the crucial step in developing efficient CSR strategies (Günther and Scheibe, 2005).

To support organisations in their efforts to change their procurement process, factors that may hamper, decelerate or even block green procurement – so-called hurdles – have to be identified, evaluated, and strategies developed to overcome them. Therefore the hurdles analysis method – a three step approach – was developed. This method enables organisations to identify, assess and overcome hurdles to green procurement and in this way manage procurement processes more proactively in the future.

Initial research: Analysing hurdles to green procurement

Considering the high potential of public procurement for fostering the production and supply of greener products and services – the public demand volume is about 12 % of total GNP – it is perhaps surprising that green procurement is not yet that common in the public sector. So the question arises, what reasons might exist for this fact? Studies (Hauschildt and Gemünden, 1999; French and Raven, 1959) indicate a number of disturbing factors – so-called hurdles – which can be responsible for hampering, slowing down or even completely blocking green procurement initiatives. It is, therefore, an important step for a public authority to identify such hurdles, both real and perceived, to make their procurement process greener.

To assist public authorities in identifying and handling their hurdles to green procurement, the hurdles analysis was developed by the Professorship of Business Administration, esp. Environmental Management of the Dresden University of Technology – Technische Universität Dresden (TUD) in co-operation with European municipalities within the EU research project RELIEF. Further improvement of the method resulted from another research project of the Professorship on green public procurement in Germany, and some case studies with administrative staff of a number of English municipalities. The result of this process was the hurdles analysis in its present form– a method to identify, assess and handle hurdles to green public procurement.

The hurdles analysis focuses on perceived hurdles, as these have the most influence on decision-makers by appearing to be most important to them. The method therefore lists a catalogue of potential hurdles throughout the decision-making process of public procurement and connects them with the key actors within this process. The different decision-makers of a public authority are questioned about their perceived hurdles with the help of a standardised questionnaire based on the catalogue of potential hurdles. Following this, the hurdles are assessed with the help of four simple assessment methods to identify the most relevant ones. To deal with these hurdles, strategies have to be developed within the public authority which can be accomplished with the help of workshops including all actors of the decision process.

From previous experiences with the hurdles analysis within the above-mentioned projects and case studies, it can be clearly stated that 'Hurdles are perceived differently in each public authority!' This is due to very different organisational structures and different numbers of actors within the process, as well as differences in the development status regarding green procurement. It was concluded that it currently seems impossible to identify 'the' hurdles valid for all public authorities alike. In fact hurdles can only be tackled by each public authority individually, together with accompanying counselling based on its framework conditions.

The results were examined for a way to overcome hurdles within public authorities themselves. As a result the online available self-evaluation tool was developed. This tool is based on the methodology of the hurdles analysis and offers public authorities the opportunity to identify, assess and handle hurdles on their own. The self-evaluation tool consists of three steps (Figure 28.1).

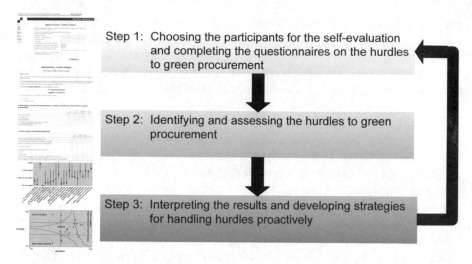

Step 1: Choosing the participants for the self-evaluation and completing the questionnaires on the hurdles to green procurement

Step 2: Identifying and assessing the hurdles to green procurement

Step 3: Interpreting the results and developing strategies for handling hurdles proactively

Figure 28.1. The self-evaluation tool

These steps, together with their benefits for and their technical realisation in the public authority, are presented in the following paragraphs.

28.2   The hurdles analysis self-evaluation tool – A tool for public authorities

Step 1: Choosing the participants for the self-evaluation and completing the questionnaires on hurdles to green procurement

Description of the step

In this first step the decision as to who shall take part in a hurdles analysis is to be made. Therefore all people who can influence the procurement process have to be identified (so-called key actors). To focus on key actors is important because they will be the ones who influence procurement decisions by determining and/or removing hurdles within the procurement process based on their perceptions. E.g. one perception could be, that there is almost no information on greener products and services available, or that such products and services are too expensive. With this perception a hurdle is created by the person, yet it might not be valid because in fact the products are no more expensive and/or information is available, but the person in question does not know where to look. Hence it is necessary for improving green procurement to firstly identify the key actors and their hurdles, and secondly to develop strategies to overcome them.

To identify such key actors within the hurdles analysis, the procurement process of an organisation has to be analysed thoroughly – which steps does it have, which departments (e.g. procurement, finance, environment, users) are involved, which persons work in these departments and who can influence procurement decisions by making their own decisions (e.g. by stating that the green product seems to be too expensive, etc.). In general the procurement process follows the steps of a decision process. But as the procurement process differs from organisation to organisation the results will be different depending on the structure and the environment of each organisation. Different steps will be identified as well as different key persons. But as a result this analysis provides the public authority with a clear picture of its procurement process. Consequently, a sensitivity for the process as a whole is achieved, because the steps of and the actors within the process are identified – possibly for the first time – and thus the interplay between the actors becomes clear. This leads to a clearer understanding of who the key persons in the organisation are with respect to the procurement process. This will help in adapting the organisational structure and increasing the identification of the employees with their organisation, by making it clear to them the important role they play within the procurement process.

After the identification process, the persons who shall be included in the survey can be chosen out of the identified key actors, so setting the system boundary. It is possible to define the system boundary very tightly and only to choose those people directly involved in the act of purchasing. But it is also possible to include all those who can influence the result of a procurement decision in the organisation (widest system boundary). This decision influences the outcome of the analysis, because it defines the assessment perspectives. By choosing a tight system boundary, only one perspective can be evaluated – the one of the purchasers. Within a wider system boundary more perspectives are assessable and comparable, and a deeper analysis is possible. But this decision depends on the objectives the public authority has for the analysis. The choice is optional within the tool.

After the setting of the boundary, all participants fill in the standardised questionnaire concerned with hurdles to green procurement, and the data of all answers is collected and stored in a database for the assessment.

Technical realisation

First of all, interested public authorities can register free of charge to get some general information on the hurdles analysis. Then the decision whether to take part or not has to be made.

After a positive decision, the next step is for the person responsible for carrying out the self-evaluation (the contact person) to register the public authority by giving the number of participants (depending on the chosen system boundary), the time span planned for the survey and a login.

After this registration the contact person will receive an email from the Dresden University of Technology – Technische Universität Dresden (TUD) giving instructions for completing the online questionnaire, including a login (user name). All participants can then use this login to answer the questionnaire online (even at the same time). The online questionnaire is therefore very practical and is an easy-to-use tool for participants. The only requirement is access to the internet.

The data of each questionnaire is stored in a database at TUD for the assessment.

Step 2: Identification and assessment of the hurdles to green procurement

Description of the step

When analysing a hurdle it is important not only to consider the relevance of it for a single person but also to look at the differences between the answers given by all participants. This is essential for upcoming strategy development and in-depth analyses.

For this reason, four simple assessment methods based on the averages, spreads and deviations of the results have been developed for analysing the perceived hurdles (Figure 28.2). These methods combine the answers of all participants and sketch the hurdles situation of the organisation's procurement process from a bird's eyes view (the view of all participants). The methods allow the authority to identify trends and sort hurdles according to their relevance for the participants. This will help the public authority to decide on which hurdle/s to concentrate their efforts.

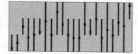 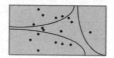 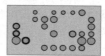

Figure 28.2. Assessment methods of the hurdles analysis

Technical realisation

In the data processing step, all the answers of one public authority are subsumed and prepared for the assessment. The data is then analysed with help of an Excel tool that produces charts of the four simple assessment methods for the local authority.

The initial set of charts shows the hurdles situation of the whole inquiry (combination of the answers of all participants). However, separate assessments of different groups of actors (procurer, finance, etc.) as well as the generation of charts for these groups are possible, so that an analysis of differences between their views can be made. Initially, these charts are in an Excel format, but they are also available in PDF format.

Step 3: Interpretation of the results and development of strategies for handling hurdles proactively

Description of the step

To interpret the results of the survey and, based on this, to develop strategies for handling identified hurdles to green procurement, workshops are recommended. They shall bring together all key persons of the procurement process within the public authority. At these workshops the results of the survey, and possible reasons for the identified hurdles will be discussed (e.g. why do different views exist on one hurdle, such as, green products are too expensive) and strategies developed for tackling them in future. This process will contribute to possible organisational improvement and strategic actions in handling hurdles. The aim of this internal discussion process is to work out a list with all relevant hurdles in order of their priority and then to compile and implement measures to overcome the identified hurdles. After some time, the success of the process can be monitored by rerunning the self-evaluation with the same participants and comparing the results.

Technical realisation

This step is accomplished by each organisation itself. The charts with the results of the assessment methods, together with a short guide showing how to interpret them, is given by TUD. The local authority organises and conducts everything else itself.

28.3 Practical applications of the method and their outcome

In the first projects initiating the development of the self-evaluation tool, hurdles analyses were accomplished by several European municipalities. In the first step the key actors were chosen by each municipality and they completed the questionnaire. Based on their answers the hurdles situation of each municipality was assessed with the help of the above-mentioned assessment methods, and interviews with some of the key persons were conducted to check on the results and deepen the analyses. Subsequently, the interpretation of the results took place within each municipality, and perceptions as well as strategies could be gained from this. The results of these practical applications of the method were summed up in the status reports of the participating cities which can be found and downloaded on the indicated RELIEF website. Further explanation and interpretation on these analyses are included in the publication of Günther and Scheibe (2004). But the most important perception gained from these applications and consequently the initial thought for the development of the self-evaluation tool was the one, that the hurdles situations vary widely from municipality to municipality and hence an individual analysis for each organisation is necessary.

28.4 Dos and don'ts

- Do analyse your procurement process thoroughly to determine all important steps and more importantly all key persons within it – key persons are persons who can influence the procurement decision with their own decisions;
- Do choose the participants in the inquiry carefully to get a representative result depending on the aim of your analysis;
- Be sure to provide all participants with an access to the internet, the URL-address of the questionnaire and the login for the survey!
- Do not include less than five participants in the inquiry. This is essential for a meaningful assessment of hurdles;
- Do not think the workshop to be less important than the assessment. It is the most important part of the analysis as the in-depth interpretation of the results takes place and strategies are developed in this step;
- Make sure that the key actors included in the workshop are aware of the importance of this step by sending them the results and a short interpretation in time, and by discussing the results in an appropriate way;
- For in-depth analysis, have the assessment of different groups (e.g. finance, procurement, etc.) handy to include them in the discussion and with that identify starting points for strategies (e.g. when different views exist it is interesting to discuss why persons/groups do not see a hurdle when others do).

28.5 Conclusion

With this simple self-evaluation tool and its assessment methods public authorities will be enabled to identify and tackle their hurdles to green procurement themselves, as well as measure and control their success by rerunning the procedure. Consequently, the method can contribute to fostering CRS the following way:

- Firstly, it makes public authorities aware of their potentials in the area of green public procurement;

- Secondly, it raises the performance of public authorities in green procuring to help them reach and accept a higher level of responsibility.

References

Günther, E. and L. Scheibe (2004). *The Hurdles Analysis – A method to identify and analyse hurdles for green procurement in municipalities*, Dresdner Beiträge zur Betriebswirtschaftslehre 80/04, Dresden.

Günther, E. and L. Scheibe (2005). *The Hurdles Analysis. A self-evaluation tool for municipalities to identify, analyse and overcome hurdles to green procurement*. CSRE Corporate Social Responsibility and the Environment. (forthcoming)

Hauschildt, J. and H.G. Gemünden (1999). *Promotoren. Champions der Innovation* [Promotors. Champions for Innovation], Wiesbaden.

French, J. R. P. jr. and B. Raven (1959). The Bases of Social Power. In: Cartwright, D. (1959). *Studies in Social Power*, Michigan.

Websites

www.tu-dresden.de/wwbwlbu/forschung/laufende_projekte/hemmnisse/en
www.wwil.wiwi.tu-dresden.de/hurdles
www.iclei.org/europe/ecoprocura/relief

29 Strategic CSR Communication: Telling Others How Good You Are

Mette Morsing

Key words: CSR communication, strategy, stakeholder information, stakeholder interaction.

29.1 Introduction to the model

A model is presented to help managers communicate their companies as ethical and socially responsible organisations to a variety of stakeholders. While managers acknowledge the necessity to communicate their corporate social initiatives to ensure positive stakeholder identification with the company and thus maintain their corporate 'license to operate', they also acknowledge that trust and responsibility are extremely difficult messages to convey. Companies' own claims about how socially responsible they are do not necessarily generate admiration or trust among stakeholders.

I present a model for strategic CSR communication that suggests that managers in addition to 'informing stakeholders' about the corporate CSR initiatives need to improve the corporate skills to continuously 'interact with stakeholders'. It is suggested that companies need to integrate both information and interaction communication strategies in the corporate repertoire for developing trustworthy CSR communication in the eyes of corporate stakeholders. Strategic CSR communication needs to enter the board room of top executives.

Stakeholder expectations

Since Freeman's legendary work on stakeholder management appeared in 1984, it has become a general assumption among managers and scholars that companies increasingly depend on their stakeholders' expectations, and that companies need to develop a sensitivity towards these stakeholder expectations. At the same we acknowledge that stakeholder expectations are a 'moving target', i.e. stakeholders concurrently change their perception of what it means to be a responsible company in modern society. For companies to follow, understand and even influence how stakeholders construct and reconstruct their expectations to the company, managers need to understand how to build and maintain an organisational sensitivity that reaches beyond the corporate boundaries.

Organisational sensitivity does not evolve by itself. Many companies have started to communicate about their CSR initiatives, and often the CSR communication is a one-way process of informing stakeholders about corporate intentions and activities. While this may improve the overall corporate transparency, it may not satisfy stakeholders' concerns and expectations. Many companies have not yet taken advantage of integrating their stakeholders in a two-way approach as part of the communication process itself. This paper argues that all companies can benefit from developing skills and routines for ongoing dialogue with stakeholders, i.e. to build and maintain an organisational sensitivity towards stakeholders' concurrent expectations – and perhaps even beyond them.

29.2 A model for strategic CSR communication

The strategic CSR communication model consists of two strategies: an informing strategy and an interacting strategy and a process: moving from one strategy to the other. 'The informing strategy' suggests on what issues to inform stakeholders concerning corporate CSR initiatives, i.e. those actions taken to display conformity to stakeholder expectations in a one-way communication process. 'The interaction strategy' suggests what two-way communicative processes the company can stage and encourage to enhance stakeholder dialogue and hereby increase understanding of stakeholder expectations. Finally, to promote the process of moving from one strategy to the other, it is suggested to structurally strengthen and tie the corporate communication to strategic management.

The model conceptualises how a company's informing and interacting strategies altogether make stakeholders themselves (employees, opinion leaders and consumers[1]) inclined to positively identify with the company as well as provides the company with sensitivity towards stakeholder expectations. The model provides a coherent and integrated conceptualisation as it demonstrates how the two communication processes depend on, interact with and extend each other in the attempt to make stakeholders positively connote to the corporate CSR efforts. Finally, the model suggests that top managerial attention and support is needed in the process of moving from informing to interacting with stakeholders.

---

[1] This paper focus on three general stakeholder groups: employees, opinion leaders and consumers, because these stakeholder groups represent important audiences for any company as they present themselves as ethical and socially responsible organisations.

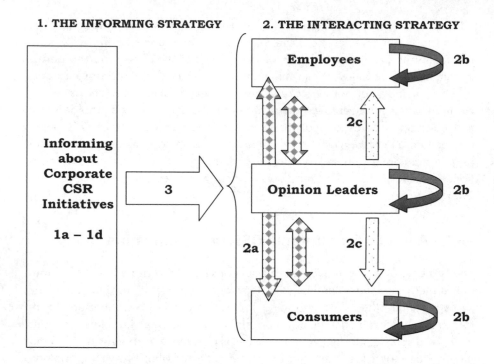

1. THE INFORMING STRATEGY   2. THE INTERACTING STRATEGY

3. THE PROCESS FROM INFORMING TO INTERACTING

Figure 29.1. The strategic CSR communication model

The informing strategy (1)

The informing strategy builds on the assumption that companies can strengthen their visibility and build trustworthy communication by integrating its internal and external communication into one coherent message that is in accordance with the corporate strategy and is able to appeal to a variety of audiences at the same time. The core concept of the message does not automatically emerge, but is a result of careful internal and external analysis. To ensure co-herent and appealing information about corporate CSR efforts, the following four issues should be integrated in the CSR information package:

- Show CSR as a shared concern (promise);
- Link CSR to the core business (proposition);
- Demonstrate organisational support (evidence);
- Demonstrate objective claims (results).

Show CSR as a shared concern (1a)

Corporate CSR messages can emphasise the company's affiliation to its stake-holders as it expresses a shared concern for or a commitment to a specific issue related to CSR and establish CSR as a potential bond between the company and its stakeholders. Keeping in mind that stakeholders' interests are diverse and changing, the shared concern must evoke a certain general interest. For a pharmaceutical company like Novo Nordisk, one of the world's leading pro-ducers of insulin, the overall shared concern is improvement of people's health, which is presumably a shared concern for most people around the world. Novo Nordisk promises as part of its commitment to help not only diabetes patients, but also to work towards preventing diabetes to develop into an epidemic[2]. But also other CSR issues are central in Novo Nordisk's CSR messages. For exam-ple, environmental issues related to saving water which is a concern in the company's local environment, gender issues such as the promotion of women to managerial positions which is considered a general societal concern well as a concern for female employees, decent care for animals in test laboratories which is a particular concern for those NGOs representing animals' welfare, and integration of ethnic minorities into the labour market which is a concern for not only those minorities but also for community leaders such as politicians.

Link CSR to core business (1b)

Companies need to propose a solid set of arguments, principles and processes, which show the integration of the corporate CSR initiatives to the core business and that CSR matters for corporate survival as well as for its stakeholders' benefit. Quite often companies launch primarily visionary and airy statements about saving the world or mention their efforts within benevolent initiatives such as environmental protection policies, employee-friendly practices or humanitar-ian sponsorships. Such communication will appeal across stakeholders: con-sumers, employees and opinion leaders as well as shareholders. However, when CSR initiatives appear to be emotionally or purely morally driven, the company runs the risk of being associated with religious or philanthropic organisations. This may not necessarily generate trust across stakeholders such as sharehold-ers. In fact, it may have the opposite effect.

The central message throughout Novo Nordisk's financial and sustainability reports is the proposition of a rational link between corporate CSR initiatives and core business. In the sustainability report 2003, the link is indicated and depicted as a link between sustainability-driven initiatives, business benefits,

---

[2] 'Our aspiration is to defeat diabetes by finding better methods of diabetes prevention, detection and treatment. We will work actively to promote collaboration between all parties in the healthcare system in order to achieve our common goals' (Novo Nordisk Sustainability Report, 2003:3).

potential financial impact and potential benefits to society. For example potential business benefits of CSR initiatives are stated as for example 'raised awareness, customer satisfaction and loyalty, employee satisfaction and motivation, new knowledge, strategic management capacity, stakeholder trust and sharing better practices' (Novo Nordisk Sustainability Report, 2003:13).

Show organisational support (1c)

CSR messages should also demonstrate organisational support behind the CSR claims. Visible managerial support is a key determinant for CSR messages to signal corporate dedication and commitment, and to make clear that the CSR initiatives are not solely a concern of the marketing or communication department but a top managerial concern. To demarcate organisational support, the message may also include employees.

Novo Nordisk's CEO and the Board of Directors are highly visible in stating and symbolising the company's CSR initiatives in all corporate communication, but also employees are part of the CSR message. Many employees appear in photos, interviews and statements or articles in Novo Nordisk's communication material. In sustainability reports, brochures and advertisements employees comment for example on the implementation of the company's CSR policies. Novo Nordisk's employees' statements and photos in corporate communication serve as evidence for the organisational support, as they show a loyalty and dedication which serves to appeal to employees, potential recruits, consumers, and opinion leaders.

Demonstrate objective claims (1d)

Analyses show that stakeholders are less likely to trust information from company-controlled sources such as advertising and corporate subjective claims, which use surrogate indicators for indicating a company's benefits or attitudes. However, these analyses also show that stakeholders are less sceptical towards corporate objective claims, i.e. technical specifications, numerical cues, and visual presentations.

Novo Nordisk has for many years provided substantial factual information in its annual sustainability reports, and while the reports embrace abstract intentions and visionary statements, they also convey objective claims in terms of statistics, facts and figures often in a sophisticated, insightful and at times almost scientific manner to support the visionary and subjective claims. Novo Nordisk addresses those issues recommended by internationally recognised guides such United Nation's Global Compact, or the Global Reporting Initiative, and the company informs the reader that it complies to these guidelines. Perhaps even more importantly the company has identified six strategic areas (values in practice, access to health, our employees, our use of animals, eco-efficiency, contribution to society) and each strategic area has its own key performance indicators, that show how much the company has improved from previous years – or the opposite, and new targets are set for the year to come (Novo Nordisk Sustainability Report, 2003:16-17).

The interacting strategy (2)

Research has shown that stakeholders' reactions to a company depend on the extent to which they know and trust the company, and 'the interaction strategy' suggests that the company needs to engage in a two-way communication process with key stakeholders to develop organisational sensitivity and to build trust among stakeholders. While the informing strategy provides the basic CSR information (promises, propositions and evidence), the interaction strategy implies a further pro-active engagement between company and stakeholders. Culture studies have shown how close relationships arise when stakeholders, including employees and consumers, engage in company-related rites, rituals, and routines and result in strong intricate and trusting relationships. For instance when consumers and opinion makers interact with the company in a significant and meaningful way, they may come to feel more like insiders than outsiders. In the following we suggest three two-way communication processes to develop increased interaction between the company and its stakeholders: social partnerships, local articulation and pro-active endorsement.

Social partnerships (2a)

Not only Novo Nordisk but also other companies like Royal Dutch Shell Group and Volvo have started to systematically engage in social partnerships with societal opinion leaders. A social partnership occurs when a company takes initiative to invite opinion leaders from for example NGOs, international organisations, universities, and political parties to dialogue on the corporate CSR initiatives. Novo Nordisk report that the company's reasons for doing so are to understand stakeholders' interests and expectations, to relate to different agendas, to identify and prioritise themes, and to manage business risks and benefit from possibilities. The company attempts to not only meet but also exceed stakeholder norms dictating desirable organisational behaviours. The company labels its strategy 'From Dialogue to Partnerships', and by doing so the company builds trust and understanding of important stakeholder concerns as well as to create a better basis for decision-making and hence solutions.

Local articulation (2b)

Local articulation is defined as a two-way communication process in which the company invites stakeholders to express their identity in close relation to corporate identity. Prior research has shown how managers and employees may serve as public relations representatives, as they are invited to talk to external audiences about for example the company's historical development, its vision, mission and principles. As managers and employees articulate the corporate statements in their own words, they are of course not free to tell the story as they like, but they could give the story a particular private turn. Most importantly they could relate their own identity to the corporate identity as they liked. Studies show how managers and employees gradually internalise the corporate strategies as they hear themselves speak about it. In this sense local articulation provides managers with an updated insight into their workplace and more importantly a sense of ownership of the corporate strategy. At the same time, local articulation creates goodwill and understanding amongst the public.

Local articulation does not necessarily make the opinion leaders less critical to the company's CSR initiatives. However, allowing for local articulation in for example the corporate annual report is likely to evoke an acknowledgement of corporate initiatives from those external stakeholders, while demonstrating an acknowledgement of other's viewpoints and an openness for dialogue with critical stakeholders.

Pro-active endorsement (2c)

Endorsement happens as the company's CSR initiatives are observed, supported, praised and even challenged by external stakeholders. Pro-active endorsement occurs as the company pro-actively seeks the support of third party stakeholders to provide a favourable public mention. It is pro-active because the company pro-actively seeks and displays an endorsement from external stakeholders rather than awaiting their comments. It happens as companies for example hire auditing consultants to audit their sustainability reports, like Novo Nordisk has asked Deloitte to audit their latest reports. The auditors produce an independent assessment of corporate CSR initiatives and provide the social reports and the CSR initiatives with an authority and credibility, which the company by itself cannot. Pro-active endorsement is also enacted as companies hire public relations agencies or communication consultants to assist them in influencing the public debate in the company's favour on issues of CSR. Increasingly CSR-related prizes are awarded and favourable CSR positions are seen in reputation rankings or image analyses, which companies themselves more or less actively can contribute to stage.

29.3   The process from an informing to an interacting strategy

Top management is the central criteria for a successful move from informing stakeholders about social initiatives to actually interaction with stakeholders. As with so many other strategic issues, top managerial attention and support is key. Visible top managerial support is needed to allow for corporate CSR initiatives to be communicated coherently and consistently and to develop a strategy for what stakeholders to interact with and how.

While there is no recipe for the individual company on how to interact with stakeholders, the strategic CSR communication model suggests that invitation of critical reflection is a decisive element in moving towards more strategic stakeholder interaction. Companies can benefit from strategically inviting what sociologists call 'the professional stranger', i.e. inviting employees, opinion leaders and consumers to comment upon what they may see as potentially burning issues for the company. It is most often such opinion leaders that form the general perception of the company's CSR initiatives. For example the media is a central stakeholder in providing companies with an ongoing self-description, and rather than awaiting the critical journalist's critical moral judgment in the morning paper, companies can themselves prepare for replying quickly and consistently when 'the critical issue' appears in the media by having an ongoing dialogue with critical stakeholders – including journalists.

29.4 Dos and don'ts

Dos

- Design a strategic CSR communication model that informs stakeholders about CSR initiatives while at the same time invites interaction with stakeholders about the corporate CSR initiatives;
- Perceive internal and external stakeholders as senders as well as receivers of the corporate CSR messages;
- Develop an organisational culture that invites critical dialogue from external stakeholders;
- Extend the communication scope from a marketer perspective to a strategic communication perspective and embed it in the organisation as a top managerial issue.

Don'ts

- Do not conspicuously celebrate your CSR efforts;
- Do not expect stakeholders to be positively welcoming your CSR communication – even if they expect your CSR efforts;
- Do not underestimate the power of engaging internal and external stakeholders in local articulation;
- Do not think that there is no quick fix to handle the managerial challenge of displaying a company as a socially responsible organisation. CSR communication is a long-term process that requires a concurrent organisational awareness of internal and external stakeholders' changing expectations.

While communicating CSR initiatives seems an attractive path, it is also a path filled with complexities for managers and employees. This paper has raised some important issues for managers to consider as they rethink their corporate CSR communication.

References

Freeman, R.E. (1984). *Strategic Management. A Stakeholder Approach*. Marshfield: Pitman.

Maignan, I. and O.C. Ferrell (2004). Corporate Social Responsibility and Marketing: An Integrative Framework. *Journal of the Academy of Marketing Science*, 32(1): pp. 3-19.

Sen, S. and C.B. Bhattacharaya (2001). Does doing good always lead to doing better? Consumer reactions to corporate social responsibility. *Journal of Marketing Research*, vol. XXXVIII, May: pp. 225-243.

Scott, S.G. and V.R. Lane (2000). A Stakeholder Approach to Organisational Identity, *Academy of Management Review*, 25(1): pp. 43-62.

Tan, S.J. (2002). Can consumers' scepticism be mitigated by claim objectivity and claim extremity. *Journal of Marketing Communications*, (8): pp. 45-64.

Website

www.novonordisk.com

Novo Nordisk sustainability reports from 2002, 2003 can be found on this web-site.

30 CSR Online: Internet Based Communication

Ralf Isenmann

Key words: Interactivity, internet, online communication, stakeholder dialogue, target group tailoring.

30.1 Introduction

Corporate social responsibility (CSR) relies on communication, outside and inside the company. Outside a company, CSR communication is the link to society and its various subsystems in which a company is embedded. Inside a company, CSR communication is based at least on communication strategy and image profile as well as organisation, staff, and infrastructure of information and communication technologies (ICT). In the last few years, CSR communication has become a topic of broader and global interest in academia, business, and government. Due to its increasing relevance to companies and capital markets, even through the eyes of investors, today CSR communication is broadening, both in its scope and quality: A narrow focus, merely communicating face-to-face with shareholders in terms of market communication or via investor relations is not sufficient anymore. CSR communication is moving away from an obviously outdated practice simply providing 'glossy brochures' often produced on print media and usually prepared as 'one size fits all' vehicles, towards an advanced online approach communicating with a number of stakeholders offering a CSR communication system. Such a system is available on the world wide web and covers a set of target group tailored, individualised or even personalised tools, e.g.: reports, brochures, leaflets, newsletters, press releases, slides, presentations, audio sequences, video clips etc. that are accessible via download and/or online, prepared for being pulled or automatically disseminated via email or other current push technologies.

30.2 Drivers for internet-based CSR communication

Current trends indicate that CSR communication is in a phase of transition, entering a new digital online stage: The field elevates from a rather 'managerial closed shop procedure' towards a 'quasi public effort' of engaging and involving various stakeholders like employees, customers, suppliers, investors, ranking and rating institutions, governments and local authorities, but also pressure groups and other non-governmental organisations (NGOs). Companies recognise that their business usually has economic, social, and environmental impacts and thus is of relevance for CSR communication. Further, companies consider that their range of influence extends across borders, and they are aware that their responsibilities also extend beyond basic compliance with national law and regulations. Hence, companies are going to expand CSR responsibilities onto a global scale.

As a result, companies need to communicate on CSR with different stakeholders via online relations, not just with shareholders in terms of market communication and via investor relations. Information supply evolves from local focus, strict monologue, and one-way company controlled exercise towards a more interactive and participatory approach, while communicating (online) with a greater audience, trying to get feedback from a number of stakeholders, or even to engage interested parties and then providing CSR communication tools exactly meeting these requirements. Such a process of fine tuning results from the fact that stakeholders are more critical of companies' business and well informed about their activities. Ultimately, stakeholders' criticism could lead to activism, campaigns, or other forms of exerting pressure on or challenging companies.

Classification framework of internet-specific benefits for CSR communication

Due to the importance of (online) communication as the basis for CSR, companies are expecting help on how to apply ICT as proper means for further improvements. They need assistance on how to use the internet for CSR communication in general, particularly to exploit the internet benefits for the provision of CSR communication tools. These media-relevant questions all involve issues of ICT, its operating internet-based online systems, information management and stakeholder online relations. The latter are to a large extent responsible for potential benefits and total costs of CSR communication. Furthermore, these issues also define added value, and facilities to provide online vehicles and other CSR communication tools in form and content in an efficient manner. In other words, companies want to know what are the unique capabilities offered by the internet and its associated technologies, services, and current mark-up languages like XML (eXtensible Markup Language) and XBRL (eXtensible Business Reporting Language) and how to make use of them for CSR communication: Is the internet merely a platform for downloads, perhaps with public access, in the sense of a medium for smart presentation or just another distribution channel? Beyond this, could the internet become a real facilitator for CSR communication that carries a number of media-specific benefits probably far from being utilised to its full potential?

As a resource for practical guidance on how to use the internet for advanced CSR communication, a generic classification framework has been developed. This classification framework arranges the various capabilities of the internet for CSR communication along four basic categories of benefits:

1. Benefits concerning the underlying purposes of communication;
2. Benefits concerning workflow and core processes along the production of communication tools;
3. Benefits concerning the contents of communication;
4. Benefits concerning the communication style.

Table 30.1. Classification framework of internet-specific benefits for CSR communication

Category of benefits	Possible realisations				
(i) Benefits concerning communication *purposes*	Resource controlling	Information, disclosure	Dialogue, two-way- communication	Learning issues and concerns	...
(ii) Benefits concerning the *workflow* along the production of communication tools	Rationalisation		Customisation		...
	Easy administration of communication tools	Efficient digital preparation of communication tools	Fast distribution of communication tools	Smart presentation of communication tools	...
(iii) Benefits concerning communication *contents*	Communication vehicles		Additional information		...
	Customised selection (data view)	Topical selection, retrieval	Internal links: e.g. CSR division	External links: e.g. guidelines, NGOs, stock exchange, ranking	...
(iv) Benefits concerning communication *style*	Online-, offline- availability	Navigation	Hypermedia	Feedback mechanisms	...

The first category covers the benefits concerning the underlying purposes of communication, e.g. improving efficiency and controlling resources, disclosing performance, enhancing reputation, learning issues and concerns of interested parties, initiating dialogue with external stakeholders, improving image, and engaging employees.

The second category includes the benefits concerning workflow and processes along the production of communication tools, e.g. automated data-based preparation and administration, multiple-utilisation of contents for different instruments (so-called single source cross-media publishing), online distribution, and smart presentation of communication tools.

The third category comprises the benefits concerning the communication contents, e.g. features to access CSR information through retrieval and search facilities, archives, tailored views, personalised communication tools on demand and various hyperlinks to guidelines, NGOs and other relevant information resources.

The fourth category contains the benefits concerning the communication style, e.g. online and offline availability, downloads, hypermedia, feature to assist stakeholders' navigation, web rides, order and feedback forms, opportunities for online dialogue like chat, forums, bulletin boards, and newsgroups.

However, exploiting the full range of internet benefits is not as simple a process as it may appear at first glance. On the contrary, CSR online communication merely becomes true when all four categories are taken into account: Purposes, processes, contents and style are to be linked and need to be considered as a total entity. One-sided solutions do not seem to be sufficient or successful.

30.3   Methodical basis of the classification framework and practical experiences

The classification framework above is an outcome of a research project on internet-based corporate reporting. This project was carried out at the Department of Business Information Systems and Operations Research and was embedded in a broader research programme 'environmental management and energy' at the University of Kaiserslautern, Germany. A goal of the project was to develop a generic classification framework on how corporate communication could benefit from internet use, which aspects are to be considered, and how to implement such a digital online approach. To gain full conceptual clarity and to present the whole potential using the internet, a comprehensive literature review of current approaches, examples and projects in corporate online communication and internet-based reporting was carried out. This analysis revealed that most proposals are more or less basic listings covering only some benefits, but lack a substantial structure and thus do not cover the full possible range of benefits using the internet taken as a whole. While some proposals highlight opportunities to prepare communication vehicles in an automated manner, some others focus on opportunities for smart presentation and dissemination.

From the pool of benefits found in literature, a catalogue of actually relevant aspects was developed. This pool was structured with the help of two powerful heuristics, i.e. the 'morphological box' and the technique of the 'four causae'. The morphological box is a tool used for creative problem solving, operations research, and computer sciences. It was introduced by the Swiss Astronomer Fritz Zwicky in the 1940s and helps to deconstruct the complex conceptualisation 'internet use' to a number of different attributes and their certain realisations. The technique of the 'four causae' goes back to Aristotle (384-322 B.C.). It provides a useful method to describe what a thing is made of (causa materialis), its form and design (causa formalis), the existence of a thing (causa efficiens), and its underlying purpose (causa finalis) and thus helps to obtain order in the number of attributes and realisations. Together, the heuristics provide a clear structure in terms of: purpose, process, content, and style when exploring the internet benefits construct in a systems approach.

The classification framework, as depicted here, is schematic, not photorealistic. However, it constitutes a helpful scheme for surveying the impressive array of benefits that ICT, particularly the internet, could provide for CSR communication in a broader sense. Further, the classification framework gives an overview of media-specific capabilities that the internet offers, bringing definite improvements in the areas of communications, information management and organisation, and perhaps smoothing the way when moving away from an orthodox stage to a CSR online communication approach. Moreover, it helps to refine companies' CSR communication while considering issues of ICT, e.g. how certain communication strategies could benefit from internet support, or what methods are to be employed for CSR online communication.

The classification framework has shown its usefulness in a number of empirical studies surveying the extent to which the internet is already being used in corporate online communication and what capabilities have already been applied. The fields that are analysed with the help of the classification framework vary from standalone environmental online communication and financial online communication to its integrated fashion as sustainability or CSR online communication.

30.4 Value and limitations of the classification framework

In order to exploit the full value of the classification framework, issues of critical importance are arranged to a list of dos:

- Do check which are the current purposes of CSR communication and decide whether CSR communication could also be linked to other fields, e.g. market communication, brands marketing, financial communication, etc. so that CSR communication may truly be incorporated in and consistent with common corporate communication;

- Do assess to what extent workflow and communication processes could benefit from internet use. Such an ICT support depends on companies' CSR strategy and existing ICT capabilities. It varies from standalone databases and other information systems to sophisticated and integrated (web) content management systems (WCMS) that are able to perform single source multiple media publishing;

- Do use the classification framework for producing CSR tools to become more precise and transparent in terms of clarifying terminology, how data are synthesised, translating measurement techniques into better management of resources, and improving standards of external audit or third party verification;

- Do put emphasis on issues of communication style; in particular throw light onto media availability, menus, search facilities, navigation, and feedback mechanisms like forums and bulletin boards, audio and video clips, and games as prerequisites to provide more interactivity, target group tailoring, and stakeholder dialogue.

Despite its overall usefulness, CSR communication supported through the internet opens up a host of questions, e.g. with respect to the target groups addressed and the ones actually reached. Among technical aspects of online communication and matters of efficient information management, a credible effort in CSR online communication has also to address issues such as the digital divide, restricted access, etc. Further, appropriate ICT infrastructure is needed at both ends of the communication link; not just with the companies communicating, but more importantly with the stakeholders who need to be actually reached.

In contrast to the binary logic of either recommending print media with a focus on real face-to-face communication, or favouring computer-based media with a preference for virtual (online) communication, as opposite means of CSR communication, a broad mixture seems to be appropriate and thus recommendable. Hence, the challenge is to develop a CSR communication system that covers all forms of communication, written and verbal tools, and to make print media and computer-based media work in tandem. Subsequently, a cross-media CSR communication approach is proposed that relies on an underlying ICT infrastructure, and is based on the internet, supporting the whole workflow along the production of the set of communication tools. Such an approach keeps companies in a position to provide a number of different target group tailored communication tools in a variety of media, based on a single data source that serves as a shared publishing basis.

The idea behind internet-based communication is that this computer-based method provides an array of media-specific capabilities opening windows for advanced CSR communication. For example, online availability, downloads, external CSR documents, interactivity, feedback opportunities, contact details, automatic order forms, CSR electronic forums, hyperlinks, graphically designed websites, navigation, search engines, web rides, regular updates, and site promotion, are just some of the style and content capabilities which companies could use. Compared with orthodox methods, internet-based CSR online communication overcomes the limitations of paper-based communication through one-size-fits-all vehicles, hard copies, print media fixation, and one-way-communication.

Verbal communication tools and face-to-face communication like public meetings, interviews, personal contacts, focus groups, open house information days, site visits, workshops and dialogue events, presentations, and business dinners are effective and proper means, but have restrictions in reaching a great and heterogeneous audience, and they are rather laborious and in several cases not feasible. Hence, it could be a useful supplement to have a readily available CSR online communication system for providing the information needed. Many of the questions asked could already be answered in comprehensive online resources. Stakeholders could extract the information they need from a publishing database, i.e. users generate their own 'tools à la carte', simply selecting key words, clicking on preferences on menus or choosing a certain guideline – perhaps creating a report in accordance with certain CSR guidelines at one's fingertips.

Because of its overall added-value-creating nature, the internet is already used by several companies and stakeholders as the pivotal platform to provide or to access information on environmental performance, social activities, and economic strategies or other related issues of CSR. In the growing information society there is a converging trend that the internet will become the prime communication vehicle of the 21st century as it has the potential to provide interactivity, customised or even personalised communication vehicles, and to offer a platform for permanent dialogue as the gateway to companies.

30.5 Implementing internet-based CSR communication

Implementation of a CSR online communication approach based on internet support requires at least three elements:

- Stakeholder analysis and information requirement analysis, representing the demand for CSR information that stakeholders are probably requiring;

- Document engineering, representing the contents a company is willing to communicate;

- Online communication system, representing a suitable ICT-architecture for cross-matching offer and demand, intended to provide a set of truly tailored tools, not just smartly polished versions of a uniformed report, while offering communication in a dialogue-oriented way.

Such a procedure helps to make CSR online communication work, with special emphasis on interactivity, target group tailoring and stakeholder dialogue, even when approaching through an incremental development. In terms of CSR, advanced internet use will improve the way in which companies give CSR information, communicate CSR issues, exchange knowledge, learn stakeholders' concerns and issues, and manage resources internally and externally, finally to the benefit of all members involved or affected, be they companies, key target groups, or other interested parties. The classification framework, as presented here, helps to exploit the internet opportunities.

References

Hund, G., J. Engel-Cox and K. Fowler (2004). *A communications guide for sustainable development. How interested parties become partners*. Columbus: Battelle.

Isenmann, R. (2005). Corporate sustainability reporting – a case for the internet. In: L. Hilty, K. Seifert and R. Treibert (Eds.) *Information Systems for Sustainable Development*. Hershey: Idea Group, pp. 164-212.

SustainAbility Ltd (2002). *Virtual Sustainability*. Print Version. London: Beacon Press.

The Association of Chartered Certified Accountants (ACCA) (2001) *Environmental, social and sustainability reporting on the world wide web: A guide to best practice*. London: The Certified Accountants Educational Trust.

Organising Accountability

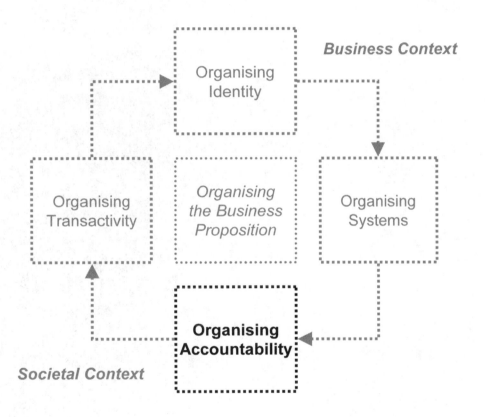

31 A Product Sustainability Assessment

Sophie Spillemaeckers and Griet Vanhoutte[1]

Key words: Integrated product management, sustainability, chain analysis, label.

31.1 Introduction

This article describes a model to evaluate a product's sustainability. The method assesses the sustainability impact of a product and its production processes. Integrated product management (IPM) has so far mainly been focusing on the environmental impacts of products. However, the framework for IPM is sustainable development. Therefore, a genuine IPM means that the impacts of a product's life cycle are to be assessed in all dimensions of sustainability: environmental, social and economic. To incorporate environmental as well as social and economic aspects, the product related LCA method is complemented with an organisation related approach. The system has been tested on several cases (refrigerator, bananas, textile, coffee …) and proved to be practical.

The model was developed by the Centre for Sustainable Development (University of Ghent, Belgium) and Ethibel in the frame of a research project on a 'sustainable development label' for products. The study was commissioned by the Belgian Federal Office for Scientific, Technical and Cultural Affairs (OSTC). The label is part of the Belgian government's policy to enhance the harmonisation of labels across Europe. To facilitate the integration of existing labels, the 'sustainable development label' was based on the Belgian social label and the European ecolabel, and contains elements of several other existing labels. The label's mission is to contribute to the reduction of the environmental and social burden of production and consumption, by offering guidance to consumers through identifying environmentally and socially preferable products, and by encouraging manufacturers to develop sustainable products and services.

The model is not only useful in the frame of the study on a product label, but can also be applied for chain management by companies. The baseline is that the subject of chain management should be a product instead of the company, because the company is also responsible for choosing partner companies that

---

[1] Both authors equally contributed to the realisation of this article.

operate in a sustainable way. A product can only be considered sustainable if all stages of its life cycle are performed in a sustainable manner, so what happens in the product's life outside the company gates should also be considered. The model can be used to assess a product's sustainability and use the results to make adjustments or it can be useful in the phase of product design to take sustainability considerations into account right from the start.

31.2   A two-fold model for assessing a product's sustainability

Presentation of the model

The following graphic shows the structure of the model that is used as framework for the label.

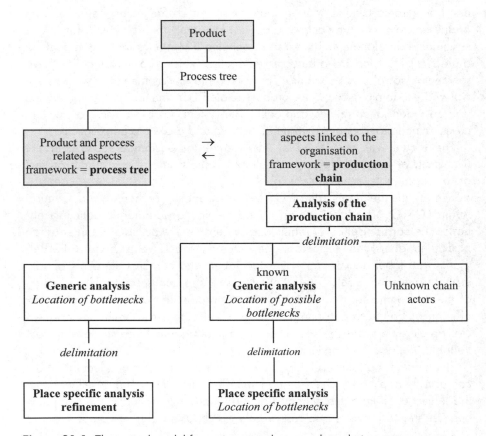

Figure 31.1. Theoretical model for an integrated approach to chain management

The framework

The sustainability of a product can be assessed through the evaluation of the various environmental, social and economic impacts associated with its life cycle (from raw materials to waste stage).

Life cycle analysis (LCA) is a widespread and accepted method to assess the environmental impacts of a product. An environmental LCA is based on the product's process tree, which is an inventory of the flows of raw materials, energy and emissions associated with the product's life cycle. The possible environmental impacts of these flows (e.g. the contribution of the emissions to global warming) are determined using software tools. The result of the analysis is an overview of the various environmental impacts and the life cycle stages and processes by which they are caused. An LCA employs an input-output model (the overview of what goes in or out the process) and usually relies on the use of generic data. No account is taken of the companies involved in the production process. Most environmental impacts are strongly related to the specific characteristics of the product and its production process. The importance of e.g. 'energy use' will be different in the evaluation of a varnish than in the evaluation of a dishwasher.

> The LCA-method is not suitable for the analysis of social and economic aspects.

If one wishes to include social and economic aspects in the product evaluation, the LCA-approach turns out to be inadequate. The social and economic impacts are related to the situation in the companies where the product is processed rather than to the product itself. Therefore, data collection for evaluation has to be done at the level of the organisation. E.g. to evaluate whether the workers producing the product receive a decent wage, the situation in the different organisations (companies) involved in the production has to be assessed. The same goes for some environmental aspects such as e.g. noise nuisance in the factory or soil contamination. Furthermore, the generic data used in an LCA can lack necessary precise information and differences can appear between the theoretical analysis and the real situation. Therefore an organisation related analysis of the environmental impacts is also recommended.

> The LCA-method has to be complemented with an organisation related approach in order to develop a method to consider all aspects of sustainability in the assessment of products and processes.

Considering these restraints, a theoretical model for the evaluation of environmental, social and economic aspects related to the life cycle of a product and its associated businesses was developed. This twofold model makes a clear distinction between aspects closely related to the product on the one hand, and organisation-specific aspects on the other. The generic assessment of the product-related environmental aspects is based on the LCA method, which analyses the product's process tree. To include social and economic aspects, the model incorporates an approach considering the organisations involved in the production chain. The analysis of the process tree only concerns environmental aspects, while the analysis of the production chain concerns environmental as well as social and economic aspects.

> A two-fold model making a clear differentiation between aspects closely related to the product on the one hand and organisation-specific aspects on the other, and between the related evaluation methods, makes a genuine integrated product assessment possible.

How the model works

The model outlines a step-by-step plan.

1. For the analysis of the product and process related (environmental) aspects the process tree is determined. This is an overview of the successive life cycle stages and production processes and the flows of materials, energy and emissions entering and leaving the life cycle.

2. The LCA method is used to make a generic analysis of the process tree. This is done by using software tools. The result is an overview of the different environmental impacts the processes in the different life cycle stages cause, based on which the bottlenecks and problem areas can be located (approximately). For example, an LCA of a washing machine indicates that compared to the environmental burden caused during the use phase (use of energy, water and washing powder during at about 15 years), the environmental impact of the production and the waste stage is relatively small.

3. It is possible that there are areas where the evaluation is insufficient. In that case, it is recommended that the results be further refined through a place-specific analysis (i.e. by collecting data on the organisations involved).

4. To study the organisation related aspects the production chain has to be made up. This implies that all companies linked to the process tree need to be identified (names and addresses of suppliers, subcontractors, manufacturers, transporters ...).

5. A first analysis of the production chain makes it possible to make a distinction between known and unknown (or changing) chain actors. Since chain management is an important feature of sustainable production, it might be concluded that the product is not produced in a sustainable way if it is impossible to trace significant chain actors. In that case, it could be considered to change the production chain to make it as transparent as possible.

6. A generic analysis of the known chain actors can be based on sector-specific or regional data: information on the general situation in companies in certain sectors and countries (e.g. in China it is not allowed to join trade unions). This facilitates the location of possible bottlenecks. Note the word 'possible': to locate the real bottlenecks, a place-specific analysis is necessary. The place-specific analysis is far more important for the organisation related than for the product and process related evaluation.

7. The place specific analysis will be carried out by a cost-efficient system including desktop screening (see also section on monitoring).

8. The chain actors where problems are most likely to occur can be identified and visited if considered necessary.

9. Chain actors are given the time to introduce corrective actions were necessary.

Sustainability themes

In order to be classified 'sustainable', the product and its production chain have to comply with certain social, environmental and economical criteria. In the frame of the label project, an extensive set of criteria was developed, again based on the two-fold model since there are both organisation-related and product-related criteria. The organisation-related criteria are the same for all kind of organisations. They are based on a literature study and stakeholder consultation, taking into account their relevance, measurability, economic and technical feasibility, policy relevance, fairness. The product related criteria are based on the outcome of LCA and are specific for a well defined product group. E.g. every company has to pay its workers a decent living wage (although the amount will vary), whereas criteria for sustainable coffee growing differ from criteria for dyeing cotton or composing a varnish. An extensive list of criteria with the corresponding evaluation method can be downloaded from www.ethibel.org.

31.3   The model in practice

Chain delimitation

An important prerequisite for applying the model is that it must be possible to draw up the process tree and the production chain. Although many companies recognise the importance of chain management and transparent chains, there are still few products with transparent chains. Organising production chains in order to make them more transparent and solid is a very important step towards sustainable production patterns. Working with long term contracts can also allow to make agreements on other sustainability themes (e.g. long term contracts including conditions on social and environmental subjects).

Chain delimitation is indispensable for example in the light of the expenses related to the monitoring, which can form an obstacle to the practical workability, especially in the frame of the label. The evaluation of the complete chain against all sustainability criteria can be too expensive and time consuming. To keep the analysis workable, in many cases the process tree and the production chain will have to be delimited.

Currently there is no widely accepted scientific model for general chain delimitation considering social, environmental and economical aspects at hand. The researchers developed an adapted system based on field experience.

The LCA of the process tree defines the environmentally precarious stages that should be included in the further analysis. For example, in the case of a washing machine, the environmental efforts should concentrate on making the use phase less harmful.

Motivating principles to include relevant actors can also be used: the components produced by the actor should represent a certain % of the weight, a certain % of the volume and/or a certain % of the costs of the assessed product. The retained chain actors in both procedures are to be linked. In the coffee case this would mean that – since according to the LCA the packing of coffee does not contribute significantly to the environmental impact relative to the entire life cycle – the companies performing the packing are not included in the analysis. Companies excluded by the LCA, might however be included if they are considered significant chain actors within the analysis of the production chain, for example if they represent a critical percentage or if the social controversies are too important. This is the case for maritime transport: while transport of coffee could be excluded in the LCA because it contributes only to a very small extent to the total energy cost of the coffee production, the existing social controversies require the inclusion of these companies.

The significant chain actors and life cycle stages are retained and those of little importance cut off using both motivating principles and LCA.

Monitoring

The data collection to prove compliance with the criteria – which is a vital part of the labelling system – proved to be one of the main difficulties of chain management. Different methods were used for product and process related aspects and for the organisation related aspects.

The first part of the monitoring is the verification of the data provided by product and process related proofs given by the company based on LCA specific criteria.

The most difficult step consists in verifying if the companies related to the production chain comply with the criteria. Ideally, the place specific analysis would be carried out by paying each chain actor a visit, but this would be far too expensive and time consuming, even with a limited chain. The number of visits could be limited using statistically sound random checks, but this implies the risk to overlook serious problems and is therefore considered too hazardous. Therefore, a more cost-efficient system including desktop screening and a limited number of visits on the spot is proposed. Desktop screening is a research method carried out according to standard written procedures. These procedures contain the search of controversies on the company by consultation of the Internet, literature and various specialised databanks. Besides that, relevant stakeholders of the companies have to be consulted, with priority to the union representatives representing the workers of the company and environmental NGO's. Note that the definition of the relevant stakeholders and contacting them can be difficult.

Based on desktop screening and the generic analysis of the chain actors where problems are most likely to occur, can be identified and visited if considered necessary. In the framework of the label project, a method was developed which classifies the companies in different risk groups and facilitates a statistically sound choice of chain actors to be visited.

A cost-efficient system is used for the monitoring of the production chain including desktop screening and a limited number of visits on the spot.

31.4 Some dos and don'ts

Transparent chain management is the future management system, but it has to be introduced gradually. The model can first be used as a companies guide for chain management. Transparency of the total production chain is a future goal all companies will be confronted with. Most companies involved in the case studies recognised the determination of the chain and the contacts with other chain actors as a very informative process. The introduction of an integrated chain management leads to better relationships with suppliers and better quality management. It gives the possibility to influence the production policy and to act preventively. This can lead to less risk of scandals. Companies can best take into account sustainable chain management at the phase of product design.

31.5 Wrapping up

Moving towards a sustainable chain management system for products is a necessary but also an ambitious objective. First mover companies are getting aware of this, but there is still a long way to go before all companies will be ready to introduce the system. In most cases the model will have to be introduced step by step, starting with partial aspects of chain management. The application on a wide scale of complete sustainable chain management, taking into account social, environmental and economic aspects, is still in the future. The introduction of the system and its advantages however should start right now.

References

Borgo, E., T. De Moor, A. Deny and S. Spillemaeckers (2000). *An integrated approach to chain analysis for the purpose of corporate chain management*. Ghent: Centre for Sustainable Development, Ghent University.

Belgisch sociaal label, 27 Februari (2002). *Wet ter bevordering van sociaal verantwoorde productie*, (http://www.cass.be/cgi_wet/wetgeving.pl).

Europees Ecolabel, verordening (EG) Nr. 1980/2000 van het Europees Parlement en de raad van 17 juli 2000 inzake een herzien communautair systeem voor de toekenning van milieukeuren, (http://europa.eu.int/comm/environment/ecolabel/pdf/regulation/001980_nl.pdf).

Websites

http://www.ethibel.org
http://cdonet.rug.ac.be

32 Drawing the Lines in Value Chain Responsibility

Johan Verburg and Sean Gilbert

Key words: Value chain, reporting, stakeholder engagement, dialogue, dilemma sharing.

32.1 Introduction

Business goes global, risks and opportunities go global, and responsibilities extend. The rapid changes in the global economy have changed business, enabling the emergence of global corporations of a size, scale, and degree of networking not previously seen. Complex business models now involve a variety of players across the value chain in multiple countries, including subsidiaries, joint ventures, suppliers or customers in developing countries. The risks to and opportunities for a company's success can lie in far-flung parts of their networks of business relationships.

New business models have changed relationships with stakeholders. Businesses are now perceived to have new responsibilities with respect to sustainable development, matching basic business concerns, such as risk reduction, market opportunities, and corporate governance. As part of these changing expectations, pressure has also grown on the strongest and most prominent players in value chains to demonstrate leadership in catalysing change across a sector or in their value chain. As one observer expressed it, they are expected to challenge even physical laws and to 'make the chain as strong as the strongest link'.

Delivering on these broader expectations – of both business as well as its stakeholders – requires managers to develop strategies for working with a wide range of relationships on issues that go beyond traditional boundaries of financial control. This new thinking requires a manager to understand where accountability lies and develop a suitable approach to stakeholder engagement and sustainability reporting accordingly. Reporting is essential for both internal and external stakeholders to make better informed decisions about value chain strategies and performance. However, how does an organisation decide which relationships are important to managing and reporting performance? Business needs new tools to manage risks and opportunities across traditional boundaries, a compass that enables management to link two dimensions: sustainability impacts and an organisation's degree of influence.

This article outlines concepts to address these issues based on the work of the GRI Boundaries Working Group. GRI is the Global Reporting Initiative; a framework designed to enable reporting on economic, environmental, and social performance.

32.2   The two dimensions of value chain responsibility

The GRI approach identifies two dimensions as key to determining how to approach measuring performance in the context of a value chain, which is depicted in Figure 32.1. The first is the scale of impacts or risks (positive or negative, actual or potential) associated with an entity with which the organisation has a connection. Second is the degree of control or influence that the organisation has over the entities of its value chain, from raw material producers to (in)direct suppliers, through to clients and end-consumers. With the two dimensions on the axes of a graph, this framework can be used to map different organisations or groups of organisations in the value chain for purposes of thinking

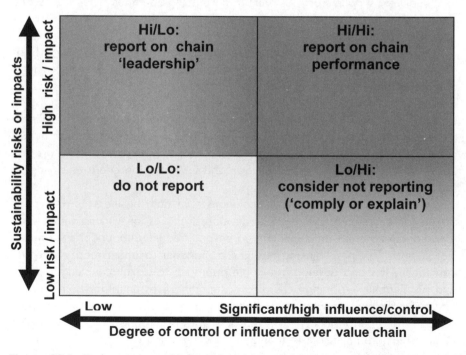

Figure 32.1. Evaluating control/influence and sustainability impact for value chain accountability

about how to measure and report performance. This mapping of impacts and relations should be helpful, since the non-complying supplier, or the critical consumer may seem to be part of the problem, however, these may also prove to be part of the solution.

For any given reporting entity, this gives four different combinations, each requiring a different strategy:

- hi/hi: entities with a high impact over which you have a high control/influence;
- lo/hi: entities with a low impact over which you have a high control/influence;
- hi/lo: entities with a high impact over which you have a low control/influence;
- lo/lo: entities with a low impact over which you have a low control/influence.

Where both impact and control are high

When the degree of control over an entity of the value chain is high, internal and external stakeholders have an interest in quantified performance information. For example, a subsidiary that is subject to the financial control and relevant for measuring financial performance is clearly also relevant for assessing sustainability performance. More importantly, its contribution to overall organisational performance should be measured and managed in a very precise and quantitative manner. According to the GRI Boundaries Protocol, control and significant influence can be determined by financial relations (e.g. percentage ownership of subsidiaries or joint ventures), contractual relations (e.g. supply requirements on food safety) or operational relations (e.g. safety standards for contractors in oil and gas operations). Control and significant influence are defined in the protocol based on financial accounting definitions.

For entities subject to control, with a significant impact, performance information should be accessible, and, if it is not, that is the sign of a problem. Quantitative data easily show trends and allow an objective assessment of the current position. The GRI provides a number of performance indicators suitable for these purposes.

Where impacts are not significant

There are other examples of entities which are subject to control, that have minimal impact such as the sales office of a major manufacturer where the environmental impacts are likely to be minor compared to a major production centre. These entities are important from the perspective of completeness, but many organisations still expend an unnecessary amount of effort in gathering and reporting detailed data on these entities (bottom of Figure 32.1). These entities are not the primary concern of most report users who seek concise reports that focus on significant or material issues and entities. The GRI Guidelines recognise this by allowing organisations to exclude indicators or entities, assuming that the exclusion does not substantively change the overall performance assessment. Just as in financial reporting, all the sustainability data should be available to management, like in the balance sheet. However, it may not be necessary to track in the same level of precision and it is certainly not necessary to report in a manner equal to major impacts. It may be limited to explanatory texts, comparable to the qualitative way financial reports handle entities under significant influence.

Where influence is below comfort level

The most challenging quadrant from the perspective of management and sustainability is where impacts associated with an entity are high, but influence is limited. As put by one businessperson: 'Those are the issues that keep me up at night'. For example, a second tier supplier with a highly polluting production technology who provides critical inputs for an organisation, but is not dependent on the organisation as a customer or otherwise susceptible to being influenced. Another example might be, owning 49% of a joint venture that is accused on multiple occasions of human rights violations. These are the situations where many stakeholders will perceive the organisation to have a degree of responsibility due its close engagement with the entity, and therefore where a strategy for defining, measuring, and reporting performance is necessary. The best approach will vary to a degree depending on the nature of the impact and the relationship. In some cases, such as the joint venture, it may be possible to use direct measures of performance aspects such as emissions. In other cases, like the second tier supplier, it may be necessary to use more qualitative measures of management performance such as audits or training.

For many companies, the greatest impacts associated with their activities may indeed lie in extended parts of the value chain and therefore require cooperation from other partners. Examples include steps such as: implementing design changes to ban the use of hazardous chemicals, sector codes to fight child labour, or conditional financing to prevent the social and environmental impacts of large project investments, e.g. on tropical forests and indigenous communities. This recognition of extended responsibility is also reflected in a number of international standards and initiatives such as the 2000 revision of the OECD Guidelines for multinational enterprises, and the emerging UN norms for business that apply to the 'spheres of influence and activities' of business.

Which quadrant do you want to manage towards?

From a management perspective, not all quadrants are equal and the combination of entities with a high negative impact/risk subject to minimal control is clearly least preferable. The organisation faces a high degree of risk with limited ability to force the entity to change its activities. Measurement is the key step towards being able to gain control of a situation and begin to manage it. Reaching this point involves a sequence of learning that starts with first recognising a challenge or dilemma. Then, the organisation proceeds through a cycle of developing a strategy, implementing policies and/or systems, and measuring progress. This requires a system of performance measurement and internal and external disclosure that is capable of supporting this cycle. GRI reporting and the approaches considered in the Boundaries Protocol offer an approach to thinking about this.

Stages of progressing influence

An organisation should report through a combination of hard numbers, its policies, its initiatives with business partners and stakeholders, or – simply – its recognition of encountered dilemmas, as depicted in Figure 32.2. So given all of the complexities, how are you expected to manage, measure, and disclose?

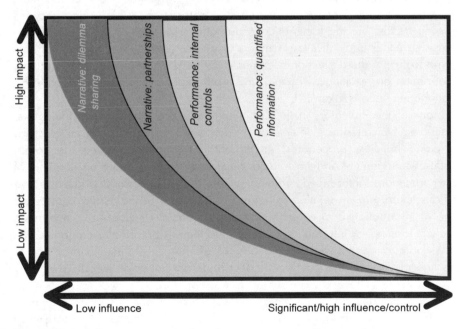

Figure 32.2. Different nature of value chain reporting in subsequent layers

Quantitative performance measurement

For entities that fall under the control of the organisation, performance expectations can clearly be defined and tracked in terms of quantitative measures, supplemented by qualitative measures and information where necessary. While challenges always exist in data gathering, managers (in theory) should have access to clear data on the state of their own operations. If they don't, it is a bad sign.

The boundaries of data gathering for quantified performance measures should sometimes be extended even in absence of full control. In certain circumstances, the size of the impacts and the resulting weight of expectations and the associated risks are so great that managers need to be able to understand and track progress in terms of precise quantitative measures of operational conditions. The same would be required for important financial risks outside formal financial control. Therefore, it makes sense to give similar instructions to the sustainability people on the 4th floor as to the financial controllers on the 3rd floor.

Qualitative performance indicators

As one moves beyond the lines of control, quantitative measures about operating conditions can become harder to obtain and, sometimes, less reliable. Performance management should remain clearly focused on measuring and improving trends, but the focus and accountability expectation may shift to emphasising either qualitative assessments or measurements of management performance. Here the distinction becomes clear between output indicators (giving information on resulting outcomes) and input indicators (giving information on management efforts taken).

Many of the indicators in the GRI Guidelines are management indicators, describing typically the elements of a company's system of internal controls, including policies, procedures, implementation, monitoring and monitoring results. Management and stakeholder decisions are then based on numbers of new procedures introduced, training given, audits performed and corrective actions taken, e.g. in relation to human rights issues in the supply chain. This type of information is also highly relevant for Socially Responsible Investment analysts looking for information to determine the risk profile of a company. It is also worth noting that while the boundaries of financial statements may stop at the line of control, the boundaries of mandatory financial reporting actually extend to entities beyond those subject to control.

In applying qualitative measures and specifically measures of management practice, a key distinction is whether the measures are designed to assess an entity's compliance with a given standard or whether they are designed to reveal the effectiveness of actions adopted to solve the sustainability problem. A simple example would be the distinction between measuring the ability of suppliers to comply with rules about employing children, compared to a measure of the number of children sent for schooling. The underlying problem is creating educational opportunity for children that will later enable economic opportunities. Many measures currently applied focus on compliance, which can sometimes undermine the ability to achieve the ultimate goal of the efforts. Research by Oxfam shows, that purchasing practices of large retailers may undermine their own codes of conduct, implemented and enforced by the audit departments of the same company. As such, there is interest within the stakeholder community for seeing value chain thinking that goes beyond setting standards and enforcing compliance, but also trying to identify emerging problems and catalyse solutions through a 'leadership approach'.

Strategic initiatives – narrative

To control risks – or more positively seize opportunities – a company, even with limited influence over entities with significant impacts may take the lead in organising a strategy. Examples here include sustainability initiatives in the food industry, e.g. the Roundtable on Sustainable Palm Oil, or in the financial sector, e.g. the Equator Principles. These strategic initiatives seek to bring together a critical mass of players in the value chain that is big enough to have an effective positive impact. In thinking about performance targets, identifying challenges for the value chain and seeking to develop a strategy that engages others can sometimes be the main opportunity and performance objective.

The larger 'brands' and multinationals are seen as stronger players in the value chain and are often expected to show this type of leadership. It often requires 'out-of-the-box' thinking to identify and take strategic partnership initiatives. The complexity of many sustainability issues necessitates openness to find new partners for effective problem solving. In many cases this may bring 'first mover' advantages. Often not only business partners, but also relevant stakeholders from civil society (e.g. labour unions), are engaged in these so-called multi-stakeholder initiatives aiming to adopt new sustainability standards in a particular sector. Sometimes the initiatives are intended to create a 'level playing field'.

At this end of the influence axis, performance may only be defined in narrative terms. Typically reporting will therefore describe the strategic initiative, the company's role in it, intended outcomes and results so far. In the context of the GRI, the elements of the GRI Guidelines address this area, e.g. the precautionary principle, voluntary initiatives, industry memberships, upstream/downstream management and the approach to indirect impacts.

Recognising dilemmas – discussion

Finally, in case of newly emerging sustainability challenges, it may be too early for strategic initiatives, management controls, and performance results to have been established. This should not be a reason to be silent about them. On the contrary, from the perspective of a stakeholder such as Oxfam, best practice sustainability management at present seriously shares dilemmas and engages stakeholders to collaborate on finding a solution. This is already called for to an extent in the context of discussing an organisation's vision and strategy and statement from its Chief Executive. However, as companies continue to evolve their stakeholder engagement systems and applying the principles of transparency and inclusiveness, more sustainability reports will also engage in this area.

32.3 Dos and don'ts

Table 32.1. Dos and don'ts

Do	Don't
Look beyond traditional financial boundaries	Draw a hard boundary where financial control ends
Engage pro-actively with stakeholders in and around the value chain	Ignore 'early-warning' signs from stakeholders who have eyes and ears close to the far sides of your value chains
Let the degree of impacts and information needs drive reporting and set boundaries	Let information availability and control be the only factors that determine your reporting
Gather quantified data on performance of value chain actors, even in absence of your full control	Restrict your reporting to your own management indicators regarding the value chain, e.g. audits of suppliers
Increase focus of reporting on what is relevant in value chains	Report indiscriminately on all indicators for the sake of compliance
Report effectiveness of problem solving in chains	Report only on effectiveness of internal control systems and compliance
See chain improvements as opportunities, chain actors as part of the solutions	See chains as risks to be controlled, with actors that just need to comply
Report dilemmas, even when undecided	Report only about decisions and solutions

32.4 Conclusion

Managers are in need of new tools to help them plot strategy and navigate an increasingly complex market where they are perceived to have a wider set of responsibilities and roles than in the past. The key to solving this puzzle lies in the ability to understand the intersection of impact and influence. Previous paradigms tried to draw a hard line where financial control ended and assume that events occurring with entities beyond that line were only of tangential relevance to an organisation's accountability. That paradigm no longer holds as organisations are penalised for actions by suppliers or other business partners, and even governments in areas where they operate.

The ultimate purpose of developing tools such as reporting and the boundaries thinking outlined in this paper, is to enable better performance management, better decision-making internal and external to an organisation, and ultimately, more sustainable development. Given the complexity of the global economy, and social and environmental problems, the only solutions will come from new modes of thinking that recognise networks, share dilemmas, and seek to identify where and with whom problems can be influenced and how to measure individual contributions towards solutions.

Websites

www.globalreporting.org/boundary
www.maketradefair.org

33 Resource Efficiency Accounting

Timo Busch and Christa Liedtke

Key words: Cost accounting, life cycle perspective, resource efficiency.

33.1 Introduction to the model

In the macro economic dimension, the de-coupling of economic growth and the use of resources has been declared as a major objective. In 2000, during the Lissabon conference, the European Council set out a ten-year strategy for sustainable development which was followed in 2003 by the publication of the European Commission's resource strategy. However, according to the Commission's Spring Report 2004 economic growth is still not sustainable enough, meaning a new development model is necessary.

What does this entail at the corporate level? Companies have an essential role to play in de-coupling economic growth from the use of natural resources. Therefore, it is their responsibility to contribute to such a new development model in their day-to-day business routines and decisions. Companies should define concrete CSR management strategies and implement the relevant tools within their organisations. A closer examination of this issue is more than worthwhile: Costs related to material and energy consumption are the major cost driver. Depending on the sector and positioning in the production chain, these costs can exceed all other cost factors up to the factor of two. However, corporate measures to reduce costs still focus mainly on labour expenses. How far strategies focusing on resource efficiency – an important part of CSR – can also contribute to cost cuts is an issue that is generally ignored in normal business practices. So what are the requirements for an adequate instrument? Fulfilling three main requirements results in an effective and efficient instrument, namely: user-friendliness (i.e. manageable outcomes), accountability (i.e. comparability and reduced complexity) and transparency (i.e. concise environmental impact assessments and identification of cost-reduction potential).

33.2 The essence of the model

Resource Efficiency Accounting (REA) aims at meeting these requirements. The objective of REA is to collect and interpret data, both on life-cycle wide material and energy inputs, as well as to define the corresponding costs within an enterprise (Orbach and Liedtke, 2002). To achieve the latter, REA uses the company's existing cost-accounting systems. In order to identify cost-reduction potential, the ensuing step focuses on the problem of cost misallocation. Based on the results, a decision is made as to how and what extent the cost accounting needs to be reorganised and adjusted. Eco-efficiency strategies can then focus either on process optimisation or on product assessment and design.

To start with, corporate material and energy inputs are considered from an environmental point of view. The specific material consumption, energy use, and flow rates are first structured and than classified and assigned to single production processes or end products (Liedtke et al., 1998). At this stage, the usual assumption is that fewer inputs always deliver better solutions in terms of improved eco-efficiency, both in view of the environmental impact as well as costs. From the financial point of view, this assumption is right in most of the straightforward cases. Reduced material or energy flows usually entail fewer costs. However, from the ecological perspective, one basic fact is inconsistent with this assumption: slimming down material or energy inputs per product or service unit does not automatically result in an improvement of the over-all ecological impact. It is not always obvious which strategy provides the optimal solution. For example, it is important that measures not only consider internal improvements. It is also necessary to analyse and incorporate the hidden inputs of preliminary or downstream production processes within the supply chain. The REA approach embraces these processes as it takes the ecological impact of the entire life cycle into consideration. This is done by the utilisation of so called material intensities that are published on the web page of the Wuppertal Institute (see web pages).

The main advantage of this approach is the simple impact assessment and the generation of comparable and manageable results. The sum of the resulting mass equivalents is described by the Total Material Requirement indicator (TMR). This indicator encompasses the following areas: abiotic material, biotic material and soil (Schmidt-Bleek, 1993). The results are illustrated by a resource efficiency portfolio, whereby the life-cycle wide environmental and according cost data are considered simultaneously. Based on this, management strategies can be analysed and investment decisions can be evaluated. The results can help the companies to find a way to achieve more sustainable growth. A differentiation can be made between:

- an eco-efficient objective function;

- cost-efficient business strategies;

- resource-efficient business strategies;

- ecologically-economically less relevant areas.

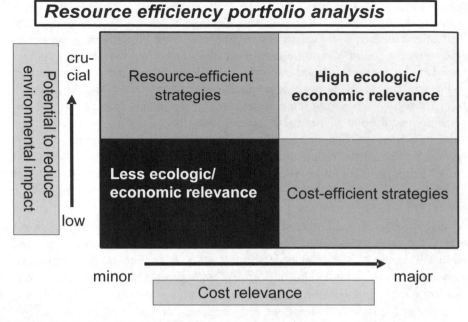

Figure 33.1. Eco-efficiency portfolio analysis (source: Busch et al., 2004)

The objective of the portfolio analysis is to provide a decision-making basis for relative comparisons of two or more product or process alternatives. The individual axes of the portfolios are described by the material- and energy-input-based cost data (X-axis) and the material input oriented, ecological data (Y-axis). The data represent company-specific information since they correspond to the relative values of the overall company.

33.3   Experience with this model in practice

The REA is suitable for any company, regardless of size or sector. The REA approach was applied in different German companies within the scope of a project funded by the German Ministry for Education and Research. Significant improvements were achieved, both in the economic and ecological areas. In the three-year project the REA-based eco-efficiency portfolio analysis was implemented on different levels within the participating companies.

For the application of REA at the process level a detailed analysis is necessary. This reveals the individual processes within the company and their relative portion of the overall costs (derived from the Profit & Losses Statement) and the relative portion of the companies TMR (derived from an input and output analysis and the material flow accounting). Processes with the highest potential for improving eco-efficiency are identified as so-called 'hot spots'. In the ensuing step, the same procedure is applied at the product level. This focuses the analysis on single output components. Usually these are end products or services that fulfil the same or a slightly different purpose for the consumer or sub-purchaser. The hot-spot analysis on this level is focused on determining products which have a relatively high total material requirement.

In the practical application of REA the following steps are helpful when identifying individual sources, accumulating different types of data, and processing the resulting information (Busch et al., 2004):

- *Definition of the production-process structure*: The structure of production processes including the connections between the individual processes can usually be identified from work plans. However, especially in small and medium-sized enterprises, it is often necessary to generate a totally new coherent structure plan;

- *Assembly of data on material and energy consumption at the company*: This type of data can be found in the profit and loss statement, bookkeeping, cost accounting, storage and purchase systems. This data can provide insight about the companies overall consumption of the main component and its related purchasing expenditures;

- *Definition of volume of consumed material, substances and energy, and allocation of figure per process/product*: Process-related material data are usually available on work plans/routings or in internal production orders. However, the internal use of energy volumes is usually not determined at the process level, especially in small- and medium-sized companies. Once this information has been gathered it can be assigned to single end-products/service units;

- *Allocation of costs per process/product*: Cost and activity accounting means that cost allocations per process or product are sometimes available. Nevertheless, it is advisable to check whether the established accounting system is working in a reliable and concise manner, especially in terms of the accurate assignment of material- and energy-related overhead costs;

- *Addition of material intensities*: Material intensities have to be added for all different kinds of used materials and the specific energy consumption. The web page http://mips-online.info provides a compilation of main material intensities and a general introduction of how to apply the concept.

33.4 Some dos and don'ts

Put together an REA team: When implementing REA a central success factor is to ensure that the topic is not discussed in separate management or specialised departments, but rather across all company departments and divisions. The team should comprise of employees who (1) possess experience and know-how in the areas of raw materials, consumption and purchasing quantities, and who are in contact with suppliers and thus have an overview of the scope of delivery, delivery times, etc., (2) have a technical overview and some years' experience with the company, thus guaranteeing precise knowledge of internal procedures, processes, operations, etc., (3) have IT experience or are in charge of operational/production control and/or (4) are involved in the process of product design and development.

Do not get put off by the volume of work: The REA method is based on detailed information about internal material and energy flows as well as the corresponding costs. Depending on the status of the established cost accounting systems within the company, specific data have to be evaluated and allocated. As this can be a rather complex process, the introduction of REA is dependent on the use of financial and personnel resources. However, the additional capacity is mainly required during the early stage of the project. If you are still concerned about the amount of work needed to get an according project started, please take a look at the model for beginners presented in the concluding section below.

Do not get confused due to the apparent contradiction between the requirements user-friendliness, accountability and transparency. In order to manage this issue, REA is based on an innovative approach that uses material intensities. Material intensities are easy to handle, as they are publicly available and utilise aggregated data. Furthermore, they give consolidated information on complex life-cycle wide environmental impacts.

Do not consider this approach as an all-round assessment of all kind of ecological aspects. The purpose of this method is to assess and improve resource efficiency. Aspects concerning toxicity or emissions should be included in the risk management. It is already mandatory to pay attention to many of these aspects, as companies have to adhere to environmental laws. However, emissions are included in material intensities, as for example in the case of CO_2 the carbon inputs of fuel and gas (Ritthoff et al., 2003). Thus, by utilising this concept in your company, the purpose is twofold: (1) optimising resource efficiency and (2) reducing the complexity of ecological economic assessments to a point where they can be managed in a simple and comprehensible way.

33.5 Concluding remarks

Start preferably with an initial analysis. The following 'wrapping up' model is particularly appropriate for companies approaching the topic resource efficiency for the first time and/or small and medium-sized enterprises with limited financial and personnel capacities.

On the process level, the goal is to improve the eco-efficiency of the entire company by means of process optimisation. To start with, material and energy flows should be determined. Usually, a complete input-output balance sheet does not have to be set up for this purpose. The company's main inputs are sufficient for a first analysis. The required annual consumption figures as well as the associated costs can be obtained e.g. from accounting documents. The total annual consumption figures can then be linked with the respective material intensities. The result is an assessment of the lifecycle-wide impacts of the most significant material and energy inputs. The next step is then to identify the internal processes that play an important role in the overall resource consumption or processing and which are presumed to have potential for improvement. In general, these are processes that also have great cost-saving potential. These processes are thus also the internal hot spots; the aim of eco-efficiency strategy is to optimise the implementation of improvements, since this could lead to the most effective result for the entire company.

When the focus is on product optimisation, it is possible to bypass the step of outlining and mapping the internal material and energy flows within the scope of an initial optimisation strategy. For the purposes of defining the eco-efficiency strategy, the main component(s) of products for which there are alternative production options should be identified first. The result should comprise specific details of the exact contents for each main component that is used for the end product. The respective product data can then be linked with the material intensities and subsequently summed up. The result describes the lifecycle-wide environmental impact of the various product alternatives. The relative profit share can be calculated to assess the economic impact. For this purpose, the production costs of each product are taken from the cost and activity accounting. If there is insufficient information in this regard, approximation values for the production costs should be determined for the previously identified main components. The difference between the selling price and the production costs can then be formulated as the profit share of each product. The profit share in relation to the respective production costs can be designated as a relative profit share. In conjunction with the environmental impact, this value forms the basis for the eco-efficiency assessment of the product alternatives. The strategy can then either be a sales increase of the product with the best economic-ecological performance or optimisation of the product with the worst REA result.

References

Busch, T., S. Beucker and A. Müller (2004). Computer Aided Resource Efficiency Accounting. In: B. Wagner and S. Enzler (Eds.), *Material Flow Management – Improving Cost Efficiency and Environmental Performance*. Berlin/Heidelberg/New York: Springer-Verlag.

Liedtke, C., H. Rohn, M. Kuhndt and R. Nickel (1998). Applying Material Flow Accounting: Eco-Auditing and Resource Management at the Kambium Furniture Workshop. *The Journal of Industrial Ecology*, 2(3).

Orbach, T. and C. Liedtke (2002). Resource Efficiency Accounting. In: M. Bennett, J.J. Bouma, and T. Wolters (Eds.), *Environmental Management Accounting: Informational and Institutional Developments*. Dordrecht, Boston, London: Kluwer Academic Publishers, pp. 83-90.

Ritthoff, M., H. Rohn and C. Liedtke (2003). *Calculating MIPS – Resource Productivity of Products and Services Wuppertal*, (http://www.mips-online.info).

Schmidt-Bleek, F. (1993). *Wieviel Umwelt braucht der Mensch? MIPS. Das Maß für ökologisches Wirtschaften*. Basel/Berlin/Boston: Birkhäuser Verlag.

Websites

http://mips-online.info
http://care.oekoeffizienz.de
http://www.sustainability-compass.net

34 The GoodCorporation Framework

Lisa Buchan and Leo Martin

Key words: Standard, certification, verification, assessment, measurement.

34.1 Introduction to the model

GoodCorporation Ltd is a private company founded in 2000. In conjunction with the Institute of Business Ethics (London) it developed a global standard of responsible business practices and a service to assess performance against the Standard. Its approach to corporate responsibility focuses on the organisation's transactivity – its relations with stakeholders – and accountability – its willingness to submit to external evaluation.

GoodCorporation is a pure 'audit' business and avoids any type of consulting to allow it to take a genuinely impartial view about a company's corporate responsibility. The Standard emphasises the principle of fairness, which cuts across differences in situations, sectors, and cultures within an organisation. If both a Mexican employee and a Birmingham supplier believe that an organisation treats them fairly, their testimony is sounder evidence than any other data that it is living up to its code of conduct. The Standard underpins ethical principles with concrete practices; assessment against the Standard evaluates how fairly those practices are working 'on the ground' from the standpoint of the stakeholders who use them.

34.2 The framework: Standard and assessment

The Standard covers six stakeholders: employees, customers, suppliers, and shareholders; environmental impacts and contribution to the community. Since the Standard is in the public domain, any organisation can adopt it as a code of conduct or use it as the basis for its own specific set of business principles.

Some 62 working practices underpin principles of business conduct in each of these six areas. For example, all companies aim to be honest and fair in their dealings with business-to-business customers. Some of the practices that demonstrate that principle in daily operations are: clear terms of business in contracts; procedure for recording and resolving customer's complaints within a defined time-scale; a process for taking customer feedback into account when developing customer policies.

Assessment against the Standard involves a mix of qualitative and quantitative measurement. It leads with a detailed review of policies supplemented by extensive interviews with stakeholders to evaluate how effectively procedures are working. On the basis of this qualitative overview, the assessor assigns grades for performance in each of the 62 practices. Grades are converted to numerical values that benchmark and capture overall performance in a metrical format. Each of the stakeholder groups can be assessed and graded using the same system. The assessment is confidential; it is up to management to decide how it will use the data with internal and external audiences.

How the assessment works

The stages in the assessment are:

- GoodCorporation aligns the Standard's 62 practices to an existing code of conduct or the organisation adopts the GoodCorporation Standard as the basis of its code of conduct. If there are key principles in the company's code not covered by the GoodCorporation Standard, they can be added to the assessment;

- GoodCorporation and the organisation develop a programme to assess a sample of business units based on the size of the work force and locations;

- The assessor reviews the procedures of the organisation in each unit and conducts extensive stakeholder interviews;

- The assessor weighs up the evidence from all the units assessed and gains an overview of performance across the organisation;

- The assessor awards one of five grades for each practice ranging from 'fail' to 'commendation' (see below);

- When there are no fail grades for the 62 practices, the organisation becomes a GoodCorporation member and can use the members' logo;

- The GoodCorporation Accreditation Council reviews all reports for consistency and quality;

- GoodCorporation re-assesses the organisation periodically as the basis for tracking progress and renewing membership.

While GoodCorporation's main activity is certification against the 62 practices of the Standard, the number of practices can be extended to meet specific concerns of the organisation. GoodCorporation also offers customised versions of the assessment using the same methodology. However, this service would confer membership only when all of the Standard's normal criteria were included and met.

Evidence review

First, the assessor checks that a policy exists in relation to each of the 62 practices. Then he/she ascertains that a system is in place to implement the policy; the organisation provides records indicating how the system is designed to work or how it believes that it is functioning.

By conducting extensive interviews with stakeholders inside and outside the organisation, the assessor can detect any differences between stakeholder and management's evaluation of how effectively and fairly practices actually work.

Stakeholder interviews

Interviews with employees, customers, suppliers, NGO groups, shareholders, regulators and community groups help to flesh out the 'bare bones' of policy-related documents. The assessor is not an opinion pollster: he/she does not restrict the conversation to a checklist of questions and multiple-choice answers. He/she can decide to ask a stakeholder about any or all the practices being assessed. For example, the assessor very likely would seek an employee's views on customer feedback or supplier relations. Interviews with management and employees are face-to-face and last on average 40 minutes; those with suppliers or customers usually are conducted over the telephone for about 15-20 minutes.

Awarding grades

Having weighed all the evidence, the assessor awards grades for each practice:

- Fail: there is no policy/system to implement the practice or it has largely broken down;

- Minor non-compliance: there is a policy/system but it does not always work in practice;

- Observation: there is a policy/system that functions but possible improvements can be identified;

- Merit: the policy/system works well;

- Commendation: the policy or system is an example of best practice.

GoodCorporation converts the grades into metrics that graphically capture the quality of performance in each practice and overall in the six stakeholder groups. The organisation's data can be benchmarked against aggregated data to enable real-world comparison. Grades in a metrical format for the practices in each stakeholder group are shown in Figure 34.1.

Suppliers and subcontractors

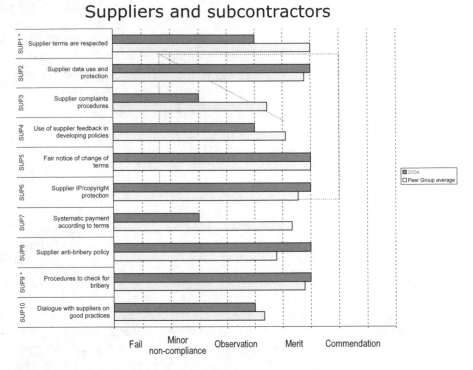

Figure 34.1. GoodCorporation assessment metrics

34.3   Company experience with GoodCorporation

ARM designs microprocessing technology used in advanced digital products. Over the past few years, the company has grown from around 600 employees to an international company with more than 1200 employees in over 20 locations worldwide. In 2004 it acquired Silicon Valley-based Artisan whose library products complement its own hi-tech IP business.

Reason for using GoodCorporation: When ARM first became involved with GoodCorporation in 2001, as Bill Parsons, Vice President for Human Resources recalls, 'We didn't have any policies. We were an unbureaucratic company, behaving ethically but with no evidence.' When it became a founding member of GoodCorporation in 2001, ARM started to use its annual GoodCorporation assessment to benchmark improvement and to identify emerging issues. It also produced its first Corporate Responsibility report based in part on its assessment.

Investor relations: ARM's engagement with Corporate Responsibility is founded on a belief that 'good business is good for business.' In line with the GoodCorporation Standard, ARM treats investor relations as part of its commitment to corporate responsibility. A FTSE 250 company, it also trades on the Nasdaq in the United States; evidence from the GoodCorporation assessment underpins some of ARM's non-financial submissions to the SEC as required by the Sarbanes-Oxley Act. It also uses the summary of grades from the assessment in its Operating and Financial Review.

Environment: Like many high tech or service-oriented companies, ARM considered itself to have relatively low environmental impacts. However, following its first GoodCorporation assessment which highlighted the absence of environmental policies, it drew up a detailed environmental footprint. This became the basis for subsequent innovations in building design, energy use, travel, paper use and waste management over the past few years.

Human Resources: For a number of years ARM has been rated as one of the best companies to work for in the UK. ARM's approach to HR has had to evolve from an informal 'around the coffee machine' style to a more structured approach in order to adapt to global expansion and deal with a rapidly changing marketplace. The GoodCorporation assessment helped to highlight specific HR issues. In the first assessment, GoodCorporation pointed out the absence of any consultation procedures. Bill Parsons recalls his reaction:

"At first we wondered why we needed a consultation process. However, the company has grown since then and has gone through some tough times. We've actually found that having an employee forum over the past couple of years now has been very beneficial."

The company receives consistently high scores for employee relations in its annual evaluation. Its innovative approach to HR goes beyond its own needs. For example, it set up the Learning Collaboration and Skills exchange in Cambridge to pool training resources of local companies, allowing all companies in the area to benefit from economies of scale and a broader offering of schemes.

GoodCorporation vs. other CSR frameworks

Many frameworks have evolved to meet the specific concerns of stakeholders or sector demands especially in the area of environmental impacts and working conditions.

The GoodCorporation Standard does not attempt to go into the same depth as some other standards that have already become the established 'marque' for a specific business practice: EMAS for environmental systems management or Rainforest Alliance to certify sustainable development in agriculture and forestry.

Although the Standard requires that companies have environmental policies and actually reduce environmental impacts over time, it does not set the criteria for achieving environmental goals. For some organisations, this may be a drawback but for others such as ARM, cited in the case study above, the observation that a service company needs to consider its impacts is enough to launch a complete environmental programme. The Standard complements sector specific frameworks because of its broad scope, which allows a company to manage corporate responsibility on all fronts and compare performance across stakeholder groups, business units and regions.

34.4   Preparing for assessment: Dos and don'ts

Independent assessment requires a shift in the way some organisations approach corporate responsibility: managers have to turn their focus away from internal processes and onto stakeholder feedback. This involves a willingness to see the organisation from the outside in, not inside out. So one of the very first 'dos' is to make clear the difference between external assessment and CSR report assurance. The assessment does not 'verify' the data and report already produced by the organisation to tell its CSR story. Instead it provides a completely independent check, a kind of 'corporate physical' by an external assessor. Assessment holds a mirror up to an organisation showing how stakeholders actually perceive the fairness and effectiveness of the way a company does business. So to use the GoodCorporation framework demands recognition by the board that if it really wants to understand how it affects its stakeholders, then it has to delegate to an external assessor the job of holding up that mirror.

Case study

> Ladbrokes, founded in 1886, is the largest cash betting company in the world. It has 2000 betting shops employing over 12,500 people in the UK and Ireland. It has operations worldwide and offers online betting and gaming in 13 languages.
>
> **Reason for using GoodCorporation:** Ladbrokes is a founder member of GoodCorporation and uses the GoodCorporation Standard and assessment as an external check on how its practices are working on the ground. As Ros Barker, HR director puts it: 'at the end of the day no matter how hard you try to self-audit, you need that external viewpoint.'

It is important to recognise the limitations of 'quantified data' in the realm of corporate responsibility. Quantified data can be helpful in some areas, like measuring environmental inputs and outputs. But the only way of evaluating corporate responsibility impacts is by talking to the stakeholders affected and measuring their perceptions. Management should see the advantage of adopting a methodology based on a highly focused and systematic set of interviews that converts 'soft issues' into numerical values for benchmarking performance.

Finally the benchmarking data created by GoodCorporation is the basis for improvement over time and comparing performance within the organisation or against other organisations assessed by GoodCorporation. The benchmarks provide a clear measurement system. However, they do not translate directly into monetary values.

34.5 Conclusion

The GoodCorporation Standard serves as a driver to embed best practice into core activities. Re-assessment adds value over time as the organisation improves on its benchmarks and highlights new issues that need to be addressed. In commenting on each practice, the assessor highlights actions that could improve a specific practice. The assessment is not just another audit but an opportunity to identify and resolve issues of importance to people engaged in the business. Grading performance provides benchmark data for 'soft' issues where measurement is otherwise difficult.

By systematically capturing performance and stakeholder feedback, the assessment provides benefits for the entire organisation. Certification against the Standard generates performance data about specific practices that a company can use in external and internal reporting. Some companies use the evidence to comply with the UK Operating and Financial Review regulations – and other implementations of the EU's company modernisation directives as well as some of the reporting requirements of the Sarbanes-Oxley Act. The results are confidential, and management maintains full control over how to use or communicate the data.

GoodCorporation only conducts assessments against the Standard. Between assessments it does not offer consulting services; it does not write assurance statements about the client's own reports nor does it audit the client's data or internal systems. In this way, it avoids conflicts of interest and preserves the genuine independence of its methodology. Since its launch, GoodCorporation has conducted over 150 verifications in 30 countries worldwide for organisations including large listed companies, small private firms, not for profit and public sector institutions.

Websites

www.goodcorporation.com
www.ibe.org.uk
www.ethicalperformance.com

35 Promoting Human Rights in the Supply Chain

Rachelle Jackson

Key words: Human rights, supply chain, labor issues, standards, compliance.

35.1 Introduction

The Global Compact and UN Norms for Transnational Corporations, among other such initiatives, render the management of labour practices in the supply chain an important and highly relevant case study. By drawing on examples from successful supply chain management practices implemented by corporations today, an effective model can be derived. This model is a road map for communication and interaction with supply chain partners. By following the map, you will have a clear indication of how to model a successful labour standards programme and how to move from model to action.

The model, as illustrated in the flow chart, includes (a) the dissemination of standards by means of contractual obligations through the supply chain, (b) assessment of risk and the subsequent prioritisation of resources, (c) the use of education to promote long term goals and achievements, (d) the use of monitoring mechanisms to assess progress and stimulate continued improvement, supplemented by (e) long-term interactions with local partners or industry initiatives.

35.2 The essence of the model

The first step in developing a supply chain labour standards programme is to define what labour standards, or code of conduct, your company will endorse for their supply chain partners, i.e. the vendors, agents, and factories that help manufacture and deliver your product to you. This code of conduct standard is conventionally linked to sourcing contracts or similar terms of business engagement. This allows the standard to be incorporated directly into purchasing practices as well as other vendor, agent, or supplier requirements.

Once the code standard has been determined and communicated, it is important to educate all interested parties on this new programme, the standards being espoused, and the expectations you have of each party, including corporate senior management, buying and quality staff, in-house compliance teams, vendors, suppliers, workers, and other relevant stakeholders. A risk assessment exercise can help prioritise interactions in your supply chain, such as education and monitoring. Those regions or products presenting the highest risk to your brand or programme may take priority in the implementation of the labour standards programme.

Finally, central to any supply chain labour standards programme knows first hand the conditions that exist in the supplier facilities. Monitoring the labour practices of your supplier partners allows you to identify if they are meeting their country labour standards, any international standards endorsed by your programme, and where there are opportunities for improvement, if any. This knowledge will allow you to, in turn, determine if specially focused engagements are needed, what long-term interactions should be considered, and the kinds of local partners or stakeholders that may be instrumental in the labour standards programme.

Application of this model ensures the up-front commitment of your supply chain partners to promoting human rights through ensuring good labour practices. It focuses your resources on your highest risk regions or products. When your supply chain partners need support to meet the agreed on standards, this model focuses improvement activities on specific areas of weakness, facilitated through education and training. In addition, this model looks to long-term local solutions by incorporating activities with local stakeholders, which help to ensure more sustainable improvements over time.

35.3   Experiences with this model in practice

Elaboration of standards

Corporations generally elaborate their commitment to international standards of human dignity and ethical trading through the exposition of a 'supplier code of conduct,' or statement of minimum expected practices regarding labour conditions. At a minimum, such codes request supply chain partners to uphold the national laws of their respective countries. Frequently, they go further and require supplier partners to also uphold international standards. These can be defined as the labour standards contained within International Labour Organisation (ILO) conventions, as well as internationally recognised documents such as the Universal Declaration of Human Rights. Corporations that have constructed such standards for their supply chains include global retailers such as Wal-mart, the Walt Disney Company, Mattel, Nike, Debenhams, and Marks & Spencer. These companies make their supplier codes of conduct available publicly on their websites.

Some companies may prefer to adopt an existing supplier code, rather than draft their own. With literally hundreds of supplier codes in existence today, it may be seen as less burdensome to the suppliers if a pre-existing standard is adopted. Such standards would include those of certification programmes, such as Social Accountability 8000, or industry association standards, such as those adopted by toy (International Council of Toy Industries), apparel (Worldwide Responsible Apparel Production, Fair Labour Association), and regional associations (Ethical Trading Initiative, Business Social Compliance Initiative).

Some companies and non-governmental organisations advocate that participation of your stakeholders, such as the suppliers and the workers they employ, is important when drafting the code. Yet the logistics of such an endeavour can be mind-boggling when the supply chain is expansive. For this reason, some companies choose to endorse the labour standards of the ILO; as a tripartite body including government, enterprise, and worker representation, the ILO labour standards are already the product of a multi-stakeholder effort.

Whether a private company code or an industry endorsed code, most supplier codes of conduct contain provisions on child labour, forced labour, freedom of association, discrimination, harassment and abuse, wages and benefits, working hours, and safety, among other things. The minimum standard set by your code will provide the philosophical guidance for your supply chain labour standards programme, setting important parameters within which your partners should operate.

Dissemination of standards

A signature page often accompanies the code of conduct, where supplier partners annually commit in writing to uphold their code as a condition of continuing the business relationship with the buyer or retailer. This provides important leverage when engaging with suppliers who are reticent to comply with the code.

Another important means of dissemination is the visible posting and communication of the code within the supplier operations. Nike has incorporated a requirement within their code of conduct asking each supplier to post a copy of the code standard in the language of the employees within the employee work areas. In addition, Nike requires that the supplier conduct training with their employees to advise employees of their rights under the code as well as under the local laws.

Use of education to promote long term goals

When striving to educate the programme stakeholders, an interactive workshop is the best format, allowing participants to ask questions, express any concerns, and give feedback related to the initial programme goals, structure, and methodology.

In addition to general stakeholder training, many companies choose to prepare and disseminate a vendor or supplier manual, containing information introducing and preparing suppliers for their role in the compliance programme.

Such manuals are important tools that allow your supply chain partners to review and understand the terms and standards of the programme. Adidas-
Salomon is one company that has prepared a range of reference manuals to
guide their supplier partners and ensure adequate comprehension of their
standards. Guidelines may include a copy of the supplier code of conduct
standards, an outline of the verification process, and examples of acceptable
and unacceptable labour practices.

Face to face training with your supplier partners is another effective way to
communicate the standards and practices of your new or changing programme.
Reebok conducts workshops with their supplier facilities to review their programme standards, provide examples of best practices, and assist factories in
developing their own internal compliance teams. Many large retail companies
may choose to train their vendors and ask the vendor to be responsible for communicating the programme tenets and standards to their contracted suppliers.

While introductory trainings often cover the entire compliance programme, it is
also valuable to utilise educational initiatives to target challenging areas uncovered during the monitoring process. Looking again to Reebok as an example, in
addition to their monitoring efforts, they may set up pilot programmes in specific
countries targeting areas of concern identified through monitoring. Through one
such pilot project, Reebok visited all footwear factories to monitor freedom of
association. Based on their findings, they designed specific correction actions to
address the issue regionally, rather than by factory. In Indonesia and Thailand,
Reebok invited NGOs to conduct training on union/welfare committees for workers in China, Reebok arranged for workers and factory managers to be trained
on the worker representative committees, provided for under the China Trade
Union Law. Subsequently, elections were held at two Chinese supplier facilities to
elect workers to the committees. This kind of targeted education can help achieve
improvements in areas of difficulty within the supply chain.

Assessment of risk

Supplier questionnaires are normally used to gather data on the size and location of supplier facilities. For example, a vendor compliance packet, containing
a contractual agreement to comply with the code standards as well as a full
introduction to the programme, may also contain forms to be completed by the
supplier disclosing the location of all facility locations. The supplier or vendor
should complete such forms, including the address of each facility, the contact
information at each facility, the type of product being produced, and even what
percent of your brand production, if any, is conducted at the facility. These
forms may be completed and submitted electronically, by fax, or by mail, depending on the level of technology available to your supply chain partners.
Companies like Wal-mart use on-line supplier questionnaires for normal busi-

ness transactions. These can be an effective means to gather the locations of the facilities used by your supplier partners.

Once you have gathered this supply chain data, you can use it to prioritise your interactions. For example, if you have a supply chain of 500 factories, you may only have the fiscal budget to carry out interactions with a portion of those factories during the first year of the programme. Let's assume that your budget allows you to engage 50 factories the first year, including educational interactions, monitoring, and supplementary interactions. In order to identify which 50 factories should be engaged during year one, you may choose to assess the apparent risk of the labour standards conditions based on several variables in your supply chain data. These may include, but are not limited to, the country where the facility is located, the product that is being manufactured, the percent of your brand label that is present in the facility, and the presence of other reputable brands in the facility.

By cross-referencing the data provided by your suppliers with the risk values you have chosen to consider, you will be able to make an informed selection of the 50 priority suppliers for your year one engagements.

Monitoring mechanisms

Monitoring may be conducted by trained internal staff, third party monitoring firms, non-governmental organisations, in conjunction with industry associations, and/or by other stakeholder groups. Many companies use diversified combinations of these, such as internal staff and third-party monitors to conduct the monitoring process and NGOs and industry associations to carry out long-term engagements or specially focused activities.

The Fair Labour Association (FLA) in the United States and the Ethical Trading Initiative (ETI) in the United Kingdom both provide examples of diversified monitoring. Each of these industry organisations brings together various companies to address supply chain labour standards. While member companies in the FLA or ETI may conduct their own monitoring activities, in addition they will participate in monitoring through the associations, in special pilot projects organised by the associations, and benefit from learning together with other member companies how best to improve labour standards in their supply chains.

Reebok presents an example of diversified monitoring. Reebok is a member of the FLA, has trained internal staff to monitor supplier facilities, and also hires external third party monitors to conduct supplementary monitoring of specific facilities. In addition, they partner with an NGO in Central America called COVERCO, which engages with one supplier facility over a period of four months to effect long-term change one-on-one. By utilising a diversified monitoring approach, Reebok is able to assess actual conditions on the ground across a large range of suppliers, place additional emphasis on specific suppliers, and even engage in long-term corrective action efforts one-on-one with supplier facilities.

Supplementary interactions

While diversified monitoring provides many opportunities for fostering targeted improvements in labour standards, additional stakeholder engagement may help propel sustainable change in different ways.

The GAP uses its membership in the ETI, Social Accountability International (SAI), and the United Nations Global Compact (UNGP) to help it expand its supplementary interactions with its supply chain. For example, ETI membership allows them to participate in industry pilot projects designed to identify effective ways of improving labour standards. Through one such project, the ETI focused on the issues and conditions surrounding home workers in the supply chain. As a notoriously exploited labour pool, the project examined different approaches to improving the labour conditions of home workers, which are frequently not protected by local labour laws.

35.4 Dos and don'ts

When implementing this model, it's important to find the right balance of participation for each of your stakeholders. This will ensure the final programme model has credibility. From the beginning, prepare to be transparent on your efforts related to supply chain labour standards and determine how you can report progress regularly to your stakeholders. Stakeholder consultations will provide important feedback at various stages throughout the development and life of your programme.

Revisit your programme goals and standards regularly to ensure they are realistic and drive you and your supply chain to constant improvement over time. If you find the bar is low compared to other companies in the industry, don't hesitate to recommit yourself to a higher standard. Don't reinvent the wheel, either. Learn from what has worked for other companies that have been managing supply chain labour standards programmes for years.

35.5 Wrapping up

In applying this labour standards model, it's important to set realistic goals. When considering what the programme should achieve initially, it's imperative to recognise that the labour conditions you will encounter are likely much worse than what you imagine. Set realistic goals with your supplier partners, such as achieving legal compliance as the first step, then progressing over time to preferred practices.

This model will work best in an environment independent from the pressures of sourcing and quality. Where possible, your company should ensure the compliance staff or division are separate from the buying and quality staff when it comes to decision making, but that they collaborate closely when it comes to supplier selection.

Finally, strong executive support is key to ensuring the credibility of your programme, ability to be transparent, and the assurance of regular financial support for continued efforts. If your senior executives are not on board, be prepared to make the business case for compliance. There are many examples out there to draw from.

References

Fair Labour Association (2004). *Year Two Annual Public Report*.
    www.fairlabor.org/2004report

Gap Inc. (2003). *Social Responsibility Report*.
    http://www.gapinc.com/social_resp/social_resp.htm

Reebok International Ltd., 2003. *Our Commitment to Human Rights*.
    http://www.reebok.com/x/us/humanRights/text-only/business/

Websites

www.bsci-eu.org
www.ethicaltrading.org

Organising the Business Proposition

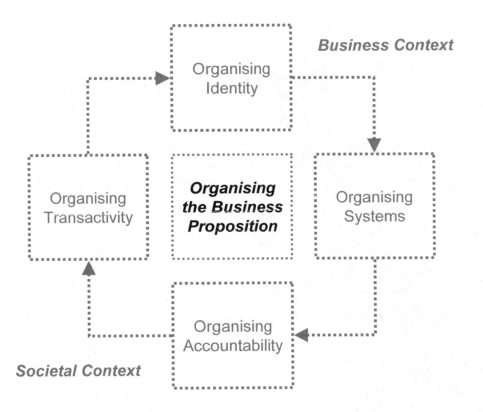

36 Assessing the Value Chain Context

Duane Windsor

Key words: Value chain, responsibility, stakeholders, drivers, profit pools.

36.1 Introduction

Corporate social responsibility (CSR) is a popular 'umbrella' label for a wide range of environmental and social issues and topics. CSR is indisputably important but lacking in specificity for business decisions. The July 2002 European Commission communication concerning 'Corporate Social Responsibility: A business contribution to Sustainable Development' calls for voluntary integration of 'social and environmental concerns in their business operations and in their interaction with their stakeholders' and promotes a voluntary European Union multi-stakeholder forum for discussing CSR choices.

Practitioners must find specific ways to cope with broader roles and responsibilities in contemporary society. The 'triple bottom line' typology calls simply for an undefined balancing among sustainability ('planet'), stakeholders ('people') and profit ('business'). CSR must be linked to the business's specific value proposition in concrete ways. The framework for defining the specific details of the value proposition and discovering linkages to sustainability, society and stakeholders is the value chain model, illustrated in Figure 36.1 of this chapter. Detailed understanding of the company's value chain—meaning how the value proposition is actually designed and implemented—is vital to business integration of social and environmental concerns and interaction with stakeholders.

Value chain analysis, widely accepted for analysis of business competitive strategy, can be used readily at business, stakeholder, industry, societal, and ecological levels. This chapter links the editors' generic CSR management model to the value chain of a business and its industry embedded within ecological, societal and stakeholder contexts. The approach is to specify the business's value proposition and to map the external linkages—industry, ecological, societal and stakeholder—to that particular value proposition.

The value chain model in Figure 36.1 demonstrates how to take the business proposition of the generic CSR management model and define that proposition concretely in relation to business and societal contexts. The generic CSR management model depicts identity, transactivity, systems, and accountability in general relationship to the business proposition and contexts. The value chain model organises the business proposition in relationship to the internal organising systems of the organisation on the one hand and in relationship to the various stakeholders of the organisation of the other hand. There is no one-to-one correspondence of stakeholders to dimensions of the generic CSR management model. Customers are addressed in identity (branding and image), systems (external communication), and transactivity (involvement). Investors are addressed in identity (drivers), systems (external communication), and transparency (auditing and reporting).

The value chain model, including revenue and cost drivers and profit pools, analyses the detailed structure of the value proposition of a business or its industry. The value chain concept originated as an extension to the focal business of industry structure theory. At the industry level, the chain concerns the inherent profitability attractiveness of an industry and the distribution of profit pools (i.e. high or low profit margins) across the interacting elements of the industry. At the business level, the chain involves where to draw boundaries of the business relative to its external environment and how to generate profit margin through cost reductions and/or price increases and/or innovations. The value chain concept has been instrumental in shifting businesses from an internal product focus to analysis of value creation along the supply and demand chains of the industry, and the value chain model provided here facilitates transition from a purely profit focus to analysis of ecological, societal and stakeholder linkages.[1]

36.2   A generic model for value chain analysis in multiple contexts

A value chain depicts a set of value adding activities (or processes). Value chain analysis has been widely used over the past two decades. What has been missing in this experience is direct mapping to ecological, societal and stakeholder environments. The value chain approach permits positioning of sustainable competitive advantage simultaneously in market and non-market contexts.

---

[1]   Michael E. Porter pioneered use of the value chain approach in Competitive Advantage (1985, 1998). Porter conceptualised an activity-based theory of the firm (1998, p. xv) as the basis of sustainable competitive advantage. A business performs some set of discrete activities (or processes). Activities (e.g., processing orders) are narrower than functions (e.g., production or marketing). Activities are 'the basic units of competitive advantage' for generating costs for the business and creating value for the buyers (1998, p. xv). The value chain concept is 'a general framework for thinking strategically about' the activities of a business. This value chain concept is an extension to the business level of the industry structure model published in Porter's Competitive Strategy (1980, 1998).

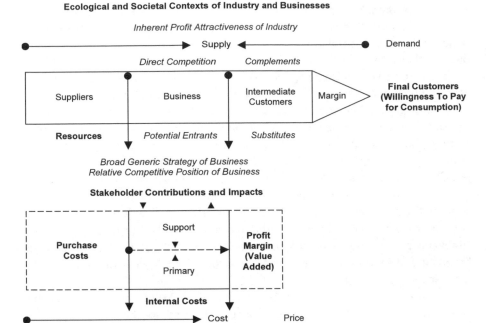

Figure 36.1. Value chain of a business and its industry within ecological, societal and stakeholder contexts

'Value' is broader than the profit margin addressed within the narrow context of a chain of business value adding activities. Interaction with stakeholders can be depicted as a value network generating a much more broadly defined 'organisational wealth' comprising the welfares of all the stakeholders of the business.

Figure 36.1 can be read left to right or top to bottom. Left to right, the figure depicts at industry and business levels flow of resources and products, services through the supply chain and demand chain to final customers. This flow is a set of value creating activities. The extension of value chain analysis to ecological and societal contexts works top to bottom. The figure organises top to bottom as follows:

- Ecological and societal contexts within which the industry is embedded;
- Inherent profit attractiveness of the industry supply and demand chains in relationship to the broad generic strategy and relative competitive position of the focal business (outputs and 'custom');
- Relationship of industry and business value chains to stakeholder contributions and impacts;
- value chain of the focal business as operational details of its particular positioning within the industry value chain.

The inherent profit attractiveness of an industry is the relationship between customers' willingness to pay and sellers' costs of production and distribution. In the upper part of the associated figure, the value chain as activity structure of an industry is shown as a linear relationship among suppliers, businesses, intermediate customers, and final customers. This generic model includes resources, production, distribution, and consumption as stages of economic activity.

As illustrated in the associated figure, the relative competitive position of any business is affected by direct competition and indirect competition. Direct competition comprises the immediate rivals of the business. Indirect competition comprises both potential rivals that might enter the market and substitute goods – services competing to attract the business's customers. Profit pools (i.e. size of margin) may vary along the value chain of an industry. Porter characterised industry structure as a relationship of five forces bearing on costs and margins of a focal business: immediate rivals, bargaining power of suppliers, bargaining power of customers, threat of potential entrants, and threat of substitutes. Complements, one form of spill-overs among companies, encourage company sales.

The lower part of the figure breaks out the business value chain of a particular company in accordance with Porter's conception of competitive advantage. The supply chain of a business is its set of suppliers from which the business purchases. It transforms those resources (or inputs) into goods and services (or outputs) for sell to customers. The business's value chain is its combination of what Porter characterised as primary value adding activities and support activities. A business may pursue a competitive strategy of differentiation (i.e. higher price resulting from some uniqueness perceived by the customer) or of cost leadership (i.e. lower cost resulting from some efficiency). The figure illustrates that price commanded by a business may be less than customers' willingness to pay.

Porter identified four key support activities

- Firm infrastructure includes all planning and control activities of the business such as accounting, finance, management information and strategic planning;

- Human resource management includes all aspects of employee recruitment, training and compensation;

- Technology development is innovation in aspects of technology (e.g., production, Internet marketing, e-commerce, and so forth) aimed at reducing costs and improving quality. Technology is often closely related to differentiation;

- Procurement is the purchasing of resources (e.g., goods, services and materials) coming from outside the business. The general goal is to obtain highest possible quality at lowest possible cost.

Porter identified five primary value creation activities.

- Inbound logistics concerns receipt and storage of resources (e.g., goods and materials) from suppliers;

- Operations concern in-house manufacture or assembly of goods and/or services by the business through transformation of purchased resources;

- Outbound logistics concerns distribution of goods and/or services further along the value chain to intermediate customers (e.g., wholesalers or retailers) or directly to final customers;

- Marketing and sales concern design and implementation of promotion efforts;

- Service includes installation, post-sales service and customer complaints, among other aspects of direct interaction with customers.

Profit margin or value added is the difference between value (i.e. cost) of inputs and value (i.e. price) of outputs obtained from those resources. Porter identifies various drivers of cost, differentiation and value. Cost of the business accumulates through purchasing, operations, logistics (inbound and outbound), marketing and sales, and service. To this operating cost must be added the cost due to support or overhead activities.

36.3   Experience with this model: Criticisms and alternatives

Value chain analysis has been used for some 20 years and connects directly to practical strategy options. A company must choose between differentiation and cost strategies at the most fundamental level. A company may engage in horizontal integration (i.e. monopolisation), vertical integration (forward by suppliers to capture margin or backward by customers to reduce cost) or outsourcing, multi-business combination, globalisation, and innovation approaches. The margin of a business can be appropriated by various stakeholders or various forms of competition and integration. The extension provided here provides linkages to ecological, societal and stakeholder contexts of the business's value proposition. Three examples illustrate how and when to use the value chain model.

The value chain concept is a workable model for assessing the ecological sustainability of products and/or processes. For example, the Novatlantis group has studied the value chain of sustainable mobility through pilot and demonstration projects in the region of Basel, Switzerland.[2] The mobility value chain

---

[2] 'Novatlantis Studies the 'Value Chain' of More Sustainable Car Use,' Environment, vol. 47, no. 3, April 2005, p. 30.

includes resources, fuel production, automobile production, and end-users. In this application, the goal is to make mobility more ecologically friendly and sustainable.

Value analysis has broad applicability to corporate social responsibility. Horizontal and vertical integration imply possibilities for monopolisation or cartelisation (by networks of businesses) and thus antitrust policy issues. Intel, Microsoft and the proposed General Electric – Honeywell merger have been the subjects of recent European antitrust actions. The basis for such actions is impact on competitors and customers. The companies should have more carefully analysed their stakeholder environments.

A business may have total product responsibility for the impacts of its products on customers and employees, as well as on nature. A business may have total supply chain responsibility for all activities feeding into its position in the industry value chain. Nike was the subject of a U.S. lawsuit, settled out of court, alleging that the company had made public misrepresentations about abuses by its contract suppliers. Unocal was the subject of a U.S. lawsuit under the Alien Tort Claims Act (ATCA) of 1789, also settled out of court, alleging liability for misconduct of the military regime in Myanmar (Burma) during Unocal's participation in a pipeline project in that country. U.S. lawsuits have attempted to bring environmental destruction by oil companies within the ambit of the ATCA.

One key criticism argues that the value chain approach implies a linear relationship between cost drivers and value drivers. Activities are linked together by complex interdependencies and overlaps (Holweg and Pil, 2004, p. 18). Holweg and Pil (2004) prefer the broader notion of a 'value grid.' Various alternatives to the value chain have been proposed, including grid, network, shop and web. What is important in value analysis is identification of the basic logic of the activities of a business or other organisation (Holweg and Pil, 2004, p. 127). As Figure 36.1 suggests, support and primary activities interact in much more complicated fashion than implied by a simple linear structure.

36.4   Some dos and don'ts

Porter explicitly held constant the role of government and by extension other environmental considerations such as stakeholders and nature as influences on industry structure and competitive strategy in order to focus on the five forces. Figure 36.1 positions the industry and business value chains within non-market ecological, societal and stakeholder contexts. One can apply traditional PEST (political, economic, social, technological factors) or STEEP (socio-cultural, technological, ecological, economic, political forces) approaches directly to the expanded value chain model. Alternatives to the value chain have been proposed that recognise non-linear complexity of business processes and relationships (e.g., grid, network, shop and web). The overarching notion is that of value configuration analysis (Stabell and Fjeldstad, 1998), for which the value chain is still the benchmark notion. If the alternative conceptions are different configurations for value creation, then businesses have a broader set of strategic options from which to choose. It is important not to neglect the possibilities of non-linear relationships in business and with the macro-environment of the business, while at the same time not neglecting the key strategic and operational insights yielded by the linear value chain model. The definition of stakeholder arguably excludes competitors, while the value network conception may include competitors.

36.5 Wrapping up: Advice for application

Norman Augustine, CEO of Martin Marietta and then of the merged Lockheed Martin (aerospace, defence contractors), views the 'toughest decisions' in business as balancing conflicts among the multiple commitments of the organisation to key stakeholders such as customers, employees, investors and communities (Paine, 1992). Augustine's experience is that fairness to multiple stakeholders requires constant practitioner work. A 'stakeholder' is anyone who makes a positive contribution to the business or who is impacted by the business. Contribution or impact occurs only through the business's value chain of value creating activities, from the suppliers to the customers of the business. A business must translate its corporate social responsibilities directly into stakeholder relationships, including governments and the general public. If not strictly speaking a stakeholder, nature is important to various stakeholders and an overriding force affecting business sustainability.

References

Augustine, N.R. (1997). Reshaping an Industry: Lockheed Martin's Survival Story. *Harvard Business Review* 75(3): pp. 83-94.

Freeman, E. and J. Liedtka (1997). Stakeholder Capitalism and the Value Chain. *European Management Journal* 15(3): pp. 286-296.

Holweg, M. and F.K. Pil (2004). *The Second Century: Reconnecting Customer and Value Chain Through Build-to-Order – Moving Beyond Mass and Lean Production in the Auto Industry*. Cambridge: MIT Press.

Paine, L.S. (1992). Martin Marietta Managing Corporate Ethics (A). Harvard Business School case 9-393-016, p. 1.

Stabell, C.B. and O.D. Fjeldstad (1998). Configuring Value for Competitive Advantage: On Chains, Shops, and Networks. *Strategic Management Journal* 19(5): pp. 413-437.

Websites

www.isc.hbs.edu
www.marketingteacher.com/Lessons/lesson_value_chain.htm
www.quickmba.com/strategy/value-chain

37 Pursuing Sustainability Through Enduring Value Creation

Peter Newman, Erik Stanton-Hicks, and Brendan Hammond

Key words: Sustainability, enduring value, mining, regionalism, partnerships.

37.1 Introduction

Sustainability as a business decision-making model gives extra dimensions to CSR by taking an integrated approach to all business activities, including those previously considered regulatory requirements or charity. Its emphasis on the long-term legacy that a company leaves requires a fundamental rethink on how corporations can be socially responsible and gain competitive advantage, stable profits and shareholder value. The Minerals Council of Australia calls this perspective on sustainability 'Enduring Value' (MCA, 2004). It requires a company to think of all of its activities in terms of their value to the region where it operates. The following model outlines one way to implement an enduring value approach to sustainability and then applies it to the Argyle Diamonds story.

37.2 The essence of the model

The model is illustrated in Figure 37.1. Essentially, if a company can prove that it contributes net-positive and 'Enduring Regional Value' in each of 'Five Values' then it is a sustainable operation with all aspects of corporate social responsibility being fulfilled.

The Enduring Regional Value model reconfigures the Sigma Project's 'Five Capitals' model to focus on value because it encourages rigorous investigation into the real worth that society places on various social, environmental and economic elements surrounding a project (Forum for the Future, 2004). The Five Values of this model enhance the normal triple-bottom-line by clearly showing what normal business practices produce: financial value created through profits and public revenues, economic value through the flow-on to household income and associated business revenue, and the technological value in the buildings, infrastructure and intellectual property contributed by the firm. However, the remaining two values are often seen as the 'intangibles' of a

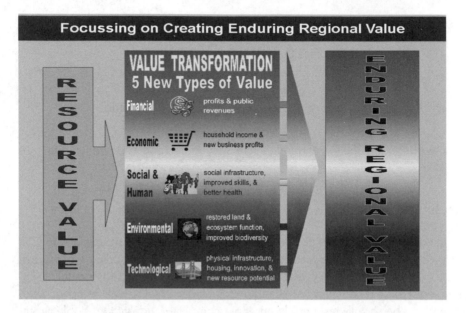

Figure 37.1. Enduring Regional Value model

business (Fiksel, 2004). By digging a little deeper, the value contribution of these elements to the company and Enduring Regional Value becomes clear. Social and human value is the legacy of skills, health and social improvements in the community that have been generated from and by the firm. The environmental value is what the firm has contributed to improving ecosystem function and restoring land in a region. Enduring Value is then measured in terms of the regional Five Value 'stocks' (akin to assets) created by the company's Five Value 'flows' (akin to cash-flow) (Forum for the Future, 2004). The importance of the model is how the Five Values can help a firm discern its real value to society. The goal is for a firm's CSR and other activities to combine to create 'net enduring value' in each of the Five Values. The firm can then show its market value and its other values at the same time in the same way. Thus, CSR becomes internalised into good business.

In order for a firm to demonstrate that it is providing 'enduring value' in these five areas, the model prescribes two processes:

1. A regional focus through some kind of Regional Sustainability Partnership;

2. the use of value indicators for a Regional Sustainability Audit.

Figure 37.2. Regional Sustainability Partnership Model

Regional Sustainability Partnerships

Value cannot be created in a vacuum. People determine values. A firm needs to establish partnerships with communities near where it works and creates value. These communities' priorities and preferences will determine where the company should focus its efforts and what value to place upon the results. The set of possible things a business can add value to while simultaneously enhancing its own business values also needs to be understood. This focus is crucial for identifying possible in-perpetuity assets. Companies can expect that it will take several iterations within the regional partnership to get a marriage of what it can do with what the region wants it to do. The scale of this needs to be carefully considered; however, regionalism is increasingly favoured around the world. Regions are large enough to encourage a systems view of impacts on society, the environment and the economy, and small enough not to lose sight of local issues. The United Nations, Canada, the European Union, the World Business Council for Sustainable Development, and Western Australia all take a regional approach to much of their work. For the same reasons, regions are also a good starting point for companies when designing their CSR strategies.

Figure 37.2 sets out the basic elements of a Regional Sustainability Partnership (RSP) and how this approach first determines and then multiplies value in a region. A clear agreement between members is a good basis for an RSP. The goal is to use the understanding created through the process of determining the Five Values, to multiply the outcomes of regional activities by identifying synergies and opportunities that add Enduring Regional Value for the stakeholder groups involved.

Regional Sustainability Audits

Asserting that a firm has created Enduring Regional Value can be supported through stories (such as the one which follows about Argyle Diamonds), but will be more powerful if it can also be quantified. A range of Five Value indicators determined by the RSP, raise the credibility of a company's CSR performance reporting in the eyes of all stakeholders. Shareholders, managers, and board members can better understand the value created through their business and CSR strategies. Employees, community members, customers and governments can gauge the real worth of their relationships with a business. Sustainability professionals and business analysts can interpret the data, finding new ways to add value that makes the company more sustainable and competitive, while doing the same for its host region.

37.3 Experiences with the model in practice

Argyle Diamonds brought in a new management team in 1998 to review the impending closure of the mine. Seven years later the mine is still running and the financial value increased from $200 million to $2 billion. During this period, sustainability has gone from a way of describing the survival of the company to becoming its primary strategic directive. Management continues to work at embedding sustainability into its planning and operations, because it recognises its business potential.

The catalyst that revealed the advantage of a sustainability approach to CSR was Argyle's success with training and hiring indigenous employees. This programme has seen the indigenous percentage of the workforce grow from less than 1 % to approximately 25 % since the late 1990s. Argyle's publicly stated goal is now 40 % indigenous and 80 % local employment by 2010. This strategy recently culminated in the signing of a partnership agreement in June 2005 between Argyle, the local indigenous communities, and the state government. Per the agreement, clear commitments now exist on indigenous concerns such as employment priority, engagement on all mine decisions, inheriting the pastoral lease, and funding. In return, the mine can now extend operations underground.

The sustainability implications are profound. As a CSR programme it delivers badly needed jobs and skills to those most in need in the Kimberley, while also offering increased opportunities for non-indigenous residents. As a business strategy, it reduces fly-in/fly-out costs dramatically, improves regional relations and acts as a catalyst for further regional business opportunities as regional economic capacity grows. It has also buffered Argyle somewhat against potentially extremely high turnover in an overheated Western Australian labour market.

Argyle's portfolio includes many CSR activities, such as:

- Employing indigenous people to assist with re-vegetation of mined areas;
- Training programmes that build skills, which increase local and particularly indigenous employment;
- Collaborating with local business to increase regional procurement;
- Creating a flexible employment schedule that can adjust to indigenous requirements for their law practices;
- Teaching indigenous children to participate in the wider economy, while maintaining their unique culture.

Each of these activities has been undertaken within a sustainability mandate. This means that each CSR activity has obvious business benefits for the economic bottom line. Argyle has made a decision to move away from investing in charity where there are no sustainability implications for the business. In doing this, it has also come to see that its sustainability is bound up in a much wider regional sustainability. Argyle is engaged in sustainable development activities across the Kimberley region, both to enhance its potential as a workforce and to leave a legacy of in-perpetuity assets. However, its strategy so far has been limited to numerous partnerships with stakeholders on individual projects. By 2004, it became clear that a consolidated internal and external framework had become crucial to further progress. This approach has been summarised here by the Enduring Value model. The goal was twofold:

1. Create a clear rationale for CSR activities that made sense externally and internally by reporting sustainability progress in terms of financial value;
2. Develop a mechanism to rationalise and enhance CSR initiatives in terms of regional and company sustainability.

To this end, Argyle is in the process of measuring its Enduring Regional Value in Five Value terms. At this point, the work on the Five Value flows is complete, and work on measuring stocks is being considered as part of the mandate for a Kimberley Regional Sustainability Partnership. These discussions are currently at an early and informal stage between key Kimberley business, government and indigenous stakeholders.

The Regional Sustainability Partnership mechanism is an extension of the logic behind the State Sustainability Strategy's call for a series of regional sustainability strategies. It is currently under consideration as a way of enhancing regional CSR programmes. It also offers the right kind of forum for assessing the Five Value stocks related to the company's operations. The ambition behind it all is to demonstrate through a Regional Sustainability Audit in twenty years that Argyle's operations have left a legacy of net-positive Enduring Regional Value, in each of the Five Values. To achieve this, management will employ a strategy of direct value creation where possible, and value creation offsets where mining will irrevocably change things such as the landscape. Meanwhile, it aims to bring new clarity to CSR objectives and greater rigour to sustainability reporting. There is no doubt that these are ambitious goals; however, Argyle anticipates returns of equal value via a reputation for responsibility and reliability for parent company Rio Tinto, and other direct business value created through a focus on value creation synergies.

Argyle's sustainability transition also inevitably produced considerable frustration for company executives. Despite continuous improvement across all measures, the company has had accusations of 'green washing' on one hand, and had difficulty explaining the business benefit to market analysts on the other. The Enduring Value approach is intended to measure sustainability performance against one scale (financial value) that both regional stakeholders and the market can trust. By aligning the market and 'intangible' values through Enduring Regional Value, Argyle hopes to end the debate over the importance of CSR and sustainability by shifting it to how best to capture the Five Value benefits simultaneously to improve competitive advantage. It hopes in this way to drive CSR and sustainability innovation by effectively making them part of the market. The effort involved is also a proactive strategy for Argyle to benefit from delivering on Rio Tinto's expectation that its '... businesses, projects, operations and products should contribute constructively to the global transition to sustainable development ... (through) ... focusing on people, the environment, resource stewardship and management systems, [to] better manage risk, create business options, reduce costs, attract the best employees, gain access to new markets and resources and deliver a better product to our customers.' (Rio Tinto, 2004)

37.4   Some dos and don'ts

The overlap between Argyle's social responsibility to the communities it works around and its business interests is the reason that the transition to sustainability has lasted through the swings in the diamond market and the present uncertainty about the mine's future. This alignment has made believable Argyle's claims that it wants to leave in-perpetuity assets that contribute to the sustainability of the Kimberley, because its own interests are so transparently intertwined with those of the region and the state. Thus, the first don't is a narrow focus on charity and the first do is sustainability.

The next step of valuing the total sustainability of the company, while simultaneously augmenting it through a Regional Sustainability Partnership, gives the company a sufficiently powerful economic rationale for CSR to no longer use the term. It hopes to do the same with sustainability, as it too becomes overtly connected to business performance. Thus, the second 'do' is to embrace a 'value' perspective on sustainability. Even if it proves too difficult initially to calculate precise financial values for a company's impacts, the perspective will enhance the rigour applied to evaluating CSR projects in terms of regional and company sustainability. Ultimately, it will also provide the basis for the collective transition to future financial valuation by markets of elements currently considered to be 'intangibles.' This is both a worthwhile effort to contribute to and an area of future opportunity for those companies with the understanding necessary to benefit from an expanded marketplace.

The last 'don't' is to attempt sustainability in isolation. Instead, the 'do' is to embrace partnership wherever interests are aligned and mutual intent is strong. To the extent that this is successful, it creates the conditions for developing a broader regional partnership group designed to identify and promote synergies. The Regional Sustainability Partnership multiplier effect on Enduring Regional Value is a powerful way to leverage greater results for the company and a region from a minimum of extra effort. This is the key to regional sustainability, and to the competitive advantages associated with CSR and sustainability.

37.5 Wrapping up and advice for application

This chapter suggests that a transition is possible from CSR to sustainability and ultimately to Enduring Value creation, particularly in the way each step along the transition enhances the regional partnership required to produce genuinely sustainable development.

CSR is a tool that allows companies to begin to engage with sustainability. However, corporate benevolence and business imperatives may only loosely align. It is far better to take the social understanding that comes from CSR activities and put them into an Enduring Value model, as a way to understand the sustainability implications for the business. As this begins to occur, the synergies between some benevolent activities and business drivers become evident and the market rationale for such exploits often becomes obvious. Adopting the language of value for this transition instils the correct mindset and offers a powerful way to evaluate the benefit of various activities across the Five Value categories. As time progresses, sustainability oriented decision-making along value lines allows a company to demonstrate its performance to markets, communities and governments alike on a uniform scale.

Whenever possible, company efforts to create Enduring Value should be augmented by overarching Regional Sustainability Partnerships. These partnerships simplify the task of the company by offering a concise view of regional characteristics and activities, while multiplying the benefits when overlaps of interest occur. The identification of new opportunities by such groups is also a matter of course. This is the raw material necessary for creating Enduring Regional Value.

References

Bebbington, J., et al. (2001). *A Full Cost Accounting – An Agenda for Action*. London: The Association of Chartered Certified Accountants.

Fiksel, J., J. Low and J. Thomas (2004). Linking Sustainability to Shareholder Value. *Environmental Management*, June.

Forum for the Future (2004). *The Sigma Guidelines Toolkit – Sustainability Accounting Guide*, (www.forumforthefuture.org).

Government of Western Australia (2003). *Hope for the Future – The Western Australian State Sustainability Strategy*. Perth: Department of the Premier and Cabinet.

Minerals Council of Australia (2004). *Enduring Value – The Australian Minerals Industry Framework for Sustainable Development*, Melbourne: MCA.

Stanton-Hicks, E., P. Newman and B. Hammond (2005). *Mining and Sustainability, Investing in Regional Sustainability Partnerships to Build 'Enduring Value' for Regions*, ISTP, Perth: Murdoch University.

Rio Tinto Limited (2005). *'Sustainable Development Policy'*, (www.riotinto.com, accessed 6 August 2005).

Websites

www.sustainability.dpc.wa.gov.au

www.argylediamonds.com.au

www.sigmaproject.org

38 Price: Earnings Ratio and Commercial Performance

Geoff Roberts and Linda S. Spedding

Key words: Strategy, risk, governance, commercial performance.

38.1 Introduction to the model

The basis of the model, supported by statistical analysis, is that companies having a superior coverage of social, ethical and environmental (CSR/CR) matters will, on average, have a higher market value relative to comparable companies within their sector. Its main application is to listed companies, but with a little interpretation it can be applied to unlisted companies as well. When looking at the commercial and CSR/CR performance of companies, the Price: Earnings (P:E) ratio has particular significance. It is defined as:

$$\text{P:E Ratio} = \frac{\text{Market Capitalisation}}{\text{Company Earnings}}$$

Figure 38.1. P:E ratio definition

Market capitalisation is the stock market valuation of the company. Earnings are the company profits after interest payments, tax and depreciation. Typically P:E ratios range from 4-30 and, within reason, higher numbers are indicative of greater investor confidence in specific companies or sectors. The P:E ratio combines two key aspects of a company's financial situation. The company's executive team is responsible for, and can influence, the company's earnings through the strategies they adopt. Market capitalisation on the other hand is set by the attractiveness of the company shares in the market. Investor views of the attractiveness of the shares are influenced by the prospects for the sector, the competitive position of the company within it, and, perhaps most importantly, by their perceptions of the competence of the executive team. Companies having a superior grasp of CSR/CR matters generally show higher P:E ratios relative to their competitors, being more favoured by investors. Consequently, CSR/CR performance can be taken as one of the indicators of executive team competence.

38.2   The essence of the model

Use of the tool requires that the company establishes its P:E ratio relative to its peers within the sector, and also benchmarks its governance and reporting systems on CSR/CR-related matters. These would include social, ethical and environmental issues insofar as they are important for the delivery of the company's strategy and strategic objectives. This analysis will position the company in one of the four quadrants of the matrix in Figure 38.2.

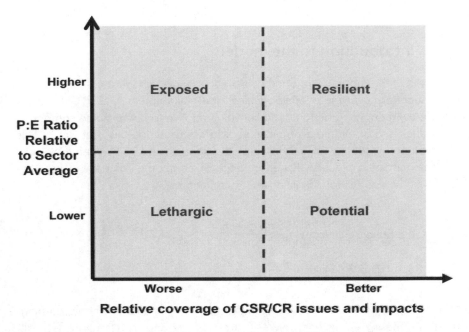

Figure 38.2. Schematic relation between P:E Ratio and CSR/CR coverage

Nomenclature within the matrix is designed to be descriptively provocative and to provide a continual stimulus to sustain the momentum of CSR/CR activities. The company position on this matrix raises different questions for the company executive team to consider as follows:

Resilient – these companies have a relatively high P:E ratio and relatively good CSR/CR coverage, indicating that they understand their CSR/CR issues and are taking action on them. Their key issues to consider here are:

- Maintaining this position as the market drivers and standards develop;
- Ensuring consistency between public statements and company actions to reduce risks to reputation;

- Ensuring that all actions and programmes are aligned with the delivery of the company's strategy and that there is no wasted effort.

Potential – these companies have a relatively low P:E ratio, but a relatively good CSR/CR coverage, indicating that they may not be capitalising on their CSR/CR activities to gain competitive advantage. Their key issues to consider are:

- Reviewing the coverage of CSR/CR topics and ensuring that they align with the company's commercial objectives;
- Cutting out the ones which do not add value;
- Leveraging the actions which are being taken to gain commercial leverage.

Exposed – companies in this position have a relatively high P:E ratio and relatively poor CSR/CR coverage, implying that they have grown to a position where CSR/CR matters should be more important, but the full scope of the issues has yet to be addressed. The matters for consideration are:

- Developing a CSR/CR strategy which focuses on reducing risks to the delivery of the company's commercial objectives;
- Setting in place an appropriately commercial CSR/CR programme, building on current activities;
- Developing a communications strategy and beginning to report on the issues and actions being taken.

Lethargic – here companies are characterised by relatively poor P:E ratios and CSR/CR coverage, which can lead to concerns that they do not fully appreciate the developing market pressures in the CSR/CR area. Such companies need to be sure of:

- Understanding the extent to which CSR/CR market drivers impact on the commercial risks and performance of the company;
- Setting out a strategy to address the CSR/CR issues which are important;
- Developing CSR/CR programmes reducing the risks to the delivery of the commercial objectives of the company;
- Developing a communications strategy to inform stakeholder groups.

More importantly, whatever position a company finds itself on within the matrix, each faces a common issue associated with possible discrepancies between a company's public statements and how it actually operates. Inconsistencies between these will lead to reputational risk, having potentially serious commercial consequences. These can affect the sustainability of the business. This is a critical factor to be borne in mind during all reporting of CSR/CR matters.

38.3 Experiences with this model in practice

The model provides some useful insights into the higher level questions which companies need to address. The approach has proved useful in prompting discussion of the more strategic issues relating to the support CSR/CR provides in reducing the risks to the delivery of the company's strategy and strategic objectives. Its prime use has been to begin to define CSR/CR programmes from a commercially strategic perspective. Frequently this has led to extensive discussions of the risks to a company's strategy, and only at the end of this process have the issues and risk countermeasure actions been grouped into something called a CSR/CR programme. This contrasts with the approach in some companies where CSR/CR is somewhat peripheral to the business, and the programmes developed are more 'bottom up' rather than 'top down.'

Applying the model to listed companies is relatively straightforward as the P:E ratio information is available through numerous sources. Establishing the sector average can either be taken from the published information in such sources as the Financial Times, or can be easily derived if the company considers that its sector peers are more specific.

An assessment of the company's relative position on CSR governance and reporting is however more subjective. Numerous questionnaire-based methodologies are available on the market, such as PIRC, EIRIS, SAM and Business in the Community. Of these the annual ranking of a large proportion of the UK FTSE 350 companies on their social and environmental performance is one of the more useful sources of comparative information. It should be noted, however, that it is not uncommon to find a company as the sector leader in one index but towards the bottom in another. This is to be expected since they frequently take a 'one size fits all' approach assuming that all issues are equally important to all companies in all sectors. Whilst this situation is improving, progress is slow. In these circumstances the advice is for companies to assess the key social, ethical and environmental risks for the sector and the company, and use these to benchmark the relative position of the company on the matrix, supplementing this with information from the Business in the Community surveys. This will provide a qualitative view of the company's relative position on CSR/CR matters.

For Small and Medium-sized companies (SMEs) a similar procedure can be followed. It is straightforward to establish the company earnings, and most executive teams will have a working estimate of the value of their company. It is therefore relatively easy to estimate a P:E ratio, which can be compared with similar companies which are publicly quoted as a rough benchmark. Companies can similarly establish their relative CSR/CR position since the executive team will have a good understanding of what is going on within the company. Benchmarking this against the competition may not be easy, especially if little information is available publicly. However, a quick comparison with one or two publicly listed companies within the sector who participate in the Business in the Community surveys and who generally publish fuller accounts of their internal activities, will provide a qualitative insight. For an SME this is all that is likely to be required in view of the need to economise in resources. Reporting, where it is necessary for an SME, should follow the principle of 'Minimum and Adequate,' since deploying any more than the minimum level of resource on this task may not be cost-beneficial.

For SMEs the supply chain pressures related to CSR/CR can also be very relevant. Frequently SMEs are part of the supply chain to larger quoted companies who themselves are seeking to align their suppliers with their CSR/CR standards, policies and practices. For this reason SMEs are advised to use the matrix to examine the CSR/CR position of their business-to-business customers, and assess what the implications for the SME might be.

38.4 Some dos and don'ts

The model is fairly broad both in its application and its general diagnostic messages. It is therefore not necessary to grind too fine on the detail. It will suffice to gain a rough estimate of the quadrant the company falls within and then take the key points. In this respect it is also necessary to take a realistic view of the company's position in relation to its competitors.

It is important not to assume that people will know what a company is doing if they are not fully informed. It is common to find more good things going on within companies than they talk about externally. However, great care should be taken when reporting and using such all-encompassing statements as: 'CSR is central to our strategy' or 'CSR is at the heart of our business' if they cannot be justified in all respects.

For example a company may state that 'Safety is paramount'. This implies that safety is the pre-eminent consideration in all strategic and operational decisions, and that the company target setting and remuneration systems reinforce this. If there is not this thorough alignment and consistency, this will lead to the potential for investors and other stakeholders to be misled as to the actual priorities within the company. Ultimately this could reflect badly on the competence of the executive team, and end up with legal proceedings against them either individually or collectively if there were a safety-related incident. Unfortunately corporate history is littered with examples of just such gaps between public statements or theory, and how a company actually operates.

38.5   Wrapping up

Overall then, application of the matrix can provide some insights into the questions around CSR/CR which a company needs to consider protecting and enhancing its commercial position. When properly addressed, the answers to these questions are likely to raise complex issues for a company to resolve since they should centre on the way CSR/CR integrates with the delivery of the company strategy. However, attempting to bolster a weak strategic position by improving CSR/CR performance and reporting will not dig a company out of its commercial difficulties. As has been emphasised throughout this chapter, it is imperative to focus on strategy, assess the risks and issues related to its delivery, design programmes to address these, and only at the conclusion of this categorise some of these as a CSR/CR programme. Approaching the topic the other way round will run the risk of CSR/CR matters being perceived as peripheral to the company's commercial position and a waste of resource.

Websites

http://www.bitc.org.uk
http://uk.finance.yahoo.com

39 A Strategy Model for Sustainable Profits and Innovation

Marcus Wagner

Key words: Environmental, social, sustainable profits, regulation, strategy.

39.1 Introduction

This analysis discusses the influence of corporate sustainability strategies and environmental regulation on the relationship between environmental and economic performance. The model presented here is supported by empirical analyses of the European paper manufacturing and electricity generation industries and of a selection of British and German manufacturing firms. The view put forward is that the potential for different industries to realise a win-win relationship between environmental and economic performance differs, but that a corporate sustainability strategy with an Environmental Shareholder Value and/or pollution prevention approach enables firms to move closer towards sustainability without jeopardising their competitiveness.

39.2 The essence of the model

This chapter discusses the influence of social or environmental regulation and corporate sustainability strategies (CSS) on overall performance. The theoretical model presented and discussed below proposes two different sets of specifications for balancing the environmental and social considerations with economic performance. In the subsequent section, the chapter looks at the effect of strict versus weak environmental and social regulation on the relationship and how it differs depending on the company approach.

Traditionally, the influence of environmental and social considerations on economic performance is expected to be negative. This reflects the view that pollution abatement activities will only increase production costs and additionally increase marginal costs. In other words, pollution abatement and environmental performance improvements are expected to have decreasing marginal benefits. It is not considered possible to make innovations in this area that are also profitable for the firm. The situation is depicted in Figure 39.1 below, where high environmental/social performance (e.g. low emissions or resource

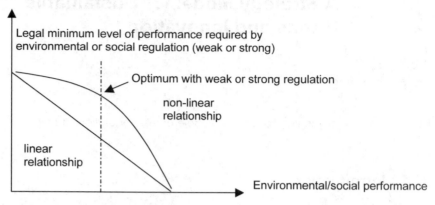

Economic performance

Legal minimum level of performance required by
environmental or social regulation (weak or strong)

Optimum with weak or strong regulation

non-linear
relationship

linear
relationship

Environmental/social performance

Figure 39.1. Traditional relationship between environmental/social and economic performance (based on Wagner, 2003; Wagner, 2005a)

inputs) correspond to low economic performance (i.e. low profitability or competitiveness), – just as vice versa low social/environmental performance (e.g. in terms of high emissions) corresponds to high economic performance. In all figures, environmental/social performance can be regarded as an aggregate index, individual emissions/inputs or an environmental/social rating. Economic performance can be regarded as an individual profitability ratio, an aggregate index of economic variables or stock-market performance. Generally, economic performance (as depicted in Figure 39.1) decreases with the increasing environmental/social performance, i.e. the slope of the curve in Figure 39.1 is always negative. In addition to this, the slope becomes increasingly more negative in the case of a non-linear relationship. The latter represents therefore the increasingly negative marginal impact of social or environmental considerations on economic performance.

Unlike Figure 39.1, the relationship in a revised approach would be that of an inversely U-shaped (concave) curve with an optimum point (i.e. a level of social/ environmental performance at which profitability or competitiveness is maximised). This curve (shown in Figure 39.2) is upward-sloping for social/environmental performance levels below the optimum (which by definition is the point where economic performance is maximised). This means that the benefits reaped from increased environmental/social performance increase continuously for lower levels of environmental/social performance. The increasing part of the curve is maintained until a certain point which is somewhere above average social or environmental performance. Beyond this point, the relationship is represented by a downward sloping curve, i.e. increased environmental/social performance corresponds to reduced economic performance.

That part of the concave curve which lies to the left of its maximum point is characterised by a positive slope but decreasing positive marginal impact on profits from increasing environmental or social performance. The part of the curve, which lies to the right of its maximum point is characterised by a negative slope which has an increasingly negative impact on profits with the higher levels of environmental/social performance.

An important aspect here is the question of how environmental or social regulation influences the model proposed in Figure 39.2. What becomes clear is that there are two distinct situations which managers may face (Wagner, 2005a):

(i) The regulatory regime is 'weak', so that the social/environmental performance level required by regulation is below the optimum level of social/environmental performance according to the curve in Figure 39.2. In this case, as shown in Figure 39.2, it would be beneficial (and thus rational for companies), to improve their environmental or social performance beyond the level required by law, since this would simultaneously improve their economic performance. This contradicts the situation depicted in Figure 39.1, where the optimum level of social/environmental performance would still be the one just achieving legal compliance with environmental (or social) regulation;

(ii) If the regulatory regime is 'strict' (the right vertical line in Figure 39.2) then the optimum level of environmental or social performance is identical to the one prescribed by regulatory compliance, as can be seen from the fact that the level of environmental or social performance which maximises economic performance is lower than the minimum level of environmental/social performance, as required by regulation. The same conclusion applies also to a 'traditional' type curve. Therefore, with strict regulation the outcome for both types of curves would be the same. The optimal social or environmental performance level to choose is that which just achieves regulatory compliance.

An example of these two situations would be to compare a firm which has just adopted a new technology enabling lower-than-required emissions at unchanged cost and a firm which has stayed with an old, 'dirty' technology. These extremes can often be found in highly regulated and environmentally intensive industries such as paper manufacturing or electricity generation.

In short, the analysis of the interaction of environmental and social regulation and the precise functional relationship between economic and environmental/social performance (as well as sustainability performance comprising both, environmental and social aspects) reveals two things. If regulation is weak then the firms' rational choices depend crucially on whether a firm faces (or

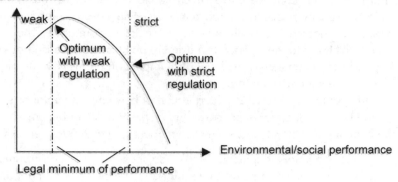

Figure 39.2. Revised relationship between environmental/social and economic performance (similar to Schaltegger and Synnestvedt, 2002; Wagner, 2005a; 2005b)

thinks it faces) a 'traditional' type (as in Figure 39.1) or a concave, 'revised' type relationship (as in figure 39.2) between economic and environmental/social performance.

When regulation is 'strict', studies show firms will always choose to just be compliant. This is regardless of whether the actual and perceived relationships differ or are the same. Given the possibility that firms cannot always establish which relationship they are facing, pure compliance seems a rational choice in many cases. For a manager, an important rule resulting from the model is that he should aim at continuously increasing environmental or social performance when facing a concave relationship and at the same time weak regulation. In this situation the chances of increased profits are highest. The cases are summarised in Table 39.1 to assist the management decision.

The analysis of Figures 39.1 and 39.2 also indicates that a CSS may have an important influence on the relationship between social/environmental and economic performance. A strategy explicitly aimed at linking environmental or social considerations with economic performance seems to be more likely to bring about a relationship as described in Figure 39.2. In particular, for the case of environmental performance, the Environmental Shareholder Value (ESV) concept (Schaltegger and Figge, 2000) provides theoretical justification for this proposition. In short, ESV stipulates, that for a defined level of environmental performance, economic performance can be improved more significantly if the environmental management activities of a company are linked to the key value drivers of shareholder value.

For example, the ESV concept finds that efficiency improvements brought about by means of an integrated pollution prevention strategy usually only require limited additional investments (compared to an end-of-pipe strategy). These improvements may well result in reduced operating costs and therefore

Table 39.1. Summary of situations which managers may face

Level of regulation is ...	'Traditional' type link (Figure 39.1)	'Revised' type link (Figure 39.2)
... strict	Optimal choice is to just be compliant	Optimal choice is to just be compliant
... weak	Optimal choice is to just be compliant	Optimal choice is to be over-compliant

higher profit margins. All of these aspects have a favourable effect on the value drivers of shareholder value and thus lead to a more positive relationship between environmental and economic performance. This explains why a pollution prevention orientation (being a special case of an ESV-oriented CSS) empirically results in a more positive relationship between environmental and economic performance. Similar arguments can also be made for social performance.

39.3 Experiences with the model

So far, a non-linear specification of the relationship between environmental/ social and economic performance has neither been used in conceptual models, nor in empirical studies. Empirically, a non-linear relationship can be ascertained based on a multiple regression analysis. This, as well as confirmation of the effects of strategy choice and regulation is the focus of this section. It concentrates on the link of environmental and economic performance and reports the results of two empirical studies.

In a first analysis of firms in the Netherlands, Italy, the UK and Germany (Wagner, 2005b; 2003) it could be shown that in environmentally intensive industries such as paper manufacturing and electricity generation, it may be difficult to bring about a positive relationship. However this is made easier by focusing on integrated pollution prevention (as a special case of an ESV-oriented CSS). This empirical analysis (Wagner, 2005b; 2003) also showed that internal factors (such as strategy considerations) as well as external factors (e.g. market settings or regulation/legislation) both have an effect on the relationship, as is proposed in the model presented in the previous section.

The study found that for firms in the paper industry a move towards pollution prevention brings about a more positive relationship between environmental and economic performance than an end-of-pipe approach. The link still doesn't show a significantly positive trend, probably because the paper industry is already strictly regulated. Nevertheless, the choice of the firm-internal strategy does play a role in the relationship in the paper industry, unlike the European electricity generation industry, which is even more strongly influenced by firm-external factors like regulation. In both cases, the results reflect the type of interaction between regulation and performance discussed under (ii) in the previous section, namely pure compliance.

The second empirical study concerned selected firms in the UK and in Germany for the manufacturing industry. Here it was shown, that for firms with an ESV-oriented strategy the relationship between environmental performance and four different dimensions of competitiveness is more positive than for firms without such a strategy (Wagner, 2005b). The dimensions were market-, internally-, profitability- and risk-related competitiveness. In this second study, the main result was that for firms with an ESV-oriented CSS an environmental impact reduction index was found to have a significant positive influence on all four environment-related dimensions.

However, all four analyses carried out on firms without a strong ESV orientation in their CSS showed no significant effect on the environmental impact reduction index for any of the four environment-related dimensions of competitiveness analysed. This means that for firms without an ESV-oriented CSS, there is no positive effect of environmental on economic performance, indicating that strategy makes a difference. In other words, firms that have an ESV-oriented CSS seem more likely to achieve a positive relationship between environmental and economic performance, while firms, which do not have such a strategy, seem less likely to bring about such a positive link. This confirms the importance of the strategy, as proposed in the previous section.

39.4   Dos and don'ts: Limitations of the model

In short, the model presented is a recommendation to companies and managers to check the alignment of their CSS with the ESV concept and the principles of the model introduced earlier. A company can screen their environmental (and social) management activities based on the value drivers of shareholder value. This establishes a bottom-up perspective of the degree to which these activities create profits and improve competitiveness. The significant differences between end-of-pipe and integrated pollution prevention activities should be a focal issue when screening environmental management activities and can help guide strategy development. Similar considerations apply also to social aspects of a firm's CSS. Knowledge of their strategy orientation allows companies to link their insights to the proposed model and the level of environmental (or social) regulation in their industry. This allows managers to make optimum choices with regard to the level of their firm's environmental/social performance.

39.5 Concluding remarks regarding the application of the model

Overall, the model and findings reported here show – that depending on the specific conditions – managers may face a positive, a neutral (i.e. insignificant) or a negative relationship between environmental or social and economic performance (or competitiveness). This means, that both theoretically derived views introduced in Figures 39.1 and 39.2 may be applicable, but under different conditions. Managers can, for example, expect an end-of-pipe strategy that focuses mainly on improving the undesired outputs of production processes (such as polluted air and water emissions) to show little positive or even negative effects on economic performance. This was found in the first empirical study reported above. Therefore, a corporate environmental strategy based on end-of-pipe activities cannot be considered an ESV-oriented strategy. However, often efficiency improvements, brought about by means of integrated pollution prevention, do not require additional investments. These may have the additional benefit of reducing operating costs and therefore increasing profit margins; they are thus ESV-oriented.

Prime examples of ESV-oriented strategies are improvements in the energy or water efficiency of a company as well as increased resource efficiency, i.e. reduced amounts of production inputs per unit of product output (Schaltegger and Figge, 2000). Corporate sustainability strategies, which focus on activities leading to such efficiency improvements thus, have a strong ESV orientation, as do integrated pollution prevention-based strategies. Managers should therefore ensure that they represent a key corporate objective.

References

Schaltegger, S. and F. Figge (2000). Environmental Shareholder Value: Economic Success with Corporate Environmental Management, *Eco-Management and Auditing* 7(1): pp. 29-42.

Schaltegger, S. and T. Synnestvedt (2002). The Link Between 'Green' and Economic Success. Environmental Management as the Crucial Trigger between Environmental and Economic Performance, *Journal of Environmental Management*, (65): pp. 339-346.

Wagner, M. (2003). Does it Pay to Be Eco-Efficient in the European Electricity Supply Industry? A Panel Data Analysis of the Relationship between Environmental and Economic Performance, *Zeitschrift für Energiewirtschaft*, (27): pp. 309-318.

Wagner, M. (2005a). *Consistency & Credibility? Environmental Reporting, Environmental Performance Indicators and Economic Performance*, Marburg.

Wagner, M. (2005b). Sustainability and Competitive Advantage: Empirical Evidence on the Influence of Strategic Choices between Environmental Management Approaches, *Environmental Quality Management*, Spring: pp. 31-48.

Websites

http://www.wi.tum.de/tim
http://www.uni-lueneburg.de/csm

40 Modelling the Business Case for Sustainability

Rachel Batley

Key words: Cost leverage, risk reduction, options creation, stakeholder preference.

'The business case is not a generic argument that corporate sustainability strategies are the right choice for all companies in all situations, but rather something that must be carefully honed to the specific circumstances of individual companies.' (Reed, 2001)

40.1 An introduction to the model

As with all business activities, there are no guarantees of success from improving sustainability performance. However, the ability to identify the risks and capitalise on the opportunities will become increasingly important with the growing pressure on companies to embrace sustainability. The most significant opportunities available through actively pursuing more sustainable approaches to business are to reduce costs, reduce risks, create options and increase stakeholder preference. The business case model for sustainability (Figure 40.1) relates key aspects of sustainability to a set of recognised business principles, demonstrating visually where the viable business case exists.

It is important to understand that this business case exists for all companies, although the specific elements vary. Thus there is diversity in the business case. For instance, small enterprises in emerging markets may focus on short-term cost leverage and options creation, while intangibles such a reputation, brand value and stakeholder preference are more significant to companies operating in bigger, more visible markets.

40.2 The essence of the model

In order to create a business case for sustainability, a company must draw on its three main pillars – natural capital, economic capital and social equity – as described below.

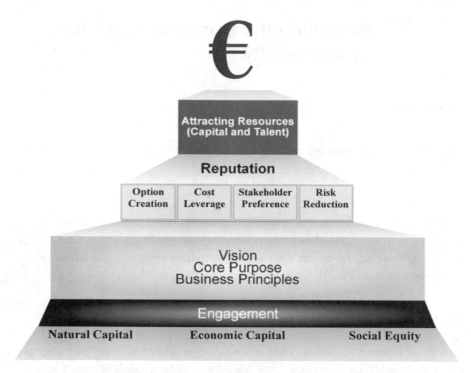

Figure 40.1. The business case for sustainability

Natural capital: the subset of all components of nature that can be linked directly or indirectly with human welfare and are valuable, vulnerable, scarce, fragile, or irreplacable enough to justify investments in monitoring.

Economic capital: produced assets that are easily assigned monetary value and sold worldwide. Some examples include appliances, furniture, automobiles, buildings, dams and other elements of the built environment.

Social equity: refers to trust, norms and networks that people can draw upon to solve common problems.

Sustainability offers a direction, not a destination. Companies that see value – and a major chance to create more value – in sustainability expect their engagement with the concept to help drive them towards corporate transformation.

We have identified four 'levers' that companies can use to derive short-, medium- and long-term value from sustainability: cost leverage, risk reduction, options creation, and stakeholder preference (Table 40.1). These levers align sustainability principles with established business management approaches and can deliver a clear premium over those approaches. In addition, they reinforce a company's reputation, adding to its ability to attract resources, both capital and talent.

Table 40.1. Benefits of corporate sustainability at a project level

Levers	Operational Benefits	Fact
Cost leverage Maximising cost savings through sustainable improvement	Avoid disruptions and delays Reduce dependency and usage of raw materials Less waste Reduce insurance premiums Reduce energy usage Operational efficiency improvements	70 % of CEOs say that sustainability is 'vital' to profitability
Risk reduction Focussing on management of long-term as well as short-term risks	Prevent show stoppers Avoid prosecution and penalties Reduce customer and regulatory retaliation Prevent supply chain disruption Improved business risk management Assure license to operate	86 % of institutional investors in Europe believe that sustainable risk management will have a significantly positive impact on a company's long term market value
Options creation Creating new methods of operation and new opportunities through penetrating untapped markets, and understanding and appealing to new stakeholder values	Competitive advantage Develop new methods of operation and new ways of working Enhance access to new market opportunities by growing stakeholder trust Pre-empt/ shape regulation Raise cost of entry for competitors	80 % of European business leaders believe that responsible business practice allows companies to invigorate creativity and learn about the marketplace
Stakeholder preference Increasing stakeholder preference through building stronger stakeholder relationships	Maintain and build relationships with stakeholders Attract best supply chain and business partners Attract resources, people and investment Employee retention Enhance employee morale and motivation Enhance reputation Regulatory approvals	Three in five people want to work in a company whose values are consistent with their own

Companies can consider whether their project portfolios are really capitalising on corporate responsibility issues by examining how well each of these four key levers are being utilised.

40.3   Experiences with this model in practice

To illustrate the application of this model we have provided some case examples above.

Case example 1: An urban transport company

The model recently underpinned work conducted by Arthur D. Little (ADL) for the Brussels Inter-Municipal Transport Company (STIB) in order to identify sustainable development actions for business strategy. The project initially set out to understand corporate responsibility expectations from stakeholders and company employees, from which a list of potential sustainable development initiatives was drawn.

The model was applied as a framework, by assigning initiatives to one of the four 'levers', in order to help cluster and prioritise actions, and more importantly to help managers understand the value of the proposed actions. Although it was sometimes difficult to assign an action to just one 'lever' the importance was that it should fit at least one category (and therefore has value for the company), and that if it fitted two 'lever' categories then the value was increased. In particular, ADL found the model brought the following benefits to the assignment:

- It encouraged actions to be elaborated thoroughly: by having to identify which lever the action fits, the team were obliged to propose actions that were more concrete;

- The process in itself was robust, which demonstrated to the more 'sceptical' managers that the actions were derived in a systematic way, which was not representative of the 'soft' way in which sustainable development is often perceived;

- By clustering the actions, gaps in levers could be identified, which warranted further brainstorming;

- The framework served as an efficient tool for prioritising actions.

Case example 2: A global beverage company

A leading global beverage company wanted to develop an effective roadmap to integrate sustainability into their business strategy within one of their regional operations. We planned and facilitated a Sustainability Master class with the company's senior management to explore what sustainability meant to the business, their current position relative to their peers and where they wanted to be in the future. A key component of the master class was to answer the question 'why is this important for our business?' The business case model was used to structure discussions around the determinants of value that could be derived through a clear strategy for sustainability. Figure 40.2 illustrates the determinants of value that were identified for each lever. These were identified as being most appropriate for their particular business.

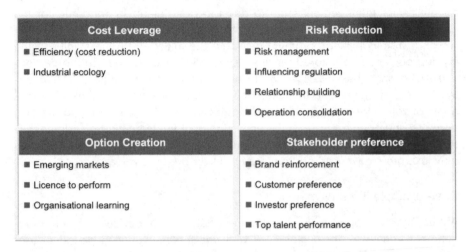

Figure 40.2. Determinants of value for each lever of the model

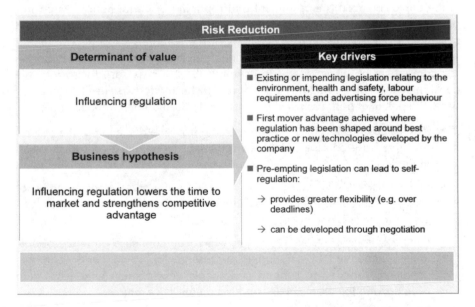

Figure 40.3. An example of how each lever can be presented in terms of the business hypothesis and key drivers

For each 'determinant of value' we then explored the business hypothesis for value creation and the key drivers of value for each determinant. An example is provided below in Figure 40.3.

This process was successful at engaging senior managers to understand the potential business value of an effective sustainability strategy. It paved the way for the senior management team to develop a sustainability roadmap for the company, enabling them to prioritise the key actions required to ensure their regional sustainability programme delivered the intended business value. Such an approach can be tailored for any organisation and can be used to demonstrate a 'generic' business case for developing and implementing a sustainability strategy. However, the limitations of this approach are that these determinants of value are not directly linked to specific activities and some levers may be more appropriate to use at the early stages of implementing a sustainability strategy, perhaps focused around delivering quick wins, whereas other levers may take more advanced approaches to deliver business value.

Case example 3: An oil major

Arthur D. Little supported the development of a sustainable development management framework for a global oil and gas major. During a period of four years, we assisted the company in the revision of its business principles to explicitly support the principles of human rights and sustainable development and in the implementation, measurement and reporting of performance. As part of our work, we undertook a systematic dialogue programme to understand stakeholder perceptions and expectations of the company as well as an intensive analysis of the implications of sustainable development for the company. A key component of this work was to establish the business case for sustainable development for the company. Each lever of the model was used to demonstrate the potential business value of sustainable development. For example:

- Reduce costs: decoupling wealth creation from the depletion of the natural resource base can lower costs by reducing dependence on raw material inputs;

- Reduce risks: Using engagement to develop a superior understanding of trends which could affect the pricing of natural and social resources lowers business risk, and costs of managing risk;

- Create options: Developing options which can capitalise on future opportunities generated by anticipated environmental, social, and economic conditions required to support sustainable development enhances value by improving the predictability and sustainability of returns;

- Stakeholder preference: Finding ways to meet stakeholder preference for a better more equitable world at the same or lower cost generates preference, loyalty, and market share.

By matching these levers to the company's strengths and competencies, the company was able to demonstrate how a combination of commitment and performance enhances reputation which in turns leads to an improved ability to attract talent and capital. Value propositions for different business units will be different and the extent to which different levers will deliver value in the short and long term will also vary. For example, most companies find that reducing costs and managing risks deliver quick wins in the short term, but deriving value through option creation and stakeholder preference can take more time to deliver business value (Figure 40.4).

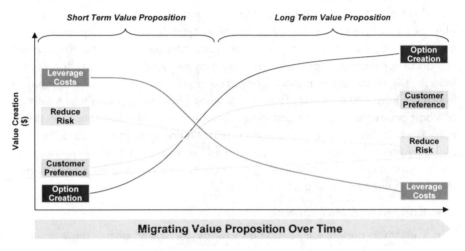

Figure 40.4. Strategic and tactical value propositions may vary by business and over time

40.4 Some dos and don'ts

The model should be viewed as a framework. In other words it should form a support for thinking and direction, rather than a prescription that is to be mindlessly followed. No business case for sustainable development will be identical, and therefore the levers, levels and attributes of the model may carry different weights, or in some cases may not be applicable. In particular, the model is a useful foundation for identifying gaps when assessing the business case.

Before applying the model it is critical to identify the stakeholders first, as they will have a strong influence over the outcomes. In addition to the ultimate outcome of reputation and resource attractiveness, one may for example want to include further outcomes in the model, such as access to new markets or innovation. Or, one may break down reputation according to stakeholder group for example.

Attention should be focussed on the four 'levers' of value companies can derive from sustainability, in order to generate and understand the way in which corporate responsibility and business principles could lead to competitive advantage or risk. Potential advantages and risks can be mapped out to understand the balance and guide decision-making. For example, if a company is considering launching 'green' products but at an increased cost to the customer, they can assess how much profit they gain from the 'low price' customers in relation to how much they will generate from premium 'green' customers.

Ideally, outcomes from the model should be quantified. A practical, balanced set of indicators can be used to translate corporate responsibility principles into measurement parameters at the project level. These measurements should link directly and transparently to your corporate policies. Recognised standards for measurement and reporting may be used where appropriate, although it is important that the organisation goes through the development of indicators from first principles to create a sense of ownership and true reflection of company results. Such measurement will inform a diverse range of stakeholders as to how the organisation is performing, and thus enable them to make informed judgements. Caution should be taken not to double-count aspects of the model. For example, if a company intends to reduce costs then it may assign this to several parts of the model:

- Cost leverage (cost savings);
- Customer preference (customer savings for lower price/ more energy-efficient product);
- Attracting resources (decreased cost of recruitment due to increase in applications).

Therefore, good practice is to avoid such double-counting.

40.5 Wrapping up

The business case is constantly evolving. Companies will need to be flexible in their approach and monitor change. It is not just companies that can take action, but also other players have responsibilities and can help to strengthen the business case. Governments in emerging markets have a responsibility to provide sound governance, investors can include companies' sustainability performance in funding selection processes, NGOs can apply appropriate pressure on companies, and customers can act on their values.

References

Reed, D.J. (2001). *Stalking the elusive business case for corporate responsibility*. World Resources Institute.

Business in the Community (2002). FastForward Research, BITC/NOP.

Nelson, T. (2001). *The European Survey on SRI and the Financial Community*.

Environic's Global Campus Monitor (2003). conducted among 1,200 undergraduates across the 20 largest economies in the world.

41 Creating Competitive Advantage: The Sustainable Value Model*

Chris Laszlo, Dave Sherman, and John Whalen

Key words: Sustainable value, stakeholder, competitive advantage.

41.1 Introduction to the model

Stakeholder value, based on a company's economic, environmental, and social performance, is a new and largely untapped source of competitive advantage that is likely to grow in the years ahead. Declining traditional sources of advantage and rising societal expectations of business are creating new strategic opportunities. Although much has been written about stakeholders, we re-frame the subject in terms of competitive advantage using an approach that systematically integrates stakeholder considerations into business strategy and operations. Such an approach can assist companies to reduce costs, differentiate products and services, develop new markets that serve unmet societal needs, and influence industry 'rules of the game.' Success in capturing these opportunities requires a new leadership vision and the courage to understand and engage a diverse set of constituencies.

The need for a new approach

A stakeholder value approach requires managers to think 'outside-in' about how their companies create and sustain competitive advantage. Outside-in thinking, which sees the world from the perspective of stakeholders, is a powerful new lens through which managers can discover new business opportunities and risks. Leaders who engage stakeholders and proactively address stakeholder issues can better anticipate changes in the business environment, discover new sources of value, and avoid being surprised by emerging societal expectations that can put shareholder value at risk (Andriof et al., 2003). Business leaders are familiar with managing financial value, whether in terms of

---

* This brief treatment of sustainable value is an excerpt from a longer article entitled 'Expanding the Value Horizon: How Stakeholder Value Contributes to Competitive Advantage,' with Jib Ellison, forthcoming in Issue 20 of The Journal of Corporate Citizenship, Winter 2005.

economic value added (EVA) or other measures driving stock price performance. They are less knowledgeable about measuring and managing stakeholder value. Because a company's impacts on stakeholders are often unintentional, it faces hidden risks and opportunities that managers can no longer afford to ignore.

To succeed in a stakeholder-driven business environment, business leaders must think and operate in new ways, shaping strategies and actions with full awareness of their impacts and implications on key stakeholders. Figure 41.1 describes company performance along two axes: shareholder value and stakeholder value. Managing in two dimensions represents a fundamental shift in how managers must think about business performance. In this framework, companies that deliver value to shareholders while destroying value for other stakeholders (or exploiting externalities) have a fundamentally flawed business model. Those that create value for stakeholders are cultivating sources of extra value that can fuel competitive advantage for years to come. Sustainable value occurs only when a company creates value that is positive for its shareholders and its stakeholders.

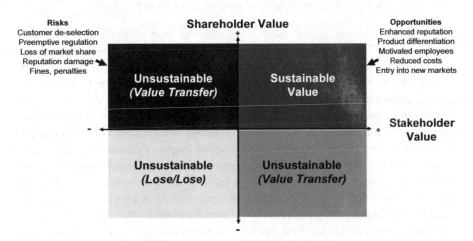

Figure 41.1. The Sustainable Value Framework

Starting in the upper left of Figure 41.1 and moving counter-clockwise, consider the following four cases of value creation:

Upper left quadrant: When value is transferred from stakeholders to shareholders, the stakeholders represent a risk to the future of the business. Leaded paint and asbestos are historical examples; today phthalates in cosmetics and toxic additives in children's toys, volatile organic compounds in carpet adhesives and paints, heavy metals in fabric dyes, and lead solder and brominated flame retardants in consumer electronics are examples of products that create risks to employees, customers and society while creating value for shareholders. Companies that avoid environmental regulations in their home markets through exporting production to countries with lower regulatory standards create similar risks. Also in this quadrant are firms that create shareholder value through a low cost strategy that tolerates management actions to cut costs through avoiding overtime pay, under training on employee safety or discriminating on the basis of gender and ethnic background. Shareholder value in these cases is created 'on the backs' of one or more stakeholder groups, thereby representing a value transfer rather than true value creation.

Bottom left quadrant: When value is destroyed for both shareholders and stakeholders, this represents a 'lose/lose' situation of little interest to either. Monsanto and its European competitor Aventis lost large sums of money by underestimating consumer and farmer resistance to their GMO crop products. Before Aventis sold its CropSciences division to Bayer in 2001, it is estimated to have lost $1 billion in buy-back programmes and other costs associated with its genetically-modified corn StarLink. StarLink was approved only for use in animal feed but was found by NGOs to have contaminated a number of human food products.

Bottom right quadrant: When value is transferred from shareholders to stakeholders, the company incurs a fiduciary liability to its shareholders. Actions intended to create stakeholder value that destroy shareholder value put into question the company's viability. Environmentalists often unintentionally pressure companies to take actions in this quadrant without realising that the pursuit of loss-making activities is not sustainable either. Avoiding offshore sourcing to protect American jobs is an example of creating stakeholder value (employee job security) while destroying shareholder value (higher operating costs). Campaigns to 'Keep Jobs in America' may create short-term benefits for American workers, but they hurt the companies who end up with uncompetitive labor costs. It is interesting to note that philanthropy, when it is unrelated to business interests and represents pure charity, is also located in this quadrant. Unfocused philanthropy is implicitly a decision to take financial value from the company's shareholders and to transfer it to one or more of its stakeholders (Porter and Kramer, 2002).

Upper right quadrant: When value is created for stakeholders as well as shareholders, stakeholders represent a potential source of hidden value. Sustainable value is created only in this case. Shaw Industries, the world's largest carpet manufacturer with over $4.6 billion in annual sales, found a way to create a new carpet backing that offers benefits to both shareholders and stakeholders. Rising concerns among stakeholders about the environmental and health risks associated with traditional PVC backing led Shaw to search for an alternative. Its solution was EcoWorx backing, in which a thermoplastic polyolefin compound reinforced by fiberglass provides the same functionality as PVC backing with half the weight, resulting in savings on shipping costs. Shaw has made a commitment to pick up any EcoWorx product at the end of its life, at no charge to the customer, and recycle it into more EcoWorx, enabling the company to use these materials in a perpetual loop. Receiving a call when the customer's product reaches end of life also presents the company with a selling opportunity for new products. Within 36 months of launch date, EcoWorx production exceeded 50% of Shaw's total tile backing production and the company ceased production of all PVC backing at the end of 2004. According to company sources, the unit cost of EcoWorx is expected to fall below that of PVC within three to four years[1].

Companies can use the sustainable value framework to think in strategic terms about their existing portfolio of products and services. Most managers are able to assess the overall value created for a business or product in both shareholder and stakeholder terms. For example, an industrial paints producer identifies solvent-based industrial paints as positive for shareholders but negative to stakeholders due to the presence of harmful volatile organic compounds (VOCs). By switching to water-based paints that are classified as non-VOC, it has the opportunity to create value for shareholders and stakeholders. By profitably recycling its water based paints, it creates a further win/win. The opportunity for industry today is to understand its impact on stakeholders, anticipate changing societal expectations and use its capacity for innovation to create additional business value from superior social and environmental performance. The managerial approach described in the next section is based in part on our work with global industry leaders seeking to capitalise on this opportunity. It provides a 'how to' guide in applying the Sustainable Value model shown in Figure 41.1.

41.2 Three key phases

A disciplined process to create sustainable value requires three phases:

The diagnosis phase

The diagnosis phase expands the organisation's view of value to include stakeholder-related risks and opportunities. It requires an understanding of the broader societal trends in the global business environment such as the advent of new technologies (genomics, nanotechnology), new warfare (bio- and cyber-terrorism), new demographics (more old people in developed countries, higher numbers of young people in poor countries), and environmental challenges (climate change, water scarcity). It also requires understanding the company's societal impacts in relation to these broader trends. Each company needs to

---

[1] Communication with Shaw Industries (March 17, 2005).

adopt a process of identifying and segmenting its stakeholders, decide which ones are important, and gain a clear understanding of the issues that matter the most to the stakeholders. The organisation must develop a clear picture of where it is creating and destroying value for them. The company must also understand value flows from stakeholders (or coalitions of stakeholders) to the company. Where and how do stakeholders impact the organisation, positively and negatively? The current state picture of value flows should be augmented by exploring how it might change in the future.

The value creation phase

In the value creation phase managers need to consider potential value from multiple levels of strategic focus. These are shown in Table 41.1.

Often companies look only at the bottom two levels concerned primarily with eco-efficiencies from reducing energy or waste; avoidance of fines, penalties, and litigation due to regulatory non-compliance; and reducing risks related to license-to-operate. The top four levels in Table 41.1 represent opportunities that are significantly larger than those represented by eco-efficiencies. They are opportunities for innovation and top-line growth based on business solutions that integrate financial and societal performance.

The Equator Principles, adopted by Citigroup and other financial institutions to set a new environmental and social standard for project financing, is an example of creating value at the business context level. Patagonia's effort to 'live its environmental values in everything it does' has led to a reputation and brand that attract customers, employees, and other stakeholders. Cemex's Patrimonio Hoy reaches a new previously unserved market of economically disadvantaged households. Toyota's Prius provides environmental and economic benefits from product use, while 3M's pollution prevention pays is a well known example of shareholder value created at the process level.

Table 41.1. Levels of strategic focus

Levels of Focus	Sources of Value
Business Context	Changing the "rules of the game" to provide competitive advantage for sustainability strategies
Reputation/ Brand	Gaining stakeholder recognition and preference including attracting and retaining talent and employee productivity
Market	Entering new markets driven by customer and societal needs (sanitation, health, clean air, water,...)
Product	Creating product differentiation based on technical *and* sustainability features
Process	Reducing energy, waste or other process costs. Security of supply of raw materials
Risk	Compliance–oriented management of risks and protecting license to operate

The value capture phase

In the value capture phase, attention is focused on the conditions for successful implementation. A key consideration is how to use actions to change the dominant mindset and embed the stakeholder value perspective into the organisation's management processes and operating model. In many cases this can be accomplished by expanding the frame of existing programmes such as Six Sigma to include the full stakeholder perspective. The ability to measure in a credible way the impact of actions on stakeholder value is critical.

Table 41.2. Summary of key questions by phase

Diagnosis	Value Creation	Value Capture
Who are your stakeholders? What are their interests? Where are you creating value or destroying value for them? What potential future developments might change this stakeholder value picture? What are the business risks and opportunities associated with this picture? Which risks and opportunities warrant action?	What actions will simultaneously create shareholder and stakeholder value? At what level of strategic focus will they create value: risk, process, product, market, brand, business context? What financial value will result: profitability, capital utilisation, lower cost of capital, growth, intangibles, market confidence? What are the critical success factors for the actions?	What existing programmes or systems could be adapted to include the stakeholder dimension? What stakeholder alignment and support is required? What social marketing is required to educate the key stakeholders? How will you train the sales force? What financial and human resources are required? How will you track progress, measure results, and share learning?

41.3 The sustainability pathway

The Sustainable Value model has been used by CEOs and line managers in Fortune 50 companies in both the US and in Europe. Experience has shown that CSR gets traction only when there is a desire by senior executives and line managers to align value creation for the business with value creation for society. The change path starts with opportunities that make financial sense today based on available technologies, processes and markets. By looking at the business through the lens of stakeholder value, line managers are able to find new sources of financial value. For example, a global retailer searching for ways to reduce greenhouse gas emissions found that it could reduce its building energy usage by 27% through readily available actions such as appropriately sized HVAC systems and better building controls. The next step on the change path is to identify opportunities that make business sense based on new technologies, new markets, new processes and product innovation. In the retail example, in store refrigeration systems could be redesigned to be more thermally isolated by using air blankets developed in clean room technologies from the electronics sector. Finally, managers need to consider opportunities to change the 'rules of the game' through lobbying government, social marketing and other actions that tilt the competitor playing field toward (instead of away from) sustainable practices. For example, some leading car companies that advocate hybrids and other green technologies are simultaneously pushing government regulators to slow environmental standards favouring those technologies. In markets in which government regulation, industry standards and consumer awareness favour sustainability practices, companies that compete on superior environmental and social performance can create significant competitive advantage.

41.4 Lessons learned

A few key lessons have emerged in how to use the Sustainable Value model. Networks of external partners are proving critical to developing innovative environmental and social solutions that reap business rewards. Companies benefit from engaging a broad range of external stakeholders in collaborative relationships, including stakeholders that initially hold critical or confrontational views. Second, listening to stakeholders – particularly societal stakeholders such as NGOs and local communities – requires a competence that is missing in most large companies. Managers often confuse stakeholder input with stakeholder dialogue, and prematurely assess what stakeholders really want. Third, organisations that begin by harvesting low hanging fruit develop credibility for a stakeholder-perspective and create the financial resources to tackle longer-term environmental and social problems.

Experience suggests that progress on Sustainable Value creation will not occur until the CEO and line managers 'own' the process. Sustainable Value efforts should not be delegated to in-house specialists such as CSR managers or external advisors who do not have profit and loss responsibility for the business. The goal is not environmental or social results per se. It is environmental and social performance that generates business value in a win/win for the company and for society. Since the target involves a new way of measuring and managing value creation, it needs to involve the whole business system. This, in turn, requires the involvement of a sufficient number of employees for the organisation to reach a 'tipping point' in its conduct of business.

41.5 Conclusion

Until the 1980s most companies believed higher quality meant higher costs. Japanese players demonstrated that it was possible to achieve higher quality and lower costs simultaneously. Today companies across a range of industries are finding that they can achieve high quality, fast speed to market, high customer service and low cost all at the same time. The leaders of tomorrow will demonstrate the same thing about stakeholder and shareholder value. Integrating the full range of stakeholders into strategic and operational decision-making will become best practice. Today, courageous business leaders can already create competitive advantage by understanding their key stakeholders' interests, anticipating societal expectations and using the insight, skills and relationships developed through this process to design new products and services, shape new markets, develop new business models, and ultimately reshape the business context itself to one that supports the creation of truly sustainable value.

References

Andriof, J., S. Waddock, B. Husted, and S.S. Rahman (2003). *Unfolding Stakeholder Thinking 2: Relationships, Communication, Reporting and Performance*. Sheffield, UK: Greenleaf Publishing.

Porter, M. and M.R. Kramer (2002). The Competitive Advantage of Corporate Philanthropy, *Harvard Business Review* OnPoint, 242x.

42 CSR Upside Down: The Need for Up-Front Knowledge Development

Jan Jonker, Marco de Witte, and Michel van Pijkeren

Key words: Theory development, CSR movement.

42.1 Looking back

The past decade has showed increasing attention to the idea of sustainability and corporate responsibility. The previous chapters provide a vivid demonstration how this growing attention has been translated into everyday organisational reality. The international harvest of a number of tried and tested management models show how a promise is turned into practice. What also appears is that CSR is not just an issue within the so-called developed countries. Although we wouldn't pretend to provide a representative overview, around the globe academic and business people are engaged in developing intelligent solutions for often-complex practical problems. The overview is the result of just one call for contributions. As far as we know this call is one of a kind showing for the first time what has been developed. As a result many of the presented models could be called 'first generation'. It is to be expected that in a few years from now new releases and adaptations will materialise. It all adds to demonstrating that CSR is a growing 'movement' gaining momentum and substance.

How the book was born

Normally we wouldn't elaborate on the 'birth' of a book. In the case of this one we would like to make an exception. The idea emerged on working an afternoon hardly a year ago when just debating the state of the art in the field of CSR. Some 'what-if's' and other hypotheses where brought to the table. 'Who is really busy developing CSR Models?' we asked ourselves. 'What are these models trying to cover?', and 'Is there more then stakeholder engagement models?' In order to find out what was really happening, we decided almost on the spot to launch a world-wide e-mail alert. In this alert we invited people to come forward with tried and tested models for CSR and sustainability. The invitation stated: 'In the past decade the field of CSR has impressively progressed. This has resulted in a number of tried and tested management models. Models that have demonstrated added value in everyday (organisational) practice. We want to harvest this experience leading to an accessible and readable volume with an overview of those models in a hands-on manner. The book will be written for a managerial – and consultants audience: people that have to deal with CSR in everyday practice.' A little naïve we were not ready for what would happen next. Within hardly two months time we received over 200 proposals, reactions and comments to this initiative, a harvest going beyond our expectations. Based on a generic management model (see also the Introduction) we structured the volume enabling us to assess the added-value of different contributions and create the needed flow in the composition of the book as it emerged. The high pace and sheer volume of enthusiastic responses convinced us – and the publisher – that this was a book that was in fact already there and just needed to be called in order to appear.

42.2 The actual harvest

Originally we started with a bit more then one hundred and twenty submitted abstracts. After a process of double reviewing and hardly one year further down the road we are able to present a book with forty-three contributions written by more then seventy authors coming from around the globe. Besides the usual editorial process we encountered one special challenge. Going through the contributed material time and again we found it demanding to position them according to our original framework that served as the foundation for this endeavour as a whole. While we thought that models were developed with a specific label covering a clear issue, it turned out that many contributions were crossing thematic boundaries, thus relating various fields. As a consequence positioning the individual contributions in the generic model as provided by us has a certain degree of arbitrariness. Still we thought it useful to keep the chosen format as it is. As a result contributions sometimes can be categorised under more then one label. Below (in Figure 42.1) an overview is provided of the authors' contributions under different headings of the model.

A second way to present the harvest of this volume is to categorise the various contributions using a concise set of key words provided by the authors. What these key words show is above all the focus in the CSR debate. What it also shows is the potential of the model we have introduced in this book. It helps indeed to better understand and discover the different issues related to CSR and sustainability in everyday practice. Furthermore it helps to explore the different functionalities of the various models, their overlap, authenticity and usefulness. It also helps in one more way. As previously explained this volume almost started off by incident. This was not a carefully planned 'book' journey, but more an inductive 'tour of discovery'. This implied that neither an explicit format nor a tested model was available at the beginning, ours was still in status nascendi. It was more like finding the 'tools' to develop the book while being busy in the process of editing it. Now that the work is done this leaves room for a number of observations.

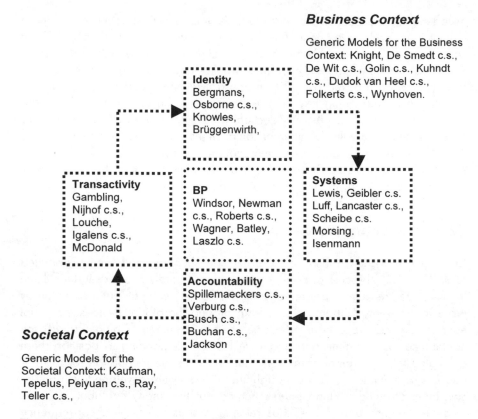

Business Context

Generic Models for the Business Context: Knight, De Smedt c.s., De Wit c.s., Golin c.s., Kuhndt c.s., Dudok van Heel c.s., Folkerts c.s., Wynhoven.

Identity
Bergmans, Osborne c.s., Knowles, Brüggenwirth,

Transactivity
Gambling, Nijhof c.s., Louche, Igalens c.s., McDonald

BP
Windsor, Newman c.s., Roberts c.s., Wagner, Batley, Laszlo c.s.

Systems
Lewis, Geibler c.s. Luff, Lancaster c.s., Scheibe c.s. Morsing. Isenmann

Accountability
Spillemaeckers c.s., Verburg c.s., Busch c.s., Buchan c.s., Jackson

Societal Context

Generic Models for the Societal Context: Kaufman, Tepelus, Peiyuan c.s., Ray, Teller c.s.,

Figure 42.1. Contributions positioned in the generic management model

42.3   Some observations from a birds-eye perspective

In this volume CSR is addressed from various functional knowledge domains such as marketing, communication, procurement, etc. As a whole a rich contribution is made to the growing body of knowledge. Still, too often CSR is seen as an 'add-on', as something that needs to be treated as yet another issue. If CSR is to be integrated in every aspect of the organisation it should not be understood as a stand-alone issue. In the Total Quality Management (TQM) movement we have experienced how long it takes to develop such an integrated perspective and get it working on the shop-floor. CSR should therefore not be delegated to one functional department such as HRM, Issue Management or the Quality Department. This observation does not imply that efforts to develop CSR should not be lead by an 'expert'. In order to flourish it definitely needs visionary leadership.

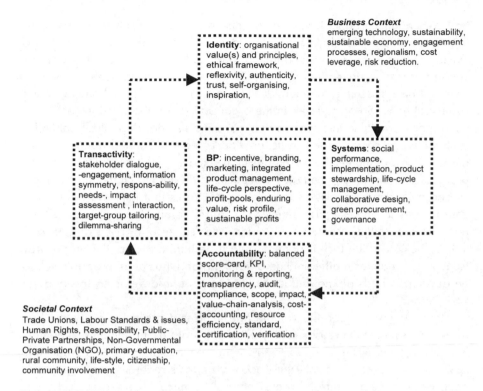

Figure 42.2. Key words positioned in the generic management model

In many cases CSR seems to concentrate on stakeholder related issues such as, dialogue, engagement or partnership. Moreover, this volume shows that specific issues like for example procurement, marketing, communication or the broader or smaller societal context are linked to the stakeholder-issues. This is the most often linkage found in the submitted management models. We think the core of the debate in CSR is to redefine the balance between the organisation and society at large. This implies that this debate should be more then developing a dialogue (how well attempted) with internal and external stakeholders. So we shouldn't go down the route where CSR is defined in a shallow way meaning simply to engage in a dialogue leading to so-called transparency, accountability and in the end compliance. There is more then just telling others how good you are in order to maintain a 'licence to operate'. Dialoguing with stakeholders is not a goal in itself. It is just a means to understand how to reconfigure the balance between a business and its societal context. It also helps to discover how a business can add value to its social and natural environment.

The presented models provide a vivid demonstration of how CSR is approached at different levels covering various issues throughout the organisa-

tion. When talking about levels we can observe different degrees of conceptu-
alisations, different levels in terms of plans, policies and strategies and also
when it comes to operations and tactics. Besides the renewed proof this observation provides in stating that CSR should be managed all through the organisation, it also underlines the multi-dimensional and multi-level character of the
issue(s) at hand. So on all levels in the organisation specific management models are now available through this volume. One size does not fit all, that's for
sure. Although some models try to provide a more integrated approach they
are certainly not main-stream. The question remains why it is so difficult to approach CSR from a truly integrated perspective. It is easy to blame the complexity and multi-dimensionality as the root cause. Yet is that fair? Maybe it is because we try to address what is new (CSR in this case) with an already existing
body of knowledge in different domains. We 'squeeze in' a bit of CSR and
then it looks as if the trick is done. Could it be that this is not the proper way
to go? CSR requires a different line of thinking and thus an appropriate still to
be developed body of knowledge. How far are we in developing this body of
knowledge?

When reading through this volume one thing that strikes the eye is the firm
roots with respect to the sustainability debate. It looks as if a majority of authors
is well educated when it comes to this issue. While started 30 years ago it is
now common practice to take into account matters regarding ecological impact, waste management and use of natural resources. Looking back the advantage of the sustainability debate – once it was discovered – has been it's
tangible character. Pollution can be measured, waste can be recycled and steel
can be re-welded. The major discovery of the past three decades is that sustainability thus becomes a 'natural' part of the business strategy, because it
leads to operational efficiency, now often called eco-efficiency. It simply pays
off to treat resources in an intelligent sustainable way. Although true, let's not
forget that it took these decades to get to this point. In hindsight we should be
grateful to Ms. Gro Harlem Brundlandt for the breakthrough perspective she
has provided with 'Our Common Future'. What then is missing in the present
CSR debate that would enable us to make a similar leap forward?

Especially this last observation leads to a final one. It remains difficult to position CSR as an 'independent' business strategy. Why then is it so difficult to
turn CSR into such a strategy? Why can't it be classified in one go with established strategies such as product-leadership, operational excellence or customer
intimacy? Going through the various contributions the harvest in this respect
remains rather modest. Could it be that what has been developed so far should
be classified as the 'first-generation' of conceptual models? Probably the real
breakthrough we are all searching for is learning to approach CSR as an indispensable component of the business model itself. The bottom-line of this obser-

vation should be that it is inconceivable to run a business without taking into account CSR as a way to create 'stakeholder' value. Many times CSR issues are studied in the context of modern organisations but much elaboration is needed to view them from the perspective of doing business in a social responsible manner. These issues can only be really effectively handled when they are embedded in a company's business strategy, plans and activities. In our view that is the real future challenge of the contemporary business enterprise.

42.4   Developing CSR upside down

Trying to fulfil this future challenge we have to realise ourselves that despite the many (research) activities that take place in academia (across the world) there is a lot of talk about organisations. It has shown that this is a rather vulnerable way of doing research. Research is than mainly set up from the outside (academics looking at organisations from a distance). It is only after results have been published that members of the relevant organisation can start putting the answers into practice and reflecting on such academic observations. This approach shows a poor ratio between the (research) efforts invested and the outcome generated. It is our belief that fundamental knowledge should be created inside organisations and preferably by the members of that organisation themselves. In other words, by helping them to build a bridge to more scientific insight. The key here is upfront knowledge development. Doing this would bring the following questions on the research agenda:

- What are the new roles for the business given a specific societal context?
- What does CSR mean to businesses?
- How is it embedded in strategies, core processes, policies and plans?
- How can the different parties in a value chain create a level playing field for CSR activities?
- How does it add value, tangible and intangible?
- What is an appropriate way to measure performance in this respect?
- How to create appropriate implementation processes?

It is impossible to answer these questions only from the 'outside'. In order to develop organisation specific answers that generate meaning and practical use these questions should be addressed from within. The key question is how to embed CSR in business, its new roles and responsibilities, its strategies. In the search for answers exchanging knowledge and experience within and between organisations is deemed crucial. It will lead to results generated within the right context and enriched through the exchange between the right actors operating in different contexts'. The growing attention being paid to CSR over the last decade(s) shows that there is a need to generate this (applicable) knowledge. We propose in addition to develop networks and platforms targeting this need. Their primary goal is to generate knowledge and experience within businesses on CSR through people working in business. Such networks and platforms will create varied benefits for the organisation, for example context-bound fundamental and applicable knowledge developed within and through the organisation. In this way it will promote the necessary capabilities to embed CSR within the core business of the organisation. To our best knowledge such platforms nowadays hardly exist.

When we trace the development of CSR, it looks as if it all has started with an 'enlightened' idea born in practice. Neither grand theories nor fundamental considerations can be traced back. Yes indeed, through time various authors have contributed to what we now call the body of knowledge in the field of CSR. But these authors have mainly been independent thinkers, certainly not presenting the main stream of scientific thinking. It is only through time almost haphazardly and by incident that ideas have been incorporated in the scientific debate. As a result we have witnessed the usual semantics, window dressing, green wash, etc. In brief, a full-fledged 'hype'. It is only during the last decade that this development has been taken serious, also by the scientific community. But, is there something new here? Dissemination of new developments over the past shows a remarkable similar pattern. How about scientific management? Process thinking? Or even: environmental management. So we know by now, based on these experiences, that the average lead time for fundamental innovations is rather considerable.

So, how practical can we be when it comes to theory development in this field? Our assumption to start with is the idea that ideas developed in practice are valid and attractive to be elaborated in academia. CSR is more then semantics, it is more than just a management hype, thus deserves to be elaborated theoretically to its application in practice. Therefore the basic way to go is to move form practice to scientific theory. This volume, a structured amalgam of management models provides a first attempt in that direction. Those that proclaim that contemporary organisational theory and its further development are irrelevant for organisational practice are overshooting their mark. Of course there is a difference between the academic world and the world of organisations. Stereotype perceptions determine the order of the day and the result is a high degree of disconnectedness. One could even go as far as to say that both worlds use their own rationales. Despite the fact that this is true elaborating CSR will require connecting both worlds.

Creating fundamental change takes a long time. The past is full of examples in that respect. When it comes to CSR that is even more the case. CSR is not just a business issue. It requires in the end a different way of thinking about how a business is run by various actors. Institutional interests originating from three different spheres of influence need to be connected before CSR becomes a mainstream issue. Across the previous pages we have talked about business leverage, academic leverage and the way these two could be connected. No need to elaborate these first two any further, but the third and final one is political leverage. In the contemporary debate just modest attention is paid to the facilitating role of societal and governmental institutions. We firmly believe that national and trans-national governments and their affiliated institutions could play a more facilitating role. In the debate so far connecting these three spheres of influence is 'unknown territory'. In the light of this thought it might be a good idea to look for possibilities leading to creative destruction. What are the institutional factors, such as laws, roles and procedures that limit the room to manoeuvre of organisations in developing CSR? Or put in other words, which factors establish the prisoners' dilemma in which businesses seem to be caught by its institutionalised context, that does not reward businesses to incorporate societal issues into their core processes. It seems that, especially multi-national organisations are forced into classical economic thinking which leads to unsustainable, and in some cases, even unethical practices. Would the identification of restraining factors not be the first issue to investigate rather than to ask companies to act, since businesses seem to be leading in this development? If those factors are then identified, maybe the time has come to connect spheres of influence in order to overcome the structural limitations to the full integration of CSR. This might offer the opportunity to make a leap forward in the contemporary CSR debate.

About the Authors

Xavier Baeten is manager at the Competence Centre Entrepreneurship, Governance and Strategy. He is responsible for the Strategic Rewards Research Centre and for the module on Stakeholder Management in the Business Ethics Course. His main research interests are Reward Management, Executive Pay, Stakeholder Management. He has also some managerial responsibilities on the level of the Competence Centre.
Contact details: xavier.baeten@vlerick.be

Rachel Batley is a Consultant at Arthur. D. Little (ADL), a leading management consultancy helping organisations create and implement innovative strategies for sustainable growth and high financial performance. She has managed a diverse range of assignments in sustainable development including: developing a stakeholder engagement strategy for a major beverage company, managing a significant project with the UK's Department for Trade and Industry to understand how emission regulations affect the rate of innovation in the automotive industry, and providing a range of verification and assurance services for a number of sustainable development programmes for a leading UK charity.
Contact details: batley.rachel@adlittle.com

Robert Beckett is a member of the Institute of Communication Ethics and a director of the private company, Communication Ethics Limited. He is a critical communication researcher presently undertaking studies in the claims made by corporations in their corporate social responsibility programmes, corporate communications, and community dialogue practice.
Contact details: rb@communication-ethics.com

Fred Bergmans is founder of Freshbusiness, international business consultant on product innovation. He had a 30 year marketing career in international FMCG companies and was the former Corporate Marketing Director of Perfetti van Melle. Freshbusiness supports companies who want to strengthen the relationship between company goals and their marketing strategy. The extended experience in business processes and change management is translated in models to bring fresh insights to business impact. Fred Bergmans is involved in CSR projects since 1999 for Van Melle, NIDO (National Initiative Sustainable Development), Ministry of Economic Affairs (scientific research) and various companies.
Contact details: fred.bergmans@freshbusiness.com

Kyla Brand is executive director of AGENDA: Social Responsibility in Scotland, a network and information exchange for all interested in sustainable relationships of business and society. AGENDA supports those promoting social responsibility and challenges those who could. It creates opportunities for conversations across business, public and voluntary sectors, within Scotland and with European partners. She also works as an independent adviser on public and private sector stakeholder reviews and CSR strategy projects across the UK. Previously she was public affairs manager with Business in the Community, London; a market research executive in the Gulf ; and a civil servant in the Department of Trade and Industry.
Contact details: kyla@agenda-scotland.org

Bart Brüggenwirth has twenty years of experience in marketing. He has a degree in marketing and is specialised in corporate sustainability. In 2003 he founded b-open, a Dutch consultancy specialised in corporate sustainability and marketing, inspired by his vision that corporate sustainability not only means doing well for society, but also offers business opportunities. It supports companies integrating corporate sustainability in their marketing policy and practice, in order to improve their market position and to create stronger brands. Bart is engaged in fulfilling his ambitions because he believes that to do so contributes towards encouraging sustainable development.
Contact details: bart@b-open.nl

Lisa Buchan holds a B.A. First Class Honours, University of Sussex and M. Phil in History, University of London. She has worked as a writer, editor and analyst for a variety of international organisations and multinational companies including: The American Petroleum Institute, the Centre for Strategic and International Studies, Esso Europe, the Economist Intelligence Unit, NATO and Vivendi Universal. She has been with GoodCorporation since 2003.
Contact details: lisa.buchan@goodcorporation.com

Timo Busch is working as an Economist at the Swiss Federal Institute of Technology (ETH) Zurich, Department for Management, Technology, and Economics. From 1999 to 2005 he was researcher at Wuppertal Institute for Climate, Environment, and Energy in the research group Sustainable Production and Consumption. The major working fields are: resource efficiency, sustainable finance, stakeholder approaches, sustainable performance evaluation, environmental related risk assessments, and climate change.
Contact details: tobusch@ethz.ch

Martine Combemale is auditor at Vigeo. She served as IIECL's (Internal Initiative to End Child Labor) Director of Auditing and has worked as FLA consultant. She has over 20 years experience in conducting social accountability audits,

development, design and evaluation of monitoring systems and methodologies in Africa, Asia, Latin America and Europe. She is the Vice President of IAS (Institut des Auditeurs Sociaux, France).
Contact details: martinecombemale@free.fr

DU Huixian (Fred Dubee) is a graduate of the European University Centre for Peace Studies. His research focus is on business, structural violence and sustainable development. A multi-lingual Canadian educated in Canada, Switzerland, Ireland, UK and Austria. Thirty years automotive industry experience, North/South America, Asia, Europe: marketing, strategic planning, training and development, general management and cross cultural team building. In 2000, he joined the United Nations, as a senior level international advocate for the Global Compact, Executive Office of the Secretary-General.
Contact details: freddubee@gmail.com

Oliver Dudok van Heel is Strategic Advisor to Enviros Consulting, specialising in corporate sustainability strategy and implementation, the business case for CSR, reporting and stakeholder engagement. He led the team that developed the sustManage methodology within Enviros Consulting. Oliver has over 10 years' experience in corporate strategy and corporate sustainability working with major multinationals.
Contact details: oliver.vanheel@livingvalues.co.uk

Henk Folkerts has been a management consultant since 1995 and is currently a partner in Rijnconsult, a medium-sized Dutch consultancy that is a member of Allied Consultants Europe (ACE), a Europe-wide consultancy. After completing his degree at Wageningen University, Folkerts worked with a number of firms and organisations in the food and agricultural industries. He advises mainly on strategy, and chain and network development, with a focus on innovation and cooperation. Folkerts is inspired by nature. He thinks in the long term, takes a pragmatic approach, is interested in the human dimension and likes to build sustainable relations and solutions.
Contact details: henk.folkerts@rijnconsult.nl

Anne Gambling is a member of Holcim's CSR/SD Coordination team. From a background of journalism and corporate communications in Australia and the United States, she joined the Swiss-based global cement producer Holcim in 1999 to assist development of their sustainability and stakeholder engagement activities. This includes the delivery of training and development workshops to sensitise and coach employees on such topics, involvement in various CSR/SD networks on the company's behalf, as well as the preparation of Holcim sustainability reports in accordance with the Global Reporting Initiative.
Contact details: anne.gambling@holcim.com

Justus von Geibler, is research fellow in the Research Group sustainable production and consumption at the Wuppertal Institute for Climate, Environment, and Energy and Coordinator of the Research Area "Government and Governance". He studied forest sciences and environmental management and policy at the University of Göttingen and the University of Lund, Sweden. The focus of research areas is: concept and tools for sustainable business development, product chain management, sustainable sectors (information and communication technologies, biotechnologies, aluminium, forestry), indicators for sustainable development as well as International Networking.
Contact details: justus.geibler@wupperinst.org

Sean Gilbert is an Associate Director for the Global Reporting Initiative responsible for its technical programme. Previous to working at GRI, he worked in the environmental field for several years in Asia. The Global Reporting Initiative is a non-profit organisation based in Amsterdam, the Netherlands that is developing a generally-accepted framework for sustainability reporting.
Contact details: gilbert@globalreporting.org

Trevor Goddard is a Research Associate and writer in residence with the Centre for Research into Disability and Society at Curtin University and in 2004 received the Vice Chancellors Award for Excellence. Trevor has been awarded a Young Australian Achievers Award by the National Australia Day Council and is a Rotary International Paul Harris Fellow. He is currently a PhD candidate with the Corporate Citizenship Research Unit at Deakin University. Trevor advocates the business case for contributing to the resolution of community issues, with business being one actor within the complex set of relationships between civil society, business and government.
Contact details: T.Goddard@curtin.edu.au

Elisa Golin, a degree in Sciences of Education, deals with training design and management; she works as HR consultant at Rainbow, the consultancy she has founded and runs.
Contact details: elisa.golin@tele2.it

Edeltraud Günther studied business administration at the University of Augsburg. After having studied languages in Geneva she became a lecturer in financial accounting. She devoted her doctoral thesis to environmental accounting. Afterwards she became a research fellow and project manager at the Bavarian Institute of Applied Environmental Research and Technology GmbH (BIfA), working closely with scientist and technicians. Since 1996 she has been a professor of business administration at Dresden University of Technology. She introduced an Environmental Management System according to EMAS at the university. Moreover her research fields are environmental performance meas-

urement, public procurement, valuation of environmental resources and hurdles´ analysis.
Contact details: edeltraud.guenther@mailbox.tu-dresden.de

GUO Peiyuan is a Ph.D. Candidate of management in Tsinghua University, Beijing, China. His research fields are sustainable development, environmental economics and corporate social responsibility. He has published several pieces of paper and been invited to attend and speak in some international conferences in China, U.S. and Switzerland. He is also the founder of China SRI website (www.csri.org.cn), providing daily CSR information and monthly newsletter with bilingual texts. He was an intern of the United Nations in 2003 and of the World Trade Organisation in 2004.
Contact details: guopeiyuan@hotmail.com

Brendan Hammond is the former Managing Director of Argyle Diamonds in Western Australia, Chairman of the Mining Petroleum Guidelines Working Group, Western Australian Sustainability Roundtable, and is a board member of the Water Corporation of Western Australia. The Argyle transition to sustainability occurred under his direction and the rest of the senior management team. His vision of using value to create a sustainable market economy is the inspiration for this contribution.

Jacques Igalens is professor at IAE in Toulouse and past- president of the international social auditors institute (IAS). He wrote a lot of books and articles on this matter and delivers lectures in many countries. He works in a French scientific laboratory, LIRHE, Laboratoire Interdisciplinaire de recherches sur les ressources humaines et l'emploi (CNRS). His last publication is about the religious roots of CSR.
Contact details: jacques.igalens@univ-tlse1.fr

Ralf Isenmann is a Research Assistant at the Institute of Project Management and Innovation (IPMI), University of Bremen, and a Senior Lecturer at the Department of Business Information Systems and Operations Research (BiOR), University of Kaiserslautern (Germany). He serves as a member of the German Expert Group on ISO 14063 "Environmental Management – Environmental Communication" and is involved in several working groups on "Environmental Informatics" of the German Society of Informatics. His research interests are the different facets of corporate communication, be it environmental, social, financial communication or its integrated fashion as sustainability communication, focused on exploiting the capabilities of current internet technologies and services.
Contact details: ralf.isenmann@innovation.uni-bremen.de

Rachelle Jackson is the Director of Research and Development at CSCC, a third party monitoring firm. Rachelle has specialised in supply chain labour standards, assisting global retailers to develop and implement socially responsible supply chain programmes. Rachelle has monitored suppliers in over 60 countries and has provided social standards trainings to suppliers in Asia, Africa, Europe, and Latin America. She has spearheaded pilot projects with corporations, including home workers in India, worker elections in China, and efforts to eliminate child labour in Central and South American agricultural commodity industries. She has a Masters Degree in Corporate Social Responsibility.
Contact details: rjackson@intlcompliance.com

Jan Jonker is an Associate Professor and Research Fellow at the Nijmegen School of Management, Radboud University Nijmegen (Holland). He has been a member of the board of the Dutch National Research Programme on CSR (2003-2004). He was coordinator of the project "Dutch corporate social responsibility and its European context" in this programme. His research interest lies at the crossroads of management and CSR, in particular with a view to the development of business strategies. He has written numerous articles and several books. He also acts as a consultant for companies regarding CSR issues.
Contact details: janjonker@wxs.nl

Alex Kaufman is Director of Operations – Global Standards, a private company dedicated to improving working conditions in the supply chains of multinational corporations. Global Standards focuses on providing auditing, consulting and training on voluntary labor standards to the private and public sector. Alex has conducted factory audits in China, Cambodia, Malaysia, Macau, Mongolia and Thailand. Prior to his current position, Alex worked as a teacher and trainer in Japan, Brazil and Thailand. Alex graduated from the University of California, San Diego with a Double major in History and Third World Studies. He completed his MSc in Responsibility and Business Practice at the Bath School of Management, University of Bath, England.
Contact details: alex@global-standards.com

Dave Knight is Founding Director of Sd3 business sustainability advisors, was a Partner Manager for Project SIGMA during 2003-2004. Responsible for guiding and supporting organisational partner contributions to the project. Dave facilitated the development of and drafted practical sustainability tools, guidelines and systems with over 15 corporations such as TNT, The Co-op Bank, Boots, RMC, Vauxhall Motors and Wessex Water. Dave's focus on delivering sustainability performance improvement through the integration of sustainability thinking into organisational strategy and process continues through his work with a wide range of private and public sector organisations. Dave has

written articles, book chapters and delivers conference sessions, workshops and training on Sustainable Business.
Contact details: dave.knight@sd3.co.uk

Richard N. Knowles opened-up and developed the Self-Organising Leadership approach to leading during his 36 years in various research and management positions in The DuPont Company. Since his retirement in 1996, he has co-founded The Center for Self-Organizing Leadership™, a not-for-profit corporation in New York. He is a Partner in The SOLiance Group USA which has helped many organisations in the USA, Australia, New Zealand, Canada and the UK to successfully develop their skills in this approach to leadership which is summarised in his book, *The Leadership Dance*.
Contact details: SOLianceRNK@aol.com

Michael Kuhndt is one of the initial founders of triple innova. He studied chemical engineering and environmental management and policy in Germany, Sweden and USA. After gaining professional experience in developing and applying environmental and social information for management decisions in the automobile industry, he worked for the European Commission on linking environmental information demand and supply in industry and science for two years. Since 1999 he has been a senior consultant for the United Nations Environment Programme and the Wuppertal Institute. At the present he is a project manager in the field of the assessing and managing eco-efficiency performance, corporate social responsibility, technology assessment, triple bottom line innovation, sustainable consumption, product stewardship and the design of corporate strategies based on multi-stakeholder approaches on company, product chain and sector level.
Contact details: michael.kuhndt@wupperinst.org

Osbert Lancaster is executive director of Centre for Human Ecology, a Scotland-based organisation carrying out action, research and education with individuals, communities and organisations taking responsibility and initiative for effective, enduring change for sustainability and justice. Osbert is also a founding steering group member of CORE Scotland: the corporate responsibility coalition. Osbert's previous work includes business advice and consultancy with the public and private sectors.
Contact details: osbert.lancaster@che.ac.uk

Chris Laszlo is a partner and cofounder of Sustainable Value Partners, Inc., a firm helping companies create value for shareholders and stakeholders. For ten years he was an executive at Lafarge S.A., a world leader in building materials, holding positions as head of strategy, general manager, and vice president of business development. Prior to that he spent 5 years with Deloitte & Touche. Educated at Swarthmore, Columbia, and the University of Paris, Laszlo earned a Ph.D. in Economics and Management Science. He currently lectures on sus-

tainability at INSEAD/CEDEP in the Executive Education programmes. His new book is *The Sustainable Company: How to Create Lasting Value through Social and Environmental Performance*, Island Press, 2003.
Contact details: Chris@SustainableValuePartners.com

Helen Lewis has worked for the Centre for Design at RMIT University in Melbourne, Australia for over 6 years, including 3 years as Director. The Centre specialises in research on ecodesign and product stewardship. Helen has spent over 15 years working on product-related environmental issues including recycling, degradability, take-back programmes and organics recovery. She has a Bachelor of Economics, a Graduate Diploma of Urban Research and Policy and a Masters of Environmental Science. She is currently undertaking research for her PhD on packaging and product stewardship.
Contact details: helen.lewis@rmit.edu.au

Christa Liedtke is head of the Research Group sustainable production and consumption at the Wuppertal Institute for Climate, Environment, and Energy. She studied biology and theology and received a Dr. rer. Nat. in Cytologie in 1993 at the University of Bonn. The focus of research areas is: development of workable concepts, tools and management systems that support economic, ecological and social sustainability in industries, enterprises and product lines. Under the head of the former Vice-President of the Wuppertal Institute, Prof. Friedrich Schmidt-Bleek, she was involved in the development of the MIPS/Factor 10 concept.
Contact details: christa.liedtke@wupperinst.org

Frederik Lippert is student research assistant in the Research Group Sustainable Production and Consumption at the Wuppertal Institute for Climate, Environment, and Energy. He is a M.A. Student of Politics, Philosophy, Public and International Law at the University of Bonn.
Contacts details: frederik.lippert@wupperinst.org

Céline Louche is Senior Researcher at Vlerick Leuven Gent Management School at the Impulse Center Business in Society where she coordinates the course on Business Ethics and Corporate Social Responsibility (CSR). She obtained her PhD in 2004 on the institutionalisation of socially responsible investment (SRI) at the Erasmus University (The Netherlands). She also worked for five years as a Sustainability Analyst for SRI at the Dutch Sustainability Research institute. In her work, she explores the way processes of change take place. A major research interest is the construction of the CSR field with a special focus on SRI and stakeholders processes.
Contact details: celine.louche@vlerick.be

John Luff advises organisations through identifying and promoting their CSR credentials. He is a frequent speaker worldwide on the topics of brand, CSR and communications. Previously John was Head of Global CSR for BT (British

Telecom). He helped BT achieve its 3rd top rating on the DOW Jones Sustainability Index. He was also Global Head of Diversity. From 1993 to 2004, John was Head of Global Brand for BT. Previous senior roles have been in the fields of occupational psychology and organisational development. He is an associate faculty member of the British Chartered Institute of Marketing. John's working life has been spent world-wide.
Contact: john@sustainablemarketing.co.uk

Leo Martin is a founder and Director of GoodCorporation. He graduated with a first class degree in economics from University of Sussex and an M.Phil from Cambridge University in development economics. He started his career as a Fellow of the Overseas Development Institute and then went to KPMG where he worked for eight years on economics and strategy for governments and companies worldwide. His clients included AstraZeneca, Rolls-Royce, KLM, EDS, Pizza Hut, as well as a number of departments of government in the UK and Hong Kong. He also worked for Lord Sharman, then global chairman of KPMG, to establish Britain in Europe, the pro-single currency campaign.
Contact details: leo.martin@goodcorporation.com

Gael McDonald is Vice-President International, Acting Vice-President, Research & Development, and Professor of Business Ethics at Unitec New Zealand. She obtained her Doctorate from The London School of Economics and Political Science, in the field of cross-cultural business ethics, and has taught undergraduate and/or graduate courses in Australasia, Malaysia, Macau, the United States and Canada in Business Ethics, International Marketing, Human Resource Management and Organisational Behaviour. In addition, she sits on the Editorial Boards of four journals, has published extensively in academic and professional journals, and consulted in the private sector. Professor McDonald is a Past President and Fellow of ANZAM (Australian & New Zealand Academy of Management).
Contact details: gmcdonald@unitec.ac.nz

Mette Morsing, Ph.d., associate professor and director of CBS Center for Corporate Values and Responsibility at Copenhagen Business School. Morsing's research interests include corporate communication in a broad sense, CSR, ethics, organisational identity, image and reputation management. She has published a number of books and articles on these issues in for example *corporate reputation review, journal of corporate communication,* and *corporate communications: an international journal.* Her latest authored book is *"Beyond Corporate Communication"*, Samfundslitteratur, 2005 with Lars Thøger Christensen and her latest co-edited book is *"CSR – Reconciling Managerial Strategies Towards the 21st Century"*, Palgrave with professor Andrew Kakabadse. She

is a member of the Øresund Environment Academy and member of the management committee and the academic board of The European Academy of Business in Society.
Contact details: mm.ikl@cbs.dk

Will Muir is a Consultant in Enviros' Sustainable Business Unit. Will primarily works in the area of Corporate Responsibility through which he continues to develop his experience in the design, implementation and maintenance of management systems, reporting systems and auditing. Will's work focuses on developing clients' CR performance; Identifying the business case for CR, developing strategy, risk management and monitoring & targeting.
Contact details: will.muir@enviros.com

Peter Newman is the Chairman of the Western Australian Sustainability Roundtable, Sustainability Commissioner for New South Wales, and Director of the Institute of Sustainability and Technology Policy (ISTP) at Murdoch University in Perth. Peter has led the development of the Western Australian State Sustainability Strategy, and is now engaged in a similar process in New South Wales. Peter is leading ISTP's collaboration with Argyle Diamonds on the Kimberley Regional Sustainability Initiative.
Contact details: p.newman@murdoch.edu.au

André Nijhof is an assistant professor at the Faculty of Business, Public Administration and Technology of the University of Twente (Enschede). Stakeholder theory, ethics of care and organisational change management are important themes in his current research. He has published in journals like the International Journal of Value Based Management, Journal of Business Ethics and the Leadership and Organisation Development Journal, besides several publications in Dutch books and journals.
Contact details: a.h.j.nijhof@utwente.nl

Nick Osborne is Programmes Manager for a national NGO in the UK and freelance management development coach. He has ten years' experience working with individual and group processes and a wide range of management experience. With an MSc in Management Development and Social Responsibility he has also trained in mediation, consensus decision-making and Neuro-Linguistic Programming. He has worked with organisations ranging from multinationals to community groups. Nick works to help participants make powerful shifts in their experience of predictability, order and what it means to be in control. His special interest is how people respond to the uncertainty which characterises the 21st Century, particularly in relation to personal transformation, corporate change and social responsibility.
Contact details: nick@response-ability.org.uk

Giampietro Parolin, economist, is researcher and lecturer in social account-ing at University of Milan Bicocca; he has been long time consultant on organi-sation and managerial accounting in the private and public sector.
Contact details: giampietro.parolin@tele2.it

Michel van Pijkeren (Mscie) is engaged in research into CSR issues as a young faculty at the Radboud University Nijmegen. His research interests lie in the field of CSR related to strategy and change management. He published articles on CSR and quality management in several Dutch journals. Besides his appoint-ment at the university he works as Quality manager at a Bosch company.
Contact details: mvanpijkeren@wanadoo.nl

Subhasis Ray is a civil engineer with postgraduate diploma from Indian Institute of Management Calcutta. He has eight years of corporate experience in sales and marketing and two years of academic experience. At ICFAI Business School, India he teaches sales and marketing. His research interest is Corpo-rate Social Responsibility and its linkage with business strategy. He is working on integrating CSR concepts in B-school environments to create sound leaders for Indian business. His articles and cases are published regularly in various magazines and journals. Some of his cases on CSR are also available at the European Case Clearing House (ECCH).
Contact details: subho@icfai.org

Martin Redfern is a freelance writer, editor and philosopher. He has twelve years' experience working with individual and group processes and a wide range of management experience. He has trained in counselling and permacul-ture and has worked with organisations ranging from public sector institutions to grassroots associations. Martin works to promote the health and happiness of human beings, the planet they live on and the wealth of nature they share it with. His special interest is the development of personal responsibility and at-tendant redefinition of the self in an increasingly secular world.
Contact details: martinredfern@myway.com

Geoff Roberts co-founded Responsible Corporation at the turn of the millen-nium following a career in the nuclear industry which covered such areas as risk prediction and management, strategic change management, and international business development. Responsible Corporation provides clients with pragmatic commercial responses to their CR issues, focussing on how CR matters support company strategy. His interests are in the area of risks to strategy, board effec-tiveness, and the quantitative estimation of the effectiveness of risk reduction programmes. He has advised numerous FTSE companies and written numerous articles on CR and risk.
Contact details: Geoff.Roberts@ResponsibleCorporation.co.uk

Deborah Rolland is a senior lecturer and programme director for the Master of International Communication at Unitec, New Zealand where she lectures in Organisational Communication and International Communication at post and undergraduate level. She is a member of Unitec's Research Ethics committee and on the editorial board of the Communication Journal of New Zealand.
Contact details: drolland@unitec.ac.nz

Lilly Scheibe studied Business Administration from October 1996 to July 2001at the Technische Universität Dresden (TUD), with specialisation in Environmental Management. Since August 2001, she has served as a Research Assistant at the Professorship of Business Administration, esp. Environmental Management, Department of Business Management and Economics at the Technische Universität Dresden (TUD). Her current projects include 'Green eBusiness (GeB)' and 'The hurdles analysis', which deals with identifying and assessing hurdles in the procurement process of public authorities and companies.
Contact details: Lilly.Scheibe@mailbox.tu-dresden.de

Esther Schouten is a PhD candidate at the Erasmus University Rotterdam, The Netherlands. Her research is about how multinational companies manage human rights across different contexts and is partly performed within Royal Dutch Shell. Before this position, she worked for PriceWaterhouseCoopers as a consultant on sustainable entrepreneurship and worked in development cooperation in Southern Africa. She completed degrees in Technology Business Administration and Development Studies and performed a six-month research project on local stakeholder dialogue of multinational companies in Guatemala.
Contact details: Esther.Schouten@shell.com

Dave Sherman is a partner and cofounder of Sustainable Value Partners where he focuses on strategies for creating both business and societal value. Dave has 25 years of general management consulting and industry experience. He served as a Vice President with A.T. Kearney and a Principal in the General Management practice of Towers Perrin. His industry experience includes positions at Chevron and Exxon. He is a Mandel Fellow at the Weatherhead School at Case Western Reserve University where he is conducting Doctoral research. He holds an M.B.A. from UC Berkeley and a B.S. in Chemical Engineering from Purdue University.
Contact details: dave@sustainablevaluepartners.com

Linda S. Spedding is a practicing Solicitor, an Attorney at Law and is also qualified as an Advocate in India. She has worked at the Legal Service of the European Commission in Brussels and the European Court. Dr Spedding provides consultancy to other law firms and to clients in both the private and public sectors. She has been particularly concerned with matters of corporate governance including environmental, CSR and sustainable development issues that affect business and has written and spoken extensively on related areas of business

risk. She is editor of "Advising Business". Her latest business manual "Due Diligence and Corporate Governance" was published in October 2004.
Contact details: Spedding@easynet.co.uk

Sophie Spillemaeckers has a degree in anthropology and studied anthropological cinematography. She was formed as ecological consultant at the 'Eco-conseil' Institute in Namur and as an SA 8000 auditor at CEP AA. She worked for several environmental and social organisations and has been a researcher at the Centre for Sustainable Development at the University of Ghent. At present, she works at Ethibel as a senior researcher on studies concerning corporate social responsibility, sustainable production and consumption and stakeholder consultation. Ethibel is a research institute specialised in research projects on CSR related topics. Ethibel developed its own methodology for screening companies on their societal responsibility (social, environmental and economic) and has a substantial experience with its implementation.
Contact details: sophie.spillemaeckers@ethibel.org

Erik Stanton-Hicks is a doctoral candidate completing a dissertation on Enduring Value, Mining and Sustainability in Western Australia. He is also a researcher involved in the Kimberley Regional Sustainability Initiative.
Contact details: E.Stanton-Hicks@murdoch.edu.au

David Teller is Deputy Director of the Committee for Melbourne, the non-partisan think-tank that created the Melbourne Model in order to facilitate relationships between non-traditional stakeholders in private and public sectors, in agenda-free and non-political settings. David is also the Global Coordinator of the UN Global Compact's Cities Programme, overseeing the Melbourne Model's contribution to business being influential in resolving complex social problems. David works to develop new mechanisms designed to achieve concrete outcomes by combining the ideas, resources, knowledge and experiences of business, government and civil society.
Contact details: dteller@melbourne.org.au

Camalia M. Tepelus is a Research Associate and PhD candidate at the International Institute for Industrial Environmental Economics at Lund University in Sweden. Her work addressing the contribution of the travel and tourism sector to support sustainable development, has won two international tourism awards in 2000 and 2003. Ms Tepelus has coordinated the Secretariat of the *Code of Conduct to Protect Children from Sexual Exploitation in Travel and Tourism* (www.thecode.org), housed until 2004 at the World Tourism Organization in Madrid. Ms Tepelus is currently continuing research on CSR in tourism, being engaged in the second phase of this project, funded by UNICEF and supported by the WTO. Ms Tepelus is based in New York.
Contact details:camelia.tepelus@iiiee.lu.se

Griet Vanhoutte is an environmental engineer and a researcher at the Centre for Sustainable Development at the University of Ghent, a multi-disciplinary research institute concentrating on policy oriented studies in a wide range of sustainability related subjects and striving to elaborate sustainable development as a social framework. She is specialised in product and process evaluation (indicators for sustainable production and consumption patterns, integrated product management, preferential product groups, sustainability assessment of products/services and policy instruments, use of raw materials). Formerly she worked as a teacher and in environmental education projects.
Contact details: griet_@yahoo.com

Johan Verburg is senior policy advisor at Novib Oxfam Netherlands, responsible for corporate social responsibility. He has a consultancy background in sustainability management in the Netherlands and in southern Africa. Novib is a member of Oxfam International and works together closely with local organisations with one goal: a just world which is free of poverty.
Contact details: johan.verburg@novib.nl

Marcus Wagner is Assistant Professor ("Habilitand") at TU Munich and Associate Research Fellow at the Centre for Sustainability Management (where he gained his PhD) researching into innovation and technology management as well as sustainability management. He studied business administration (MBA) and economics (Dipl.-Volkswirt). Marcus is a visiting lecturer at Luneburg University where he teaches on the MBA "sustainament" and lecturer/author at Hagen University (microeconomics; growth, distribution, business cycles; environmental accounting and performance indicators; environmental economics). He has work experience in the chemicals and semiconductor industries and in 2001 was Scientific Advisor to the Global Reporting Initiative.
Contact details: mwagner@uni-lueneburg.de

Holger Wallbaum is freelancer at the Wuppertal Institute for Climate, Environment and Energy and Director of the research and consulting company "triple innova", Germany, managing partner of the mipsHAUS-Institute for Sustainable Construction as well as Scientific consultant for the Trade Union for Building, Agriculture, Forestry and the Environment (IG BAU), Germany. He studied Safety engineering at the University of Wuppertal, and Maitrise 'Gestion des Risques' at the University of Mulhouse, France and received a Ph.D. in Architecture at the University of Hannover. The focus of research areas is: sustainable enterprises, water and building related material flows, life cycle analysis, sustainability indicator systems, management tools for decision support.
Contact details: holger.wallbaum@triple-innova.de

René Weijers has worked as a management consultant since 1986 and is currently a senior partner at Wagenaar Hoes Organisatieadvies, a medium-sized Dutch consultancy for private-sector and public-sector organisations. René advises firms and public-sector organisations on corporate philosophies, strategy, management structure, governance and leadership. He focuses on the human dimension of change and development. He is pragmatic, resolute, averse to passing fashions and driven by sustainable results. After completing a degree in civil engineering, he took a number of national and international postgraduate courses in strategic development and management consultancy.
Contact details: rene.weijers@wagenaarhoes.nl

John Whalen is a partner and cofounder of Sustainable Value Partners with over 20 years of management consulting experience in business strategy, operations strategy, business process design, supply chain integration, change leadership, and sustainability. Prior to SVP, he led his own successful consulting business focused on leadership development, strategy, and organisational transformation, and was a senior consultant at CSC Index where he helped to develop its business re-engineering practice. He holds a Masters from the University of Pennsylvania and a B.A. from the University of Notre Dame.
Contact details: john@sustainablevaluepartners.com

Duane Windsor is Lynette S. Autrey Professor of Management at the Jesse H. Jones Graduate School of Management, Rice University, Houston (Texas), where he has taught since 1977. His current research interests include corporate social responsibility and stakeholder management. He has published many scholarly papers and several books, including *The Rules of the Game in the Global Economy: Policy Regimes for International Business* (Dordrecht: Kluwer Academic Publishers, 1992, 1997) with Professor Lee E. Preston. He teaches leadership and business ethics in the MBA programme for executives; he previously taught strategy and business-government relations in the MBA programme.
Contact details: odw@rice.edu

Monique de Wit is Social Performance Advisor for Shell International B.V. She advises Shell companies how to better manage the social impacts of their operations. She previously worked as technologist in Oman, facing various issues with communities. She is one of the founders and ambassador of Shell's Project Better World; a volunteer initiative involving employees in environmental and community projects in partnership with NGOs. Previously she worked in Shell Global Solutions as energy consultant and on Curacao, performing a co-generation market survey for Dynaf Energy technology. Monique has a degree in both Mechanical Engineering and Technology and Society.
Contact details: monique.dewit@shell.com

Marco de Witte is an Associate Professor and Research Fellow at the University of Groningen (The Netherlands), Faculty of Management and Organisation and lecturer at the Academy of Management for courses on 'Change Management'. He has written numerous articles and several books, especially on the subject of the bridge between organisational design and change management. He also works as a management consultant. His key competence is coaching managers and management teams and leading 'inquisitive' discussions which often result in new insights and solutions for the course participants. Contact details: dewitte@hgrv.nl

Ursula Wynhoven is the Human Rights Adviser and Special Assistant to the Executive Head of the Global Compact Office. She has worked with the Global Compact Office for approximately 4 years. Her background is in domestic and international human rights law. Prior to joining the United Nations, she worked in government human rights agencies and in private legal practice in Australia and the United States. She also spent a year working in the OECD Secretariat on their corporate responsibility initiative: the OECD Guidelines for Multinational Enterprises. Contact details: Wynhoven@un.org

YU Yongda is a professor in Tsinghua University. His research fields are regional development, international finance, and corporate social responsibility. Several books and papers in these fields have been published, such as Conflicts in World Economy, China Antidumping Report. He has also been invited to visit George Mason University, Columbia University of U.S., and University of Bonn of Germany since 1990s. Contact details: yuyongda@tsinghua.edu.cn

Index

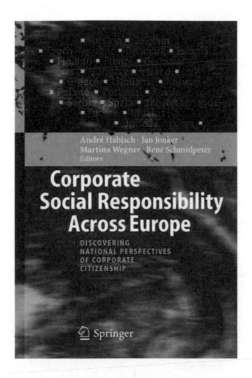

Habisch, A.; Jonker, J.; Wegner, M.; Schmidpeter, R. (Eds.):

Corporate Social Responsibility Across Europe

2005, XVIII, 397 p. 7 illus., Hardcover
ISBN: 3-540-23251-6

Corporate Social Responsibility (CSR) has become an increasingly important topic in our global society. **Corporate Social Responsibility Across Europe** is the first volume of its kind to bring together twenty-three national perspectives on this issue. Thirty-seven European researchers worked on the book, which provides a comprehensive and structured survey of CSR developments and progress at national levels. An overview and analysis is provided for each country. Topics addressed include business and societal mindsets in the different cultural settings, national drivers for the current development of CSR, and prospects for the individual countries in the future. Furthermore it contains three comprehensive pan-European analyses. The chapters also contain practical information and references to the Internet as well as relevant literature in order to support further research and stimulate business activities in this field. The result is a rather unique collection of essays on the topic of CSR across Europe.